SOCIAL CHALLENGES AND ORGANISING CAPACITY IN CITIES

The European Institute for Comparative Urban Research, EURICUR, was founded in 1988 and has its seat with Erasmus University Rotterdam. EURICUR is the heart and pulse of an extensive network of European cities and universities. EURICUR's principal objective is to stimulate fundamental international comparative research into matters that are of interest to cities. To that end, EURICUR coordinates, initiates and carries out studies of subjects of strategic value for urban management today and in the future. Through its network EURICUR has privileged access to crucial information regarding urban development in Europe and North America and to key persons at all levels, working in different public and private organisations active in metropolitan areas. EURICUR closely cooperates with the Eurocities Association, representing more than 100 large European cities.

As a scientific institution, one of EURICUR's core activities is to respond to the increasing need for information that broadens and deepens the insight into the complex process of urban development, among others by disseminating the results of its investigations by international book publications. These publications are especially valuable for city governments, supranational, national and regional authorities, chambers of commerce, real estate developers and investors, academics and students, and others with an interest in urban affairs.

| Euricur website: http://www.euricur.nl |

This book is one of a series to be published by Ashgate under the auspices of EURICUR, the European Institute for Comparative Urban Research, Erasmus University Rotterdam. Titles in the series are:

Governing Metropolitan Regions
Leo van den Berg, H. Arjen van Klink and Jan van der Meer

Urban Tourism
Leo van den Berg, Jan van der Borg and Jan van der Meer

Metropolitan Organising Capacity
Leo van den Berg, Erik Braun and Jan van der Meer

National Urban Policies in the European Union
Leo van den Berg, Erik Braun and Jan van der Meer

The European High-Speed Train and Urban Development
Leo van den Berg and Peter Pol

Growth Clusters in European Metropolitan Cities
Leo van den Berg, Erik Braun and Willem van Winden

Information and Communications Technology as Potential Catalyst for Sustainable Urban Development
Leo van den Berg and Willem van Winden

Sports and City Marketing in European Cities
Leo van den Berg, Erik Braun and Alexander H.J. Otgaar

Social Challenges and Organising Capacity in Cities

Experiences in Eight European Cities

LEO VAN DEN BERG
JAN VAN DER MEER
PETER M.J. POL
European Institute for Comparative Urban Research
Erasmus University Rotterdam

EUROPEAN INSTITUTE FOR COMPARATIVE URBAN RESEARCH

ASHGATE

Published by
Ashgate Publishing Limited
Gower House
Croft Road
Aldershot
Hants GU11 3HR
England

Ashgate Publishing Company
Suite 420
101 Cherry Street
Burlington, VT 05401-4405
USA

Ashgate website: http://www.ashgate.com

British Library Cataloguing in Publication Data
Social challenges and organising capacity in cities :
experiences in eight European cities. - (EURICUR series)
1. Cities and towns - Europe - Growth - Case studies 2. City
planning - Europe - Case studies 3. Municipal government -
Europe - Case studies 4. Urban policy - Europe - Case
studies
I. Berg, Leo van den, 1948- II. Meer, Jan van der, 1947-
III. Pol, Peter IV. EURICUR
307.1'16'094

Library of Congress Cataloging-in-Publication Data
Social challenges and organising capacity in cities : experiences in eight European cities
/ edited by Leo van den Berg, Jan van der Meer, and Peter M.J. Pol.
     p. cm. -- (EURICUR series (European Institute for Comparative Urban Research))
Includes bibliographical references and index.
ISBN 0-7546-3454-X
     1. City planning--Europe. 2. Urban policy--Europe. 3. Cities and
towns--Research--Europe. 4. Urban impact analysis--Europe. 5. Social
structure--Europe. 6. Europe--Social policy. I. Berg, Leo van den. II. Meer, J. van der.
III. Pol, Peter. IV. Series.

HT169.E97 S63 2003
307.76'094--dc21   2002028370

ISBN 0 7546 3454 X

Printed and bound in Great Britain by MPG Books Ltd, Bodmin, Cornwall

Contents

List of Figures and Schemes

List of Tables

Preface

For the third time the city of Eindhoven has taken the initiative, as member of the Eurocities Association, for an international comparative investigation into the organising capacity of urban regions. The first study was devoted to metropolitan authorities (van den Berg, van Klink and van der Meer, 1993), the second focused on the organising capacity in developing major urban revitalisation projects (van den Berg, Braun and van der Meer, 1997). The valuable and stimulating experiences with the first studies resulted in a call for a further study into the organising capacity with regard to social challenges. The observation that social exclusion is highly concentrated in the larger cities and persistent, owing to the accumulation of social problems there, made the need for a study into the organising capacity of social strategies even more pressing. The question crops up: what factors and conditions determine the success or failure of a city's 'organising capacity' in social revitalisation? The exchange of experiences in this field is considered useful for public authorities and other public and private organisations involved in developing and implementing social strategies.

As with the first and second studies, the European Institute for Comparative Urban Research (EURICUR) was invited to carry out this international comparative study. Organising capacity is defined here as the capacity to develop and implement the comprehensive strategies needed to respond to fundamental changes in society, and to create conditions for a sustainable metropolitan development. Organising capacity incorporates public and private networks to reach objectives that are difficult (or even impossible) to obtain by the public sector alone. Other important elements are vision, leadership, political and societal support, communication, and monitoring and evaluation of results.

The investigation consists of the analysis of strategies aiming to combat social problems by trying to link solutions to (economic and physical) opportunities. Eight cities decided to participate because they are convinced of the importance of the subject. Thus eight social strategies have been analysed according to a theoretical framework of organising capacity elaborated for this study.

The eight case studies have largely been accomplished by interviewing more than 90 representatives of municipalities (from various departments), urban districts, NGOs active in the social field, (social) housing corporations, local residents and business associations, programme and project managers, etc. Without their help and information the investigation could not have been accomplished at all. We want to express our great appreciation of the welcome we received in the participating cities and the willingness to share valuable information with us.

The research has been carried out under the supervision of a Steering Committee chaired by Mr Philip Werner (on behalf of the city of Eindhoven) and furthermore composed of representatives of sponsors of the research, Mr Bert Harmsen, representing the Ministry of the Interior and Kingdom Relations, and Mr Alfons Kemper, representing the Ministry of Health, Welfare and Sports, and representatives of the cities involved: Ms Marleen Melis, Mr Tarik van Ballaer and Mr Tom Meeuws for Antwerp, Mr Marko Karvinen for Helsinki, Mr Mats Andersson for Malmö, Mr Jos Dams and Mr Theo Eikenbroek for Rotterdam, Mr Stig Hanno and Mr Mats Granath for Stockholm, Ms Jeanette Couval for Strasbourg, Ms Cate Kervezee and Mr Ton Hegeman for Utrecht and Mr Ron Pullen, Mr Erik van Merrienboer and Mr Anton van Gerwen for Eindhoven. Mr Pullen and Mr Van Merrienboer also took care of the preparation and organisation of the study project.

Besides the members of the Steering Committee, Mr Henk Geveke and Mr Edgar van Leest, representing the B&A Group, a Dutch consultant specialised in social strategies, were engaged as special advisers to the investigation.

The authors thank the members of the Steering Committee and the B&A Group for their valuable remarks and pleasant cooperation. We would also like to thank our colleagues Ms Laura Capel-Tatjer, who assisted in producing the case studies of Helsinki, Malmö, Stockholm and Strasbourg, Mr Alexander Otgaar, co-author of the case study of Eindhoven, and Mr Paulus Woets who produced the tables with statistical information. Finally we would like to thank Ms Attie Elderson-De Boer for promptly translating and screening the text, Ms Ankimon Vernède, the EURICUR secretary, for her 'general assistance' during the investigation and Ms Pat FitzGerald for preparing the text for camera-ready copy.

Leo van den Berg
Jan van der Meer
Peter M.J. Pol

Chapter 1

Introduction and Theoretical Framework of Social Organising Capacity

1.1 Introduction

Globalisation and the transition to a knowledge and information society have considerably strengthened the position of cities as nerve centres of the 'new economy' (see, for instance, Castells and Hall, 1994). Cities, with their diversified economies, often form the incubation environment for new developments and economic innovations (Jacobs, 1984). They provide the daily context for the increasingly global and footloose interactions within economic, social and cultural spheres. However, globalisation and informationalisation of society have also sharpened urban competition: cities behave in a logic of competition in a highly dynamic and complex environment. Urban policy is at the focus of attention at all administrative levels; competition for mobile investments, citizens and companies induced not only the cities themselves but national and regional governments too to pay explicit policy attention to urban development. The European Commission has also expressed the need to make better use of urban development potentials in the context of its regional policy (see Geddes, 2000; Liebfried, 1993).

However, in many cities economic progress is accompanied by a pile of social problems, boosting the emergence of a dual society and, among other things, raising feelings of insecurity. In the cities, large underprivileged groups are continually developing as an essential characteristic of changing urban economic and social structures (Cheshire and Hay, 1989; Bhalla and Lapeyre, 1997; Madanipour, 1998; Eurocities, 1993, p. 4). Where poverty in the Western metropolis used to be largely residual or cyclical, embedded in working-class communities, geographically diffuse and considered remediable by means of further market expansion, it now appears to be increasingly long-term if not permanent, disconnected from macroeconomic trends and fixated upon disreputable neighbourhoods of relegation in which social isolation and alienation feed upon each other as the chasm between those consigned there and the rest of society deepens (Byrne, 1997; Levitas, 1998; Mingione, 1996; Young and Lemos, 1997; Wacquant, 1999, p. 1640). There is an increasing social polarisation, that is, a growth in both the bottom end and the top end of the socioeconomic distribution, for example an increase in the proportion of households with low skills or low income (many of whom are immigrants) and at the same time an increase in the proportion of people who are highly skilled or the number of households with high incomes (Clasen, Gould and Vincent, 1997; Perry, 1997; Musterd and Ostendorf, 1998, p. 2). This is not only unacceptable from a societal point of view, it also threatens the (economic) attractiveness of cities. To stimulate urban revitalisation and to attract (and retain) economic activities, residents and visitors, serious efforts are made to make cities *attractive*. Obvious problem areas do not contribute to such an image.

Cities are observed to switch their focus of attention from urban *hardware* (tangible facilities like locations, labour, infrastructure) to *software* (intangible qualities like safety, ambience, quality of life) and *orgware* ('organising capacity', the capacity to deal adequately with *hardware* and *software*). To enhance the effectiveness and efficiency of social policy is, in that context, often considered a major challenge for urban governments. In practice, social policy does not have a reputation of being very effective and efficient. This seems inherent in the extremely complex and stubborn nature of social problems (and their solutions). Furthermore, results are hard to measure because of the lack of unambiguously-defined indicators. However, a change can be observed from the traditional problem-oriented approach to an opportunity-oriented one. According to Michael Porter, in many cities social policy has put economic policy in the shade and the economic potential of urban areas has all too often been neglected by public policy makers. 'Social programs will continue, but they must support, not undermine a coherent economic strategy for the inner cities' (Porter, 1995). One point to keep in mind in social policy is that it should not rob people of their own initiative. Welfare support should not take away (too much of) the stimulus to people to take their own future in hand. That approach seems to be increasingly adopted. In Europe, the traditional concern of welfare state policy since the 1950s has been the establishment of an adequate 'safety net' for individuals and families in employment and retirement. While this has played a vital role in sustaining those most in need, many of whom were to be found in the most run-down neighbourhoods within the major cities, it was not until the 1980s that serious attention began to be paid to the longer run incentive effects or to the fiscal cost (OECD, 1996, p. 22).

To develop comprehensive policies to combat social problems (in reaction to an ad hoc, problem-led approach), the formulation of a vision and the development of a strategy are of critical importance. Social problems usually have a physical dimension (unattractive, badly maintained dwellings and a depressing living area) and/or an economic dimension (unemployment, low spending budget). An adequate approach to social problems therefore demands cooperation and coordination between institutions that happen to function alongside each other. Education, house building, spatial planning and economic development are domains that have considerable influence on combating social problems. The ability to set up social programmes and projects in a more strategic, comprehensive way is an important part of a city's *organising capacity*.

Organising capacity is understood here as the ability of those responsible to solve a problem to convene all partners (public and private, internal and external) concerned and jointly generate new ideas and develop and implement a policy that responds to fundamental developments and creates conditions for sustainable economic growth. Elements of organising capacity are: vision on long term sustainable development (for strategies, programmes and projects to hold on to); formulation of concrete, measurable objectives; strategic and coherent thinking and acting; leadership qualities to manage processes and projects adequately; creating and supporting strategic networks of relevant partners, needed to develop and implement policies successfully; creating political and societal support and emphasising communication strategies both within the city administration and as external communication (to citizens, companies, public bodies, and so on).

In the social sphere, organising capacity is closely bound up with the strategic networks of the parties involved. Public authorities play a dominant role because it usually is their first concern to take care of the sustainable well-being and prosperity of their citizens. But within the municipal organisation all kind of sectors and service departments (social services, economic affairs, spatial planning, real estate, health service, education, police, housing) that are not always accustomed to cooperation, are directly or indirectly involved. Bureaucratic organisation principles, traditional policy field classifications (often related to political portfolios), lack of market incentives (subsidies are fixed) and lack of result-orientation do not usually contribute to comprehensive and innovative thinking and acting. Next to the internally divided public actors a variety of institutions, mainly nonprofit organisations, are engaged in social care, education, job mediation, social housing, and so on. Even some segments of the commercial sector seem to realise that it is to their own advantage to prevent or reduce social tensions that threaten the urban revitalisation process in general. An increasing number of companies, understanding that the public sector and the 'social care' organisations by themselves cannot adequately solve the problems, are considering or reconsidering their societal responsibility, not as 'charity' but as a form of 'enlightened self-interest'.

These considerations have induced eight cities to participate in an investigation aiming to apply the concept of organising capacity to policy programmes and projects in the social sphere, an important reason being that so far results of social policy have not always given rise to much optimism. Much money may be spent on solving a problem without effective progress being accomplished. Cities keep trying to develop ideas for new approaches that hopefully will have the desired results. Never before has so much time and effort been spent in tackling problems and seizing opportunities, for instance in the field of unemployment, integration of ethnic minorities and physical, economic and social revitalisation. There is an increasing need for research in this field which can adequately support policy choices. So far, studies were often based on single policy fields and/or comparisons within country borders. The study of social policies on which this paper is based is in this respect quite unique. The comprehensive and cross-national perspective makes it possible to judge social policies in a much broader way.

1.2 Problem Statement, Objectives and Methodology

The problem statement of this research is: what social strategies do urban actors develop in response to social problems and how are they implemented to contribute in an effective and efficient way to a sustainable economic and social revitalisation? By trying to answer this question we want to achieve two objectives. Firstly, to deepen the theoretical knowledge of 'organising capacity' in cities confronting social challenges; and secondly, to generate practical knowledge by which cities can strengthen their 'organising capacity' on behalf of social revitalisation.

Methodology

The method used is an international comparison and evaluation of experiences with strategies (programmes, projects) in the social sphere. For the analysis a theoretical framework has been drawn up, based on international literature and the results of previous empirical research into the organising capacity of major metropolitan projects in European cities (van den Berg, Braun and van der Meer, 1997). This framework has been elaborated for this study and agreed upon by experts in the field of social policy and by representatives of the cities involved. The eight cities involved submitted a local programme or project for the analysis. The analysis of the cases is based on written documentation and on interviews with more than 90 key persons involved in social policy in the eight participating cities. A draft version of each case study could be commented on by the interview partners involved, as well as discussed among the members of the Steering Committee. During an international conference held in Eindhoven in April 2001 the final report has been the subject of discussion and reflection by internationally reputed academics in the social field and by representatives of the cities involved.

Selection of Cities

The city of Eindhoven, the initiator of the study, had proposed to conduct an investigation into the organising capacity of social policies among member cities of the Eurocities network. Seven other cities, Antwerp, Helsinki, Malmö, Rotterdam, Stockholm, Strasbourg and Utrecht decided to participate, the main reason being that they were convinced of the need to improve the organising capacity of their social policies. The selected cities offer a interesting mix of experiences with respect to, among other aspects, city size and population growth (growing versus stagnating populations), economic structure (port and industrial cities versus capital and service centre cities), economic performance (affluent cities versus cities whose economy is trailing behind the national average), local competence in the formulation and implementation of policy (rather autonomous cities versus cities more dependent on higher layers in the administrative hierarchy) and schemes to deal with social problems (cities much beset with them and others for which social segregation is a newish phenomenon). Table 1.1 presents some facts and figures about the cities included in this study.

Limitation

Programmes and projects in the sphere of social policy should offer solutions for (multiple or cumulated) complex social problems in cities. The present investigation does not cover the entire social policy field in the eight cities. The programmes or projects investigated follow submission criteria like a

Table 1.1   Demographic data of cities involved in this study

City	Population city	Share foreign extraction* (%)	Population urban region	Year	Growth population city (%)	Year
Rotterdam	593,000	44	1,080,000	1996	+2.9	1981–1996
Strasbourg	264,000	14	451,000	1999	+6.5	1990–1999
Antwerp	456,000	14	1,161,000	1995	–2.5	1991–1996
Malmö	247,000	11	618,000	1996	+1.1	1991–2001
Stockholm	762,000	10	1,762,000	1996	+11.0	1981–1996
Helsinki	539,000	5	1,155,000	1998	+10.2	1980–1996
Utrecht	234,000	29	548,000	1996	+1.0	1980–1996
Eindhoven	202,000	20	700,000	2000	+1.0	1980–1996

Note: These percentages have different definitions. The Dutch definition includes: ethnic minorities (based on native country of person him/ herself, his/her mother or his/her father from a selection of typical migration countries) and non-natives from other countries. The other percentages refer to non-nationals.

Sources: European Commission, 2000a and 2000b; van den Berg et al, 2001, p. 4.

minimum duration (two to three years at least), sufficient critical mass, a substantial scope including a multitude of policy fields and/or actors and preferably an innovative approach or innovative aspects. A major part of the social problems (and the policies addressing them) had to be left out of consideration. Nevertheless an attempt has been made, with the help of well-chosen examples, to find an answer to the problem statement and attain the objectives of the research. The limitation of the relatively small number of cases should be considered while interpreting the results of the study.

1.3   Theoretical Framework of Social Organising Capacity

Figure 1.1 displays the framework for the present research. It is based on the analytical framework of *Metropolitan Organising Capacity* as developed by van den Berg, Braun and van der Meer (1997). Organising capacity refers to the entire process from the identification of certain needs, through development of strategies and policy, to implementation of the policy and monitoring the results. This analytical framework has been elaborated and adapted to the specific features of social-revitalisation policies.

To our mind the key elements of organising capacity for policies of social revitalisation are the organisational 'tools' (the instruments with which to achieve an adequate social policy) and the policy process. The tools are relevant to all phases of the policy process. The explicit introduction of the metropolitan context (upper part of Figure 1.1) refers to the possibility that other factors than policy intervention, like a changing metropolitan context, can change problems and opportunities. The *output* of the policy process, that is the results of the policy intervention, and the *outcome*, that is the effectiveness of the entire process, may be influenced by a changing context. For instance, a policy oriented on empowering unemployed people to (re)enter the labour market will probably be more successful during a period with severe tension on the labour market than during periods with growing unemployment figures. The elements of the research framework will be described below.

General Metropolitan Profile

The metropolitan context is a strong determinator of economic and social opportunities and threats. Knowledge of the specific metropolitan context is necessary for understanding regional social problems and opportunities and policies pursued to fight or to seize them and to be able to draw lessons from

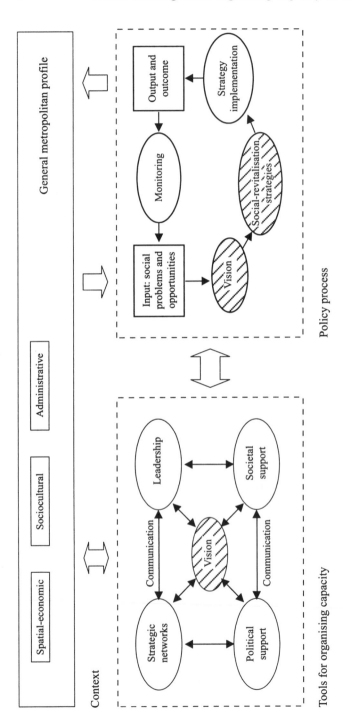

Figure 1.1   Theoretical framework of social organising capacity

social revitalisation policies of other cities. This knowledge can also help to understand the urgency of social problems. Changes in the metropolitan context can have a strong impact on the outcome of the policy process in the social sphere. Moreover the administrative context influences the preconditions under which actors (can) cooperate with each other. For a better understanding of the regional context of social-revitalisation policies, we have distinguished three relevant aspects: the spatial-economic context; the administrative context; and the sociocultural context.

For each case study, the general metropolitan context has to be investigated, including information about size, growth, demography, economic structure and economic development. Affluent cities will probably be better equipped to develop a policy of social revitalising and become less dependent on the support of, say, other governments. However, social problems in prosperous regions are often disguised by relatively high average prosperity figures. Social policy in less prosperous cities, on the contrary, will be more likely to need support from the national or European government or organisations outside the public sphere.

Moreover, some understanding of the administrative structure is important, since the government, and especially the local government, often has a key role to play in policies of social revitalising. Is any form of neighbourhood management practised, and if so, what are its competencies? Neighbourhood administrators can flexibly respond to initiatives from the bottom up. We need to know how effective and efficient such administrative organisations are, and what their culture is? National governments tend to develop broad frameworks for (new) urban social policies, but do not always provide corresponding financial support to local governments. The European authorities may also issue specific policy measures that stimulate local actors. The granting of means from the European Structural Funds, for instance, depends on local co-financing.

In the context attention is also given to social problems. Many metropolitan areas are subject to voluminous immigration flows from other countries. The presence of a variety of cultures (ethnic groups) may be fraught with specific problems. In the frame of this investigation they should be recognised. To be able to analyse the impact of social strategies or projects, it is first necessary to describe the relevant social problems together with their causes and backgrounds.

Tools for Organising Capacity

Vision It is assumed that vision is the key element of the tools for organising capacity. Without a vision of how to link social problems with opportunities, social policies will not lead to lasting results. Vision is the embodiment of the opportunity-oriented approach of social policies. It manifests itself on different levels: a broad general vision on the future development of the entire urban region; a vision on the social policy field; and visions on the level of social programmes and projects. On all levels the vision, the idea to combat social problems or to take social advantage of opportunities is the principal element. That is the reason why vision has been indicated as the central policy tool as well as the starting point for the policy process. A vision of social policy should ideally be evolved on the basis of the overall vision of the urban region. Social policy is traditionally oriented to the solution of social problems. An opportunity-oriented approach responds to chances. However, chances are often found in other fields, for instance in that of the economy, spatial development, housing or quality of living. Characteristics of an adequate vision on the level of social policy are multidisciplinarity and surpassing of the narrow policy field. Failing that, a vision will have to be developed just for the social policy field as such, without being embedded in a wider perspective.

A vision is a prerequisite for the integration of different aspects and the prevention of inconsistencies (van den Berg et al., 1997, p. 13). A vision helps to formulate objectives and strategies. In principle, the vision must be based on the interests and aims of all actors involved. Among the greatest obstacles to overcome on the road to social revitalising is the adequate formulation of the problem. Such an analysis should in principle have general support. Parties tend to define the problems in different ways.

Strategic networks Strategic networks can be conceived of as patterns of interaction between mutually dependent actors that evolve around policy problems or projects. A network consists of the total of relations linking (public and private) organisations, the relations being marked by a degree of two-way dynamics (van den Berg et al., 1997, p. 11). Networks among and within organisations have to be identified. As pointed out, to 'un-fence' the segments within organisations is of the essence to social policy. The aim is to find out who cooperates with whom in the development and implementation of social policies, and how and to what extent this cooperation takes place. Certain executive bodies actively engaged in the solution of social problems maintain direct formal relations with the local government. Others operate in formal independence and have to find another way to cooperate with the local government. Another matter to inquire into is whether there are incentives to cooperate, and if so, what incentives? Are they due, for instance, to subsidies or to mutual interests? On the other hand, lack of cooperation, agencies working in separate cocoons, are aspects that should be elicited as well.

Leadership Every organisation, programme or project needs a leading actor to initiate, continue and complete it. The assumption is that leadership of key actors contributes substantially to the successful design, development and implementation of projects. Leadership is a necessity, whether relying on specific competencies (the position in the administrative hierarchy, financial capabilities, specific know-how or other powers) or on the charisma of public or private individuals who successfully 'drive' the project (van den Berg et al., 1997, p. 12). An important aim of our case studies is to find out to what extent a particular type of leadership is crucial for the success of social policies and how this leadership arises.

Whereas good leadership is required on all levels, the necessary operational skills and the tactical and strategic insights vary among levels. A comprehensive approach makes high demands on the communicative skills of programme leaders. In a comprehensive approach within a divisional structure, leadership on the level of programmes requires intensive consultation, negotiation and adjustment with other programmes and with the public and private parties involved. Communicative skills are crucial in such a situation. Leadership is important not only on the level of a project leader or motor, but also on that of, say, the envisaged target group or neighbourhood. Leadership on the project level is focused on implementation; it should be operationally strong, and have a well developed relational component, because of the direct contact with the customers.

Leaders often occupy an essential key position between the rank and file and the institutions (for instance with respect to integration problems). A prominent aspect of leadership is stimulation with administering incentives. A project is initiated and propelled to achieve certain objectives. In a business company the objective is to yield a profit; the object of metropolitan projects can be to realise a new city quarter (and that implies setting distinct financial or economic targets). With social projects, the objectives are often less tangible and harder to measure. The commitment and enthusiasm of the actors involved often need to be stimulated otherwise. Because the results are less manifest, special efforts are needed to engage the actors' activity for a long span of time. To focus more explicitly on results may then be advisable. In matters of social policy, the part of director is often assumed by the government, but it may also be taken on by other organisations, such as NGOs (nongovernmental organisations).

Political support Social policy frequently depends on the political will to tackle social problems. Politicians are often key actors when new social programmes are to be introduced. Local politicians as well as national and even supranational ones have a voice in matters of social policy. Programmes drawn up on the higher government levels can serve as catalysts for the development of social programmes on the local level. Programmes of social policy initiated on the (supra)national level (such as the European Community Initiative Urban) often call for local sponsors, thus stimulating local commitment to social policy. The relative intangibility and invisibility of social policy makes it difficult to enlist political support.

Most politicians are keen to 'score' on certain themes. If the results of social policy are charted better, there may be opportunities for politicians to enhance their profile. Representative bodies can do much to create political support for the tackling of social problems. A municipal council, for instance, can put pressure on the proper authorities to deal energetically and decisively with certain problems. This can stimulate the actors involved in the project implementation.

Societal support No matter how valuable a project might be for sustainable metropolitan development, lack of support from those directly involved (the 'clients' or 'customers') or interested parties, notably inhabitants or private investors) may curtail the chances of successful implementation (van den Berg et al., 1997, p. 13). One point to keep in mind is the need to get people more committed to their own neighbourhoods and to develop 'local pride'. In cities, the residents often lack such involvement. Societal support for measures to overcome social problems depends on the active involvement of citizens/ target groups. In the United States, and also in the Netherlands, there is a growing interest in approaches that underline the importance of social networks (networks of civic engagement) as a condition for successful social policy (community empowerment). That is why the creation and maintenance of social networks in cities is so important.

Communication While *vision* is the starting point of everything, *communication* is needed to convey the message of the vision to the networks involved: the (potential) leaders, the politicians and the society; and the very important target groups of the social policy. Much communication will proceed through the regular media channels (newspapers, regional/local radio/TV and the Internet). The actors involved in the social policy should make proper use of those channels to create social support. Excessive media attention for occasional disturbances and instances of pointless violence can build up strong incidental support for the solution of certain social problems, but 'regular' measures of social policy, which draw less publicity, could well do with some more positive attention.

The local government and other relevant actors will have to work out an adequate communication strategy to explain the importance of social problems and of the policy to be conducted to the population at large. Adequate mutual communication between the 'social partners' and the population appears to be a crucial success factor for (policies) of social revitalisation. Communication helps to chart the social problems and to reinforce the political and social support for the policy.

The Policy Process

Policy implementation and output Policy development implies the translation of the strategies into the 'right' policy measures. The objectives must always be clearly formulated so that their suitability in the broader vision and strategy of the urban region can be judged and their effects, after some time, evaluated. All dimensions of the social policy have to be considered: object, functions, scale, domain, method, and the mutual relationships of the actors involved. The implementation of policy consists in the acquisition of means, the allotting of partial tasks, and the execution of the strategy. Of particular interest is the output: how adequately has the strategy been implemented? Were there sufficient financial and human resources available for the effective execution of the measures as proposed in the strategy? Quality criteria will not be thoroughly treated here. Cities have much experience on that score and we do not want to lose into a surfeit of details. Ultimately the success of social policy depends on the proper implementation of measures introduced to achieve the aims envisaged. To that end, the right actors have to be activated and good feedback instruments must be at hand for constant monitoring.

Monitoring and outcome The orientation of social policy is observed to shift from input to result. The implication is that more attention should be given to evaluation and monitoring. That is useful to gain insight into the degree to which the formulated objectives of social strategies have been attained. The outcomes of monitoring enable those in charge whether the strategy should be cancelled, adjusted or continued. Without periodic monitoring there is not much that can usefully be said about the success of a social strategy. The outcomes of monitoring permit comparison of the actual results with those envisaged or with the benchmarks formulated in the strategy. Measuring the performance makes feedback to the actors possible. Should shortcomings come to light, then the organisational instruments and/or products need to be adjusted. Did the problems diminish, did nothing change or did they even increase?

1.4   Social Strategies and Projects

Programmes and Projects Submitted for Analysis

The following programmes and projects have been submitted by the cities involved (see also Table 1.2):

1   Rotterdam: *integrated area approach* for the borough of Hoogvliet, regarding conditions set by the national *Major Cities Policy*, including a large-scale house demolition and rebuilding project making use of past experiences with urban renewal.
2   Strasbourg: *implementing a new management scheme* to improve the organisation of social intervention in order to make it more customer-oriented and to promote partnerships between the organisations involved.
3   Antwerp: *organisational reforms* and a well-formulated social strategy as prime conditions for an opportunity-oriented comprehensive social policy, according to the objectives of the Flemish *Social Impulse Fund*.
4   Malmö: innovative attempt at *integration and employment* in the subdistrict of Hyllie by enlisting capacities of immigrants and using an integrated approach, as part of the national *Metropolitan Initiative*.
5   Stockholm: *innovative opportunity-oriented ways to fight unemployment* in the subdistrict of Norrmalm by mobilising relevant local players, following the concept of the European *Territorial Employment Pacts*.
6   Helsinki: a *strategy to prevent social exclusion and segregation* by promoting strategic partnerships between relevant partners, both within and outside the city administration, and by supporting citizens' initiatives.
7   Utrecht: establishment of a *district service centre* in Northeast Utrecht aiming to improve customer orientation by bringing the municipality closer

Table 1.2   Strategies submitted by the cities

City	Programme name	Sponsors	Functions
Rotterdam	Integrated Area Approach	National government City	Physical renewal, social investment, employment
Strasbourg	Masterplan for Social Intervention	City National government Département	Reorganisation, physical renewal, employment
Antwerp	Social Impulse Fund	Region City	Reorganisation, integrationemployment, physical renewal
Malmö	Metropolitan Initiative	National government City	Employment, integration, education
Stockholm	Territorial Employment Pact	European Union City	Employment
Helsinki	Strategy against Social Exclusion and Segregation	City	Employment, stimulating partnerships
Utrecht	District Service Centre	City	Reduction of distance between city-citizen
Eindhoven	Chain Approach to Addicts	National government City	Reintegration, reduction nuisance

to the citizens. Questions regarding municipal and social services (housing, and even police) are physically combined in a 'social shop'.
8   Eindhoven: *Handles for Recovery*; a network project aiming to reduce drug-related nuisance and to promote social reintegration of addicts by offering them a chain of services and involving citizens and business companies.

The order chosen is in line with the scope of the programmes and projects submitted: from broad comprehensive programmes to individual projects with a more limited scope.

Actors Involved in Social Policy

This investigation is concerned with the organising capacity incorporated in social programmes and projects in cities. In principle, therefore, the organising capacity will be considered of all actors involved within an urban region. Not only public parties, but also, for instance, business companies and NGOs, will be included. What organisations are actively involved, what are their respective roles and how does networking among them proceed? Business actors show an increasing inclination to participate in actions to revitalise (social structures in) urban districts.

   The actors involved have certain perceptions of present levels of well-being and prosperity among the population of their urban region, and also certain ambitions on that score. They want to reduce the discrepancy between their ambition and the levels they perceive. However, the population groups differ among themselves in the perception of discrepancies. Together the relevant actors will have to arrive at a satisfactory formulation of the social policy to be implemented.

1.5   Structure of the Book

Chapters 2–9 are devoted to the case studies. These chapters have more or less the same format. Each case study starts with an introduction. Next, a concise general metropolitan profile is presented, containing some socioeconomic and administrative characteristics and an overview of social problems in the city and, in some cases, in a specific city district. The following section is a description of the social strategy, programme or project in that particular city. An important topic in this section is the introduction of the actors involved and their respective contributions. The next section is the analysis itself: the confrontation of the social strategy with the elements of the research framework. In this section both the policy *tools* and policy *process* will be dealt with. Each case study chapter is completed with a summary of the main conclusions.

Chapter 10, the synthesis of the study, is written as an 'executive summary'. It can be read separately; it summarises the successive parts of the report: the motive to undertake this exercise, the problem statement and the eight case studies. The principal part of the synthesis is the analysis based on the elements of the theoretical framework. For both the policy tools and the policy process the main findings of the case studies will be recapitulated and assessed in a comparative way. The analysis of the case studies also resulted in what we have indicated as an evolution in the approach to social policies. The synthesis is concluded with a condensed summary of the main findings.

Chapter 2

Integrated Area Approach in Rotterdam-Hoogvliet

2.1 Introduction

Since the early 1980s the harbour city of Rotterdam has suffered from a high rate of unemployment and related social problems inherent in metropolises, through the decline and loss of several port-related basic industries. While an energetic approach has changed Rotterdam's economic position and physical aspect in a positive way, the social dichotomy is still very much in evidence. The Integrated Area Approach (IAA) has heralded a new phase of urban and social renewal in Rotterdam, a phenomenon with which the city has already had a lot of experience. The new approach aims at the integrated economic, physical and social revitalisation of Rotterdam's backward neighbourhoods. Six out of the 13 boroughs are selected for the IAA, among which is the borough of Hoogvliet, the subject of the Rotterdam case study. The efforts in Hoogvliet concentrate on a thorough physical restructuring. One quarter of the low quality, post-war apartment buildings will be demolished and replaced with more attractive housing. Hopefully, the operation will also make the whole area more attractive as a place of residence, and to that end much attention has been paid to the social aspects of the demolition and rebuilding process, aspects that have often been neglected in the past. Another important issue of this case is the relation between the municipality of Rotterdam and the borough of Hoogvliet. The data of the metropolitan profile of Rotterdam are summarised in Table 2.1.

2.2 Social-economic Profile of the Rotterdam Region

Situation in the Randstad Conurbation

Rotterdam is located in the Rhine delta, on Europe's busiest river and is connected with the world's busiest sea. The Rotterdam region has approximately 1.1 million inhabitants and is situated less than 30 km from

Table 2.1   Data of metropolitan profile of Rotterdam

Characteristic	Rotterdam
Population of the city (1996)	593,000
Population of the urban region (1996)	1,080,000
Growth of the urban population (city, %, 1981–96)	+2.9
Share of the population of foreign extraction (city, %, 2000)	44
Proportion of population of working age in employment (city, %, 1996)	53
Unemployment rates (city, %, 1996)	7.2
Proportion of employment in industry (city, %, 1993–97)	18.2
Proportion of employment in services (city, %, 1993–97)	81.7
Number of administrative tiers (including state and boroughs)	3
Borough Boards	Yes

Sources: van denBerg, Braun and Meer, 1998, p. 257; Centrum voor Onderzoek en Statistiek, www.cos.nl; European Commission, 2000, Vol. 1, p. 122; idem, Vol. 2, pp. 110, 186.

the regions of The Hague (700,000 people), Delft/Westland (250,000) and the 'Drecht' cities (Dordrecht region, 210,000). The Rotterdam region is part of the Randstad conurbation, together with the city regions of Amsterdam, The Hague, Utrecht and some smaller urban regions inbetween. The Randstad (including the 'Green Heart') covers about one-quarter of the Dutch territory and houses about two-fifths (6 million) of the Dutch population. It has no formal status, extends across three of the 12 provinces and covers a large number of independent municipalities. The recently published national spatial planning memorandum emphasises the forming of a strategic urban network called 'Delta Metropolis', a new name for an old idea, but now considered a chance to cope with changing international competitive positions resulting from globalisation and the emerging information society (Ministry of Housing, Planning and the Environment, 2001). As well as one of the world's largest seaports, Rotterdam has a small regional airport (which is mainly used for business flights) and is a prominent transport and distribution hub for rail, road and water traffic. Rotterdam Central Station will be connected to the high-speed rail link Amsterdam-Schiphol-Brussels-Paris/London in 2005.

Demography

Rotterdam, the second city of the Netherlands, recorded 593,000 inhabitants in 1996. Since the end of the nineteenth century (when industries such as shipbuilding, dock work, petrochemicals and wholesale trade were flourishing), Rotterdam's population had rapidly grown to a peak of 740,000 residents by 1965. From the 1970s onward, the increased prosperity and shifting housing preferences, smaller households and a national housing policy favouring spatial deconcentration, caused a net population drop of some 175,000 in 20 years. The highly selective suburbanisation process, together with the effects of the energy crises of 1973 and 1978, resulted in serious social-economic problems in the early 1980s. Drastic policy changes on the national and local level (allotting housing schemes to big cities and not only to selected suburbs; state participation in large scale urban revitalisation schemes), coupled with new economic chances for cities, helped to turn the tide. Since 1985 the population has been growing again. The present number is 593,000. More than 28 per cent (160,000) of the inhabitants belong to 'ethnic minorities'. The largest groups among them are people from Surinam (50,000), Turkey (40,000), Morroco (30,000), the Antilles (16,000) and Cape Verdia (14,000). Moreover, 90,000 inhabitants (15 per cent) are foreigners, adding up to a 44 per cent share with a non-native Dutch background. The population in the suburban ring rose from about 275,000 in 1960 to 574,000 in 2000. The regional growth in the period 1970–2000 was between 2,000 and 3,000 annually. The number of dwellings in Rotterdam increased from 201,000 in 1960 to 284,000 in 2000. In the region as a whole the increase was from 273,000 to 522,000. The average occupation size in Rotterdam dropped from 3.6 in 1960 to 2.1 in 2000.

Economy

The seaport complex is the pillar of the regional economy. Rotterdam ('Gateway to Europe') serves as an important international logistic node and centre of trade. In 1999 transhipments amounted to 323 million tonnes, considerably more than those of its European competitors. The total (direct and indirect) contribution to the national economy is estimated at nearly €28 billion annually (RCDC, 1998). Until well into the 1960s the Rotterdam (and Dutch) economy expanded so fast that 'guest labourers' (from Turkey and Morroco mainly) were attracted to those (simple and dirty) vacant jobs for which Dutch workers were hard to find. From the middle of the 1960s industrial development stagnated. Shipbuilding and ship repair ran into difficulties and new growth sectors were poorly represented in the city. As people became more aware of the environment, Rotterdam acquired a bad reputation as far as quality of the living environment was concerned. The vulnerable Rotterdam economy suffered heavily under the economic recession of the early 1980s. Unemployment in the city quickly rose to one-fifth of the active population (about 60,000 people were unemployed).

In the 1970s an extensive urban-renewal programme, almost entirely publicly financed, had been staged and to a great extent carried out (predominantly rehabilitation of the social residential function), and through investments in the port, Rotterdam managed to consolidate its position as main port. From the mid-1980s onward, the economy started to grow again, helped by an energetic urban revitalisation policy. Companies such as Unilever, ING (banking and insurance), Stad Rotterdam (insurance), Robeco Group (investment company), Mees & Hope (banking), Nedlloyd (shipping) and Crédit Lyonnais (banking) invested in new offices in the town centre, often of striking architecture. The office space increased from 2.5 million square metres in 1986 to 3.6 million in 1999 (COS, 2000). A new World Trade Centre was completed as well as a casino, a new conference venue linked to the concert hall, exclusive high-rise apartment buildings, new shopping opportunities, etc. The large-scale revitalisation scheme *Kop-van-Zuid*, connected with the city centre by an eye-catching 140 metres tall landmark bridge, provided space for city centre expansion in former dock lands. Here, too, public and private investment in offices, residential functions and leisure activities is going on. The metamorphosis gave the city its modern identity and international character. In recent years the city has developed more and more explicitly into a city of art and culture. Its nomination as Cultural Capital of Europe (together with Porto) in 2001 confirms the ambition not only to be known as a port city but to change its image into that of a diversified, modern European city.

Since 1996, employment (especially in business and health services) has grown substantially, but the Rotterdam economy still lags behind that of other Dutch cities (like Amsterdam) and the national average. The officially registered unemployment figure decreased from 38,000 (17 per cent of the active population) in 1994 to 18,000 people (7 per cent) in 2000 (COS, 2000). Comparable national figures are 8 per cent in 1994 and 3 per cent in 2000, which is less than half that of the Rotterdam percentages. According to municipal statistics people looking for a job, the nonregistered included, amount to 34,000 (16,000 more than the 'official' figure). Moreover, 50,000 persons are entitled to social allowances. The participation degree is 59 per cent (working people as a percentage of the population between the ages of 15 and 65), which is rather low.

Because the port and transport are no longer major employers, the Rotterdam authorities try to support the diversification of the economy by stimulating some promising clusters, such as ICT, media, health care and tourism. However, most policy attention is still focused on port and port-related activities. Table 2.2 shows the present employment structure of Rotterdam.

Table 2.2   The employment structure of Rotterdam (1999)

Sector	Employed persons	Per cent
Agriculture	618	0.2
Industry	30,406	10.3
Public utilities	1,501	0.5
Construction	16,116	5.5
Trade	40,541	13.8
Transport/communication	40,214	13.6
Financial institutions	17,686	6.0
Business services	54,612	18.5
Public services	72,998	24.8
Hotels and catering	8,440	2.9
Culture, leisure and other services	11,618	3.9
Total	294,750	100.0

Source: 'Kerncijfers Rotterdam', COS, 1999.

Administrative Framework

Compared to most other European countries, municipalities in the Netherlands are financially strongly dependent on general and specific payments by the State (more than four-fifths of the municipal income), but local authority is fairly free to formulate its own policies and spend its own budget. Many policies are decentralised, which gives cities the opportunity to develop integrated strategies. The Grotestedenbeleid (GSB, Major City Policy), initiated by the state in 1994, is a clustering and coordination of city-oriented grants, subsidies and city policies from nine ministries. The cities involved in the programme have to draw up an integrated social strategy that has to be approved by the state. On the basis of the implementation and evaluation of the strategy, contracts are signed between the local and national authorities.

In the 1980s, discussions started (again!) on reforming the administrative organisation by forming metropolitan authorities in the seven largest urban regions. However, in – unofficial – referenda held in Amsterdam and Rotterdam an overwhelming majority of citizens voted against that initiative. The national authorities withdrew their plans and what is left is a formalised regional cooperation body in which autonomous municipalities are committed to reach agreement about the planning and execution of a restricted number of regional, mainly space-related tasks.

Role of Boroughs

To better conduct affairs of direct concern to communities on district level, the two largest cities in the Netherlands have a system of subdistricts or boroughs (*deelgemeenten*). Boroughs have their own elected local governors, who concern themselves with affairs directly affecting citizens. The borough has no complete package of public tasks, but it is practice that the municipality consults the boroughs in all matters that are of interest to them. Boroughs are responsible for local welfare policy and for the management (less for the implementation) of projects. Boroughs are better informed about local needs and because of their restricted size they can operate in a more coherent, integral way. They are financially dependent on the municipality. They receive funds for implementing policy in the fields of employment, borough economy and safety, but they are more or less free to decide how to spend their budget. The Amsterdam boroughs are more independent than the Rotterdam ones. Contrary to the situation in Rotterdam, they can carry out works themselves (by their own departments). They can also decide to work together, for instance to reach scale advantages.

Borough of Hoogvliet

Rotterdam consists of 13 boroughs (the city centre included), averaging 45,000 residents. One of them is Hoogvliet, located in the south-west of the city. Hoogvliet is one of the six Rotterdam boroughs hit by severe social problems and selected for the 'integrated area approach policy'. Hoogvliet was built in the 1950s as a satellite town of Rotterdam, to provide housing for port workers in a rather open and green environment. The Shell Company built houses for their own workers. However, Hoogvliet did not grow according to the plans, which envisaged a 'final' population of 60,000. National spatial policy stimulated the growth of nearby Spijkenisse. Today Hoogvliet has 37,000 inhabitants. Many of the original settlers still live there. This has resulted in a high share of senior citizens. Since the 1970s many people of foreign descent moved into Hoogvliet, especially from Surinam and the Antilles. By now 30 per cent have a foreign background, most of whom live in the North-Hoogvliet quarter (43 per cent of foreign extraction).

2.3   Social Problems in Rotterdam

In the Netherlands, the most severe social exclusion problems are concentrated in the four largest cities that form the Randstad. Among them, Rotterdam has been traditionally one of the most affected by problems such as unemployment and immigration. Registered unemployment in Rotterdam during the 1990s was twice as high as the national average. Almost 47 per cent of the job seekers were of ethnic origin and 74 per cent had little or no skills (Miedema en Oude Engberink, 1999). As mentioned before, the port and its related activities have always been the main source of employment in Rotterdam. This has influenced the social structure of the city, which is characterised by a broad base of 'blue-collar' workers of low education, a weak middle class and an almost nonexistent upper class. The great concentration of ethnic minorities in the city (28 per cent) is related to this working profile.

In the 1960s, as fast industrial growth boosted the demand for labour, the first workers from abroad began to arrive, especially from Italy and Greece, followed later by workers from Turkey and Morocco. To accommodate all those new inhabitants, the municipal government began to build new neighbourhoods at the eastern and southern outskirts of the city. At the same time, a process of suburbanisation took place as the younger and more mobile families began to leave the city, leaving behind a scene of impoverishment and degradation. In 1975 the former colony of Surinam gained independence, and many Surinam citizens flocked to the Netherlands, especially to Amsterdam and Rotterdam, having free access as Dutch nationals. They tended to concentrate in the old neighbourhoods and quickly joined the ranks of unemployed people drawing social assistance. Those were the years that determined the social structure of the city.

Under the economic recession of the early 1980s, unemployment in the city rose to one-fifth of the active population, the ethnic minorities being most affected. In particular, the number of Turkish and Moroccans unemployed rose sharply. Again by the mid-1980s, as the city began to rehabilitate its economic structure, the immigrants and other low-skilled groups were to suffer. There ensued a distinct polarisation between those participating in the new information society and those left behind, huddling together in the meaner town quarters. Socially vulnerable groups are old-age pensioners, one-parent families, long-term unemployed and households of foreign ethnic origin. In 1999, about 17 per cent of the Rotterdam population were dependent on some kind of social benefit. In 1996, the average disposable income was 20 per cent below the national average. In this respect Rotterdam takes the 569th position of the 572 Dutch municipalities (COS, 2000). Associated with unemployment and relative poverty are the well-known big-city problems of exclusion, crime, alcohol and drug abuse, etc.

Social Problems in Hoogvliet

From the Hoogvliet Strategic Note, when the GSB was initiated in 1995, the key problems were: a high crime rate in certain neighbourhoods; youth problems (caused in particular by young Antilleans); tension between groups of foreign and indigenous extraction and between old and young people; the hardships suffered by young single (Antillean) mothers; a higher-than-average rate of unemployment; hard-to-let flats; a distressingly low average level of education and skill; poor chances for inhabitants to improve themselves socially; an obvious downward spiral in some neighbourhoods; and a poor image (Deelgemeente Hoogvliet, 1999). The situation in some neighbourhoods was defined as 'tragic'. A few years of GSB-policy and a favourable economic tide have by now achieved some positive development, but weak points and threats still abound.

2.4 The Integrated Area Approach

Urban Policy in Rotterdam[1]

The programme of the city council, which was in office until 2002, built on to Koers 2005 (Course), a vision of the future in which Rotterdam has laid down its ambitions to take its place as a service city and regional core of culture, entertainment, shopping and tourism, as well as to make the city more attractive to entrepreneurs, residents and visitors (Van der Vegt, 1998). The council's four-year policy programme 'Met raad en daad' (which can be translated as 'By council and action' as well as 'By counsel and action') translated that vision into 10 implementation programmes (see Table 2.3). Recently, the city council presented a new vision (Visie 2010) in line with the programme of the council.

Table 2.3   Themes of the Rotterdam council programme 'Met raad en daad'

Theme 1: Strong city
Economy and work: more work and a sound urban economy
Sustainable city: Rotterdam as strong city with future value
Space for Rotterdam people: Spatial Plan Rotterdam 2010 and Attractive City

Theme 2: Valuable neighbourhoods
Neighbourhood approach: Major Cities Policy and social activation proceed in unison
Clean and in good repair: Rotterdam should be appreciated as a clean city
Safe: more safety in Rotterdam

Theme 3: Concerned citizens
Fight against social exclusion and poverty: a 'one-hundred-percent poverty policy'
Growing up in Rotterdam: youth policy including education

Theme 4: Enterprising government
Government 2000+: friendly approach and citizens' participation

Source: 'Met raad en daad; Council's programme, 1998–2002', City of Rotterdam, 1998.

Integrated Area Approach (IAA)

The intention of this approach is to tackle the difficulties of backward neighbourhoods (unemployment, educational arrears, poverty, drugs trade, crime, lack of safety) by a combination of existing sectorial policy and implementation practices. The idea is to combine available means and channel them to specific zones of the town. On behalf of the IAA, three types of measure are combined.

1   The Dutch Major City Policy (GSB), which sets out to create new employment in major cities, reinstate safety in the streets, stimulate the integration of migrants and bring the standard of living up to par. The Minister for Major City Policy has defined it as follows. GSB in the Netherlands combines expertise, money and human resources to take in hand a town's economic, social and physical problems as well as its prospects in an integrated manner. The objective is to accomplish 'the complete town', a town in which everybody feels at home, which has economic vitality, provides employment to whoever wants it, a town where the living is good, the neighbourhoods clean and the streets safe, where all

residents are participants and no-one is left out or behind. GSB distinguishes an economic, a social and a physical pillar. Three aspects can be perceived: the need to integrate policy practices (integrality), a bottom-up approach (decentralisation), and evaluation of the policy by measurable objectives.

2   Urban Renewal, another nationwide policy (Ministry of Housing, Spatial Planning and the Environment), meant in particular to boost the competitive power of the living and working environments in urban areas. Central to this policy is the integrated approach to the physical-spatial structure.

3   Social investment, aiming to increase citizens' empowerment. Social problems and their solutions are defined by key persons in their own neighbourhoods. Priority number one is investing in people, to enable them to become self-supporting and making them not or less dependent on social assistance. Safe, clean and intact areas, special youth programmes, upbringing support, single mothers support, etc. are among the subjects of this programme.

On the national level, the GSB policy is looked upon as a means to coordinate and combine several (partly available) means for the integral tackling of urban problems. Rotterdam has added the aspects of Urban Renewal and Social Investment to GSB to arrive at an integral area-oriented policy. Moreover, Rotterdam has incorporated the European programmes Objective 2 and URBAN 2, as far as funds from those programmes can be used for the benefit of designated boroughs.

It should be stated here that the IAA is a temporary programme and that regular, mostly national programmes in the field of social policy are carried on normally. It means that on the municipal level, IAA is considered a 'side' programme, although a very important one. Indeed, policy choices made in the context of the IAA are not a directive for the regular programmes.

The total costs of GSB policy for all 25 towns involved in the 2000–2004 period are estimated at €46 billion. Of this amount, the state accounts for €7.5 billion, of which about €4.5 billion go to the four largest cities (G4). The costs of GSB policy in Rotterdam are estimated at €6.1 billion, of which the state puts up €1.5 billion. The whole sum is distributed as follows among the three pillars recognised in Rotterdam: €3.7 billion for the physical pillar, €2 billion for the economic pillar, and €400 million for the social pillar. So, in terms of money, physical policy is by far the most important element of GSB policy in Rotterdam.

IAA Policy Intentions in Rotterdam

The policy intentions pay considerable attention to the social aspect; the social pillar is the core of the Urban Vision and the IAA. Great importance is attached to the consolidation of social networks and citizens' commitment to and solidarity with their city. In that vein of thought the following objectives of the IAA, based on social principles, have been formulated:

1   to invest in the 'heart' of Rotterdam on the basis of the ideas among inhabitants themselves. The town should respond to and make use of their potentialities, ambitions and insights;
2   to use the power of individual differences. The distinctive properties of individuals, groups and areas offer a fertile basis from which to build up a structure of opportunities;
3   cultural expression as an element of self-esteem. For a successful IAA, one should have an eye open for any cultural values residents have to offer in the form of customs and traditions, stories, music, arts and crafts;
4   to catch on to and make use of social networks to initiate progress. To develop themselves, individuals appear to draw more support from social networks than from official agencies. Therefore, to stimulate such networks seems an effective way to prevent social exclusion;
5   an approach geared to mutual profit – a complex of measures which allows people to develop their capacity eventually to go forward under their own steam. A great challenge would be to find out how the results of exertions and investment in one sector can be transferred to others;
6   to carry the urban concept over into the borough: a good division of tasks between borough and municipality, and a city-feeling in the boroughs. Metropolitan provisions should serve the boroughs, and the heartbeat of the city should be felt there too;
7   organisation: the role of the government, and that of the citizens, social institutions and private sector. The government should take a position somewhere in between wielding the power to change society and laissez-faire. Some serious thinking about the optimum reach of government intervention is warranted.

So, the variety of needs and opportunities of the residents, their social networks and their involvement with the neighbourhood and the city are thus prominent objects of the Rotterdam IAA. How far the policy intentions are, or can be, translated into practical policy measures, and whether the policy accents are adequately reflected in the division of means, remains an interesting question.

The Hoogvliet IAA Project

The IAA plans for Hoogvliet are laid down in the investment plan 'Hoogvliet, a Proud City', drawn up by the borough itself. Within a decade, the borough wants to:

- raise the quality of the housing stock considerably;
- create a fully-fledged city centre with attractive provisions;
- enhance the image;
- attract more economic activity;
- improve the educational services;
- improve the leisure services (connections with the *Oude Maas* river and the green belt);
- create more opportunities for migrants;
- strengthen the social cohesion.

For the 2000–2010 period, some €90 million in financial support was allocated to Hoogvliet in the framework of the IAA. The total investment envisaged is a multiple of that amount.

In its management vision for the period 1998–2002 the borough formulated its mission as follows: 'Together with residents, entrepreneurs and NGOs in the social field, realise a proud city within the region.' From that formula, the IAA mission for Hoogvliet can be derived as: to ensure that Hoogvliet develops into a normal, vital borough of Rotterdam, capable of advancing under its own steam, offering an appealing housing and business climate, along with good educational services and a tight social fabric. Five programme objectives have been formulated:

1 being housed to one's liking;
2 a feeling of togetherness in housing and living;
3 education and work;
4 safety nets and care;
5 favourable location climate.

The rather ambitious programme has been worked out into some 60 projects, distributed across the physical, social and economic pillars.

Physical Pillar

The core of the programme is the replacement of a major portion of the housing stock. In the whole of Hoogvliet, one-quarter of the existing dwellings will be demolished (4,500 out of the 17,500 dwellings). In principle, an equal number of housing units will return. In the first instance, investment will be mainly in social housing. Later, houses 'for the market', now in short supply, will be built. In November 1999, a start was made with the demolition of the *Waaier* (fan), the neighbourhood where Shell used to house its employees. For years a symbol of Hoogvliet's decline, this zone has now become the symbol of the borough's renewal. In the neighbourhood North-Hoogvliet one-third of the housing stock is being demolished; the unattractive and very small houses registered an average vacancy of more than two years. The new houses will be much more to the taste of the residents, who in particular want more spacious dwellings. The objective is to give Hoogvliet residential accommodation appealing and varied enough for the residents who want to stay in Hoogvliet, even when their housing requirements change. Hoogvliet should offer opportunities for a 'housing career' that until now have hardly existed: attractive and spacious dwellings were in short supply, as were owner-occupied houses. An inquiry into the quality of the housing supply disclosed that seven out of 10 Hoogvliet residents wanted to move out because of the poor quality of the available houses.

The policy of demolishing houses and replacing them with more appealing ones has been pursued for some 10 years. Now, an explicit choice has been made to try and do so while preserving the social coherence. The Housing Corporation Maasoevers is rebuilding half the number of demolished premises, and the present inhabitants will be the first eligible for the new houses.

In the course of the years, many relatively affluent people have left Hoogvliet for the neighbouring municipality of Spijkenisse, where suitable owner-occupier houses could already be bought and a subsidy was granted to those wanting to settle there. All over the Netherlands there is a clear trend towards a wider choice of tenancy houses. The greater variety on the tenancy market stretches to the more expensive segments. Failure on the part of Hoogvliet to offer a competitive choice of houses has a distinct push effect on the local population, as has indeed been manifest for some time now. The intention of the policy now adopted is to turn the housing supply into a pull factor for new inhabitants and a keep factor for the present residents. Hopefully, an inflow of more affluent citizens will raise the status of the borough and be an incentive for a more adequate and varied supply of services.

Social Pillar

Reinforcement of social structures. The inflow of several groups of immigrants as well as the impending demolition put the social structures under heavy pressure. Projects are being set up to nurture more mutual understanding and more involvement in the environment among the populace. The initial design set up was to make the primary school the heart of the neighbourhood. It was to be the focal point of all manner of actions supposed to reinforce the social coherence of neighbourhoods. That thought is now being abandoned in favour of efforts on the one hand to widen the target group (the neighbourhood is more than just parents and children) and on the other not to put too heavy a burden on the schools. Actions to strengthen the social fabric are now undertaken from community centres and meeting places in the apartment blocks are being made available (by the housing corporations, for instance) to facilitate neighbourhood meetings.

Education and work Hoogvliet has an alarmingly low educational level. A prominent problem is that many 4-year-old children are backward in cognitive and social skills. This problem forms Hoogvliet's major social challenge, certainly while the IAA is an opportunity-oriented approach. The educational services will have to be much improved to remedy that situation and other deficiencies. Adult education should also become more widely available. Those involved (schools, associations, welfare NGOs and others) have concluded a covenant committing them to raising the quality of education. Four spearheads have been distinguished: day school for the two- to four-year-olds; improved primary education; a more comprehensive type of school; and reduction of premature school leaving.

Attention to people who have trouble fending for themselves in society Three groups in particular are at stake: single mothers (in North Hoogvliet, 45 per cent of the families with children are one-parent ones), senior citizens whose dwellings are being demolished, and the relatively large inflow of Antilleans (who often have a poor command of the Dutch language and hardly any schooling). From the local population has sprung the idea of 'mothers meet mothers' (teenager and 'normal' mothers). Next in importance to trying to get children on the track, is the idea to invest in mothers, in the hope that a better education will keep the children from going astray. A special project in progress for some time is the private initiative of Schildkamp's boxing school. Efforts are made to teach young people not only the art of boxing but also imbue them with a sense of accepted norms and values. In the early 1990s there was rather a lot of crime in North Hoogvliet, in which Antilleans were often involved. With the help of European subsidies and other resources, projects have been started to take the problems in hand, with good success. With more Antilleans in Hoogvliet than before, criminal actions among them have diminished. A 'care and safety net' package has enabled the borough to get closer to the problems and relieve the anonymity in which Antilleans tended to live.

Economic Pillar

By the creation of attractive provisions Hoogvliet hopes to attract and bind more business companies and (affluent) residents. At present, Hoogvliet still boasts relatively few well-to-do inhabitants, which reflects on the (rather low) level of services. That in turn affects the status of the borough, which is quite negative among outsiders, though remarkably enough not among the residents themselves. The borough's closeness to port and industrial zones and the rather monotonous apartment buildings may be to blame. The most important element of the economic pillar is the revitalisation of the centre, where quite a lot of open space is available. The idea is to give the area greater appeal by infrastructure operations and by filling the empty spaces with new buildings for offices and business companies, the leisure industry included. The plans also envisage a reduction in the number of shopping precincts in Hoogvliet from eight to five, which will be made more attractive by, among other things, a more up-to-date infrastructure and well-appointed public space. Neighbourhood shopping centres that stand to lose their retail function will be converted into local industrial centres.

Main economic locations for Hoogvliet are the business park *Gadering* and the office location by the new city-railway station of the same name. There is quite a healthy demand for those two sites. Both are considered to be of prominent significance for the economic development of Hoogvliet. One branch thought promising for Hoogvliet is the ICT-sector, notably port-linked logistic ICT. Efforts are also being made to strengthen tourist activity along the river Oude Maas.

International Building Exhibition

A project that is separate from the investment programme in the IAA framework but that fits perfectly into the policy of raising Hoogvliet's low status, is the proposed International Building Exhibition (IBT). This long-term project endeavours to respond in an innovative way to a new challenge covering a wide area. The ambition is to follow the example of a comparable project in the German Ruhr Area (IBA-Emserpark), where former business parks and industrial buildings were given new functions. However, while the German exhibition was devoted to physical aspects only, the Hoogvliet planners have a broader scheme in mind. As well as to architectural aspects they want to give attention to the social and community effects of spatial-physical intervention. Preparations for the exhibition have recently been started, following the positive outcome of a feasibility study.

Monitoring, Evaluation

Deliberate efforts have been made to choose objectives that are measurable, as is required in the context of the GSB, the Major Cities Policy. For each partial project the objective, the present state of affairs, the budget, the planning and the consistency with other projects have been laid down. Progress is reported on twice a year. In cooperation with the Ministry of Health, Welfare and Sports, through a special programme *'Heel de Buurt'* ('All the Neighbourhood') a 'quality-of-life' monitor has been constructed, by which several implementing agencies (municipality, borough, housing corporations, etc.) jointly measure the satisfaction among residents. The information this makes available is actively passed to the actors involved. Together with other data collections, the monitor provides the basis for progress measurement. Within the national GSB policy, a – mandatory – first evaluation has been carried out for the 1996–98 period. The GSB monitor indicates that North Hoogvliet is on the right path. The area scores positively on the aspects economy, quality of life, safety and citizens' participation. On school absenteeism the area lags behind the targets.

2.5   Actors Involved in the IAA

A comprehensive approach to neighbourhood problems demands the cooperation of actors on the municipal as well as the borough level. Figure 2.1 shows which administrative organs, services, and specifically created institutions are involved. Before paying attention to some public actors, the principle of 'complementary administration' will be explained.

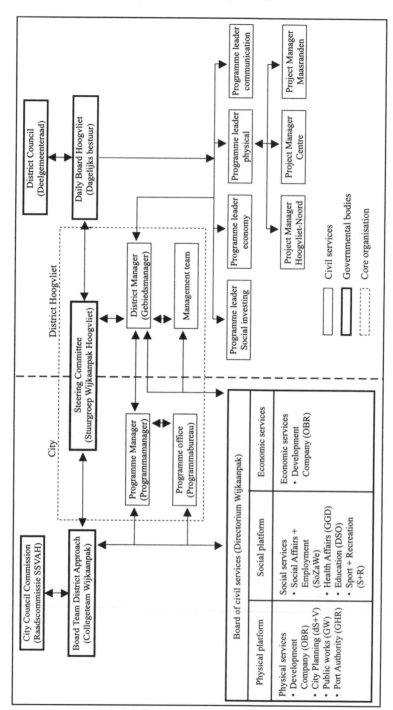

Figure 2.1   Public actors involved in the strategic district approach at city and district level in Rotterdam

'Complementary Administration'

IAA is an example of complementary administration, which is evident in Figure 2.1 by the placing of municipality and borough on one level. Both the municipality and the borough have tasks on the level of IAA. By the Plan of Approach, the two administrative organisms work closely together, alert to solving the problems and seizing opportunities, and complement each other by the means and competencies mutually put in. The key officer is the area manager. He/she is chair of the management team on the area level. The area manager is first and foremost a process manager, who takes care that matters are properly taken in hand and well-adjusted. He/she does not act as the leader of specific projects, but selects officers from the agencies involved (the municipal departments) to do so.

The complementary administration is reflected in the composition of the Steering Committees of the IAA areas. The chairman of the Hoogvliet Daily Board officiates in the Hoogvliet IAA Steering Committee, alongside the 'adoptive' alderman (comparable to deputy mayor, see below). The borough chairman and the alderman constitute the decision-making part of the Steering Committee; the area manager acts as its secretary. The Steering Committee answers for its management to the borough council and the municipal council (and through the municipality to the central government). The Steering Committee has to find consensus about the programme and its implementation. Next the public administration should in theory be capable to carry out the implementation in the most effective and efficient way. The Plan of Approach (1998) suggests an inverted organisation chart, with the area with its residents and entrepreneurs at the top and the other parts of the organisation in supportive positions. In that perspective, the municipal organisation enables the area manager and the associated implementing organisation to function properly.

Area Approach Board (the 'Board Team IAA')

For each of the six boroughs coming under the IAA, an 'adoptive' alderman has been appointed. Together with the municipal Programme Manager the adoptive alderman sits on the IAA Board, which is responsible for the directive administration of the implementation programme on the municipal level. The adoptive aldermen have been designated to bridge the distance between the municipality and the borough, and involve themselves more than before in neighbourhood development. The structure is also supposed to stimulate an integral approach to neighbourhood problems, since the adoptive aldermen are apt to be confronted with problems from the portfolios of their colleagues. However, since an adoptive alderman has no competence over other portfolios than their own, their overcoming the partitions will largely depend on the individual way they fulfil their functions. In Hoogvliet, the adoptive alderman – an alderwoman! – functions as a kind of supervisor. She keeps her distance, and though dedicated, leaves the development and implementation of policy to the local actors, who report monthly on the progress and results of the projects. The idea prevails that the adoptive alderman has not yet become a full-fledged liaison officer between the borough and the municipal board. Besides, the phenomenon of adoptive aldermen is still new and unfamiliar to the public at large, and the social pressure exerted on them by their 'adopted' boroughs does not yet carry much weight.

IAA Programme Office

For the implementation of the IAA, an IAA Programme Office has been set up within the Department for Urban Planning and Housing (dS+V). This office is responsible for the policy development and coordination of the IAA on the municipal level. In theory, the IAA Office is a separate body, but in practice it has a close bond with the boroughs covered by the IAA policy. Some associates of the Programme Office are assigned directly to specific neighbourhoods and indeed posted with the boroughs concerned. For the implementation of the IAA the Programme Office, like the boroughs, depends on the municipal departments. The Programme Manager is a significant link between the Area Approach Board Team and the Municipal Departments, but has no directive power in that context. His role is mostly concerned with coordinating and facilitating.

Municipal Departments: Programme Implementation

The municipal departments are the ones to carry out the various projects eventually, which makes them a crucial link. Eight relatively large-scale and a few administrative departments are involved (see Figure 2.1). The boroughs are obliged to leave the execution of their proposals to the departments. Any capacity or directive problems evolving within the departments could affect the continuity of the policy, for a chain is no stronger than its weakest link. That is why it is of the essence that the departments are efficiently managed.

The managers of the departments involved have seats on the IAA Board of Directors, as have representativse of the borough clerks, the Urban

Programme Manager and the Secretary of the IAA Board Team. The Board's tasks are to harmonise, on the municipal level, the input of the departments in the areas, to solve bottlenecks and to promote the exchange of 'best practices' in the various policy fields. Moreover, the departments have the support of three municipal platforms related to the economic, physical and social pillars. They are supposed to give advice, but to whom remains unclear: the municipality, the municipal council, the borough or the borough council?

Other Hoogvliet Actors Involved

On behalf of the execution of the IAA plans, a covenant has been concluded between the public parties (municipality and borough), the two local housing corporations, the entrepreneurs' association and the joint residents' associations. The relevant actors from Hoogvliet are very much at one in the matter of the proposed operations. Nearly everybody accepts the necessity of the envisaged changes, drastic demolition and all. Indeed, the commitment seems very general.

Housing corporations The housing corporations, a Dutch phenomenon, are the providers of social housing in the towns. As foundations, they do not need to strive for profit, just to be self-supporting with the help of a relatively modest subsidy. Latterly they have become self-supporting and as a consequence turned more market-conscious. In Hoogvliet, there are two large housing corporations at work: *Maasoevers* and *Estrada*. Maasoevers is having some 4,000 dwellings of its stock demolished, *Estrada* some 800. For North-Hoogvliet, Maasoevers is the most important. As in other Dutch cities, the trend is for housing corporations to sell a portion of their stock on the argument that the proportion of tenant dwellings is too great. At the moment, only one-fifth of all dwellings in Rotterdam are owner-occupied, and the ambition is to raise that proportion to 30 per cent by 2005. The rebuilding of the houses is partly financed from the sale of a portion of the corporations' stock.

Shell Company Hoogvliet traditionally has a special relationship with Shell. It was developed as a new growth nucleus to accommodate employees of Shell's adjoining petrochemical complex. Shell has always remained committed to the development of Hoogvliet. Only a motorway separates the petrochemical complex from the borough. However, over the course of years, Shell has greatly reduced its manpower, from 8,000 to a mere 700. Shell and Hoogvliet are both trying to improve their image, and can help each other in that respect. A covenant has been concluded between Hoogvliet and Shell, stating that the number of houses in the northern part of Hoogvliet will be reduced, and that Shell will contribute to the creation of the International Building Exhibition, by financing leisure areas and a youth centre, among other things.

2.6   Analysis of the Organising Capacity

Vision

The vision expressed in the IAA is an opportunity-oriented one, because it is aimed at individuals developing themselves by making use of their own ideas. The city should respond and make use of the potential, ambitions and insights of its inhabitants. To carry out this vision, social networks and increasing self-esteem are considered basic elements. This vision is geared to mutual benefit; people should be supported to go forward at their own pace. The effect will be that the number of those inhabitants dependent on social support will decrease.

IAA as part of the municipal vision   The current agenda of the Municipal Board lists four spearheads, among which are 'Neighbourhoods of Value' and 'Concerned Citizens'. The first one divides into three implementation schemes, among which is the IAA. The second aims at youth policy, including education. On the basis of its current agenda – which builds on the municipal strategy 'The New Rotterdam' and the 'Social Revitalisation Strategy' – the Board has published its 'Vision 2010; Rotterdam on Track' (2000) in the framework of the national Major Cities Policy. That publication maintains the same four spearheads. Within the spearhead 'Neighbourhoods of Value' the IAA takes a prominent position. 'The IAA has to be a paragon of joint endeavours, efforts that remove partitions, open the way to the overall orchestration of agencies, and achieve a whole that is more than the sum of parts' (*Vision 2010*, p. 99). In that vision, measurable beacons to be reached by 2003 have been formulated. The Vision devotes about half a page to the borough of Hoogvliet to describe the principal proposals. The same is more or less true of the draft 'Spatial Plan Rotterdam 2010', the spatial projection of the 2010 Vision. Relatively little attention is given to Hoogvliet and the other five IAA boroughs. So, the vision on strategic and spatial development of Hoogvliet forms itself mostly on the borough level.

IAA vision: developed mostly within borough The vision and strategy for the IAA in Hoogvliet have been developed mainly on the borough level, with the 'Vision 2010' as guideline. The municipal IAA Programme Office has left most of the development of ideas to the Hoogvliet actors. Basically, Hoogvliet is to be aided by the IAA, but the more ideas are developed on the borough level, the better. The mission of the borough reads: 'In cooperation with residents, entrepreneurs and the social institutions, realise a proud city within the region.' Some borough objectives follow from that definition. One objective is to enhance the weak status of Hoogvliet, changing it from a bleak and colourless area into a city with an aspect of its own, able to proceed on its own account. That can be achieved in particular by improving the quality of the housing supply and the services. As to the latter, the area should have 'metropolitan' services, in line with one principle formulated by the Rotterdam municipality, that boroughs and neighbourhoods should be metropolitan in status and nature ('the city in the neighbourhood'). To that end, all relevant actors should be involved. Since in Hoogvliet the feeling of solidarity is stronger than in other problem areas, a joint approach should be within comfortable reach. However, the 'metropolitan status' seems not really to apply to Hoogvliet, as it is more or less detached from the city.

Lessons from the past: physical intervention based on social preferences The municipality of Rotterdam has drawn lessons from the urban-renewal policy carried out during the 1970s and 1980s. One point that emerged from it was that physical restructuring is an insufficient condition for achieving acceptable living conditions. Rotterdam has invested quite generously in physical undertakings, but relatively little in keeping social structures alive. The new vision is that efforts are now being made to make individual needs and the 'human factor' a priority for physical restructuring. Physical planning following dweller's behaviour is the innovative way of the Hoogvliet approach: esteem for occupants and social tissues, neighbours who prefer to move together, special requests by teenage mothers, elderly persons, groups of youngsters, etc. Problems encountered during renewal processes have been instructive as well. Those in charge are now intent on watching any negative developments attending the gradual dismantling of neighbourhoods (displacement, crime, pollution, etc.).

Strategic Networks: Cooperation of the Actors Involved

Networks play a crucial part In June 1999, the borough, the housing corporations, the Hoogvliet Entrepreneurs' Association and the Association of Residents' Councils signed a declaration of intent for the joint achievement of a rather ambitious plan. Although one can doubt the level of ambition, the solidarity displayed in the planning for the Hoogvliet IAA is considered a high trump card. Notably the Borough Administration and the emancipated housing corporations are at one with respect to the tackling of social problems. Both have a stake in improved and varied housing stock. The peripheral situation of the zone to the rest of the city is in some respects a weakness, but seems to produce significant advantages, which manifest themselves in particular in the organisation of the drastic restructuring plans. Because Hoogvliet operates as a more or less independent entity, the important role of some actors is very evident. The actors in turn show a deep commitment to the ideas for the improvement of the area. In other backward neighbourhoods, embedded in urban built-up areas, the situation can be quite different.

Relation with municipality and municipal departments Because the organisation of the IAA is rather complicated (due for one thing to the required integral approach) and the distribution of tasks among the levels (municipality, borough) and parties (municipal departments) involved is not always perfectly clear, a lot of communication is necessary. Our conversation partners marked this situation as an 'embodied polder model'[2] or 'one great communication circus of all actors involved'. The impression is that the actors are disproportionately engaged in mutual adjustment and communication. There seems to be a fundamental quandary: too little communication could starve certain links of necessary information and thus lead to tension between actors; too much could delay and frustrate the implementation of policy. Inevitably, actors must communicate if they are to give substance to a complementary administration, but the usefulness of certain links seems doubtful. For instance, the three platforms that are supposed to coordinate the input of the municipal departments, in fact have no clear advisory competency. The communication lines between municipal departments seem rather long. Often the communication is in writing, which may give rise to disturbance and delay. In sum, the present organisation cannot cope satisfactorily with the envisaged comprehensive approach.

The suggestion has been made to put more responsibility on the level where the action is (the borough). In the present configuration, boroughs are obliged to buy services from the municipal departments. The alternative would be to leave them a choice between buying from the municipal department or elsewhere. That might induce public departments to adopt a more demand-oriented attitude. Moreover, the departments would no longer be confronted with excess demand from boroughs (that might cause delays). The expectation is that basically the municipal departments, with their inherent advantages, would have the edge of external parties: their mutual connections and expertise, no need for the transfer of VAT and continuity of the products delivered. Some prominent advantages of a free choice for the purchase of services are that the departments will be encouraged to supply a constant quality and that, should the municipal departments fail in capacity, the boroughs could purchase services elsewhere and thus ensure the implementation of their programmes.

Division of tasks between municipality and borough More clarity about the division of tasks between the municipality and the borough is of the essence. The present lack of clarity can be a source of tension, since both parties strive for greater competency in local matters. However, there seems to be a taboo on discussions of the subject. Hoogvliet, jealously guarding its independent position, tends to look askance at municipal intervention in its policy making. Complaints are heard about too much municipal control of the boroughs, and the suggestion has been made that municipal approval should be given on the level of programmes rather than of projects. Actors involved in projects claim that there is too much municipal interference with details. Every single project has to be submitted to the city council, which may considerably delay implementation. The municipality, on the other hand, believes that for the sake of coherence, it should keep a firm hand in with strategic policy efforts, such as the IAA and the reinforcement of the economic location climate. The question remains: how to find the right balance between bottom-up and top-down?

Leadership

The elected chairman of the borough who was in charge during the period 1991–2002, had undoubted leadership qualities. As the representative of a local interest party he was considered by most Hoogvliet actors as the real representative of the borough. Thanks to that strong leadership, planning and policy implementation enjoy strong political support. There is moreover great commitment on the local level to the plans coming under the IAA. Other directly involved parties, such as the housing corporations, fully subscribe to and support the process set in motion. Within the Steering Committee, in which the municipality of Rotterdam is represented by the adoptive alderman, consensus prevails about most policy plans. Since the final decision has to be made by the adoptive alderman and the borough chairman together, a good understanding between these two seems crucial to the implementation of the policy. In the case of Hoogvliet, the adoptive alderwoman conceived of her role as that of a 'governor', willing to leave most of the control to the borough council as long as that body seems adequate. That seems in line with the principle behind the IAA, represented by the inverted organisation chart (bottom-up control), and is appreciated by the borough chairman. However, since the two administrators have resigned, no clear way out of the quandary can be expected.

Communication and Support

Hoogvliet considers an adequate communication policy of major importance. Good communication serves two major goals: exchange of information about the physical restructuring scheme, and the enhancement of the area's image. To do justice to the subject's importance, a separate communication programme leader has been appointed (see Figure 2.1).

'Demolition can be fun!' The saying is that the greatest restructuring scheme of the Netherlands is at the moment in progress in Hoogvliet. To create sufficient support for the drastic demolition plans, the borough does its utmost to draw in the local population. One principle is that an ominous message such as the imminent demolition of their houses should be cleverly presented to the community as a golden opportunity for improvement of their living environment. The message to be broadcast should be that demolition is indeed a reason for celebration. At the end of 1998 the demolition plans were made public once the actors involved had come to an agreement about them. All residents were visited and informed of the plans by the district and the housing corporation. The feeling was that the message could best be brought to the residents by a neutral party. The municipality and the housing corporations were direct stakeholders and might be considered not neutral enough by the residents. For that reason, the 'Welfare Foundation' (a private NGO) was enlisted to carry the message to the residents.

An information centre has been opened for that purpose. A booklet has been written to indicate for which houses the rents would be frozen, which would go on being let, and which would be sold. A demolition permit is granted only when 50 per cent of an apartment building has fallen vacant (which can take three to four years). Once it has been granted, residents have a claim to a removal bonus. Care is taken that the units with frozen rents remain habitable and presentable. The population is explicitly involved in the planning; they can submit and vote for alternative proposals and express how they would like to be accommodated in a new living environment. Neighbours have a possibility of moving together to another building, thus preserving their social networks. They may also ask for additional provisions such as a room for leisure pursuits. Excursions have been organised to show how people are living elsewhere. All this has been done to strengthen the social support for the drastic changes and show the residents how and by what means their living environment can be upgraded. That the involvement of local residents in the demolition planning has clearly been successful can be concluded by the absence of important protest actions.

Some tension has admittedly risen at locations where nothing is happening, adjacent to the houses to be demolished. Many people are leaving those premises because they are considered to become the next least attractive residential locations of Hoogvliet, once the doomed houses have been demolished. There is also considerable anxiety among those living in houses to be demolished at a later date. They cannot be sure about the demolition timescale, for the borough, dependent as it is on other parties involved, is unable to give them the exact date when their dwellings are to be pulled down. The borough will indeed have to tread very cautiously to keep its credibility, which is of the essence for the physical restructuring.

Improving the image Hoogvliet has two different images: one among outsiders and another among residents. Outsiders judge this borough mostly by the behaviour of criminal Antilleans, the odour of the petrochemical industry, the peripheral situation in respect of the (inner) city, and the nuisance produced by the motorway. Hoogvliet's own population on the other hand perceives Hoogvliet as a green, spaciously designed borough with a close community, with immediate access to the pleasant leisure areas along the river *Oude Maas*.

By recent soundings, Hoogvliet has by now become one of the three safest boroughs of Rotterdam, yet outsiders still look upon Hoogvliet as one of the most unsafe. The second objective of the communication policy is to raise Hoogvliet's status, in particular among outsiders. The initiative *'Briljantjes in de wijk'* ('Small Neighbourhood Diamonds') serves that purpose by trying to get individual Hoogvliet residents to play at being an ambassador for their own neighbourhood. They should exert themselves to spread their own positive perception to the outer world. Along with that, a dedicated marketing campaign for Hoogvliet will be organised. The International Building Exhibition will also contribute positively to Hoogvliet's image.

Policy Development and Implementation

Lack of clarity of the IAA concept on the municipal level On the level of the borough, the IAA concept seems clear. The objectives are well-defined, and there is clarity about who are and who are not involved in the programme. Furthermore, the IAA is given political priority. It is the policy programme, to which other schemes are subordinated.

On the municipal level, the objectives of the IAA seem to be less transparent, however. There is no well-defined concept from which to base the implementation. In principle, the IAA is a demand-oriented, integral approach. The municipal departments do not show clear understanding of what that integral policy means in practice, and who exactly are the demanders in the IAA. To try and remove partitions is all very well, but even integral policy calls for choices. Rotterdam wants to achieve a whole range of objects by its integral area approach. A comprehensive package of measures has been proposed, but their integral realisation remains questionable in view of the human and financial resources available. The IAA approach seems to be overambitious in its intention to turn the municipal organisation into a demand-oriented, comprehensively operating organisation. Not everything can be carried out at the same time everywhere and with everybody. Priorities are missing and on the municipal level they do not follow naturally from the initiated IAA measures.

A prominent difficulty for the municipal departments is that the IAA is but one of the many policy programmes for which they have to render services. It comes on top of the regular programmes. The departments do not always recognise the IAA as a directive instrument for their policy implementation by or division of capacity, because it is coordinated with other programmes. The theory of the inverted organisation chart does not seem to work on the level of the municipal departments. To them the IAA represents an additional task, whose urgency moreover seems to be differently estimated by the individual departments. Some of them already have their work cut out in their regular tasks, and the IAA does not replace one of those but comes on top. Although the four social departments have appointed a so-called 'change agent', hardly any extra manpower is made available to carry out the IAA, so that there are inevitable bottlenecks at the municipal level. For sheer lack of capacity no sufficient attention can be given to the IAA. Hoogvliet for one has had difficulty purchasing extra capacity from the departments.

Evaluation and Monitoring

The need to learn from experience The municipality of Rotterdam has for some time had experience with the IAA, and has had the opportunity to draw lessons from it. Several improvements have been carried through. One important lesson from the urban renewal was that physical changes alone may not suffice for structural neighbourhood upgrading. More attention for the social component has proved essential. Instead of the 'input-controlled' method of the early days a 'result-oriented' approach has come in vogue.

Although the IAA is an attempt at integrality, integral evaluation processes and instruments are still lacking. Every public body involved (such as European DGs, state departments, municipalities, boroughs) has its own responsibility and calls for separate evaluations. One disadvantage of the ensuing spate of evaluations is that much is measured, but hardly anything is done with the results. Little knowledge is distilled from the evaluations to bring forth better programmes and projects.

The City Council has drawn up a programme of ten partial objectives. For each policy field, the ambitions and 'beacons' (measurable objectives) have been determined. According to our discussion partners, not all of these targets have been adequately formulated, nor are they duly associated with (political) consequences. If good, achievable 'beacons' could be formulated, directives for policy might also be derived. The beacons might be coupled with the position of those who are politically responsible. One obstacle seems to be the dependency on the policy effects of other factors, such as the favourable economic development. In practice, there is no such thing as a *ceteris paribus* condition, 'everything else being equal'; there is always some change to make the margin between the output and the performance of the policy uncertain.

To avoid flattered figures at benchmark moments, the beacons ought to be measured at reasonable intervals. For instance, if the set target is to reduce the number of premature school-leavers by 3 per cent, evaluation should be monthly rather than twice a year. In that way a more or less continuous incentive for active policy in that particular field would be generated. Some beacons are relatively simple to formulate, such as the number of houses to be built within a certain timespan. But a beacon concerning safety is already much harder to define. The indicator chosen is a mark given for the perception of safety among a random sample of residents (not a permanent panel, which would probably show the increase or decrease of safety perception more clearly). One specific difficulty is people's sensitiveness to incidents, in particular when extensively spelt out in the press. A recently committed crime can considerably colour the results.

To identify distinct policy priorities, it seems advisable not to set too many beacons, representing clear and univocal policy objects to be striven for. For successful monitoring and to prevent camouflage of certain developments, the entities evaluated should preferably be not too large. At first, a subdivision into two areas, North and South Hoogvliet, was envisaged for the evaluation. However, that turned out too crude for a good impression of the initiated changes and the lessons to be drawn. For instance, after some business companies had been attracted to business park *Gadering*, things suddenly went very well in North Hoogvliet. However, that had nothing to do with the IAA in this zone, which by rights should be the object of the evaluation. The new division into neighbourhoods promises a better insight into IAA-initiated changes. It follows that the success of the IAA for an entire borough should be treated with great caution.

2.7   Conclusions

Since the mid-1990s, fighting social exclusion has become a political spearhead of Dutch national policy. Within the Ministry of the Interior, a Minister for Urban Policy and Integration of Ethnic Minorities has been appointed, whose first task is to coordinate payments and policies targeted to cities that suffer from social problems. Rotterdam is among the cities with the most serious social problems. In many respects (disposable income, educational level, unemployment, crime, etc.) the city belongs to the most disadvantaged areas of the country. Within Rotterdam, six out of 13 boroughs have been classified as 'three star' problem areas, indicating that on physical, as well as economical and social indicators they score considerably below the municipal average. Among these boroughs is Hoogvliet, located close to the port area and once built as a residential area for industrial and port workers. A few years ago the situation in some of Hoogvliet's neighbourhoods was defined as 'tragic' in many respects.

The Integrated Area Approach is an opportunity-oriented strategy, combining existing divisional policies (physical, economic and social) and implementation practices to tackle difficulties in backward neighbourhoods. The IAA demands intense cooperation of actors on the municipal as well as the borough level. Both levels have tasks and responsibilities. The municipal departments are the ones to carry out the various projects in the boroughs.

Elements of Organising Capacity

Vision According to the principle that ideas should preferably be developed at the borough level, the vision for the Hoogvliet IAA has indeed been elaborated on the borough level, with the municipal vision as guideline. The Hoogvliet vision is 'to realise a proud city within the region', which emphasises the special status of Hoogvliet as a kind of 'independent' part within the city. The detached location has brought some valuable advantages (such as the high commitment of the local actors to the new (social) policies), but also some drawbacks (such as the lack of city feeling). The idea prevailing in Hoogvliet is that to solve social problems the quality of life has to be improved considerably, among other means through the demolition of the old, unappealing housing stock and its replacement by more attractive and varied dwellings. Without such drastic changes, opportunities to turn the tide are hard to find. To improve educational services and levels, fight crime, improve borough centre provisions and enhance the poor image are some other IAA objectives. In this case study most attention was given to the new housing schemes, indicated by the citizens as the most urgent problem to tackle.

Strategic networks Two different aspects should be considered: networks on the borough level and the partnership between the borough and the city. On the level of the borough communication lines are short. The few key actors consult regularly with one another about the implementation of policy. Because these actors all recognise the importance of the IAA and from the beginning have been involved in the planning, they show a deep commitment to the policy implementation. So, networking is well developed among the partners on this level.

Networking between the municipality, the borough and the municipal departments raises more questions. The complex organisation of the IAA is regarded as an obstacle. A multitude of municipal bodies are involved, which need to communicate frequently and extensively. The communication lines tend to be long. The involvement with local problems is much less on the municipal level than in Hoogvliet itself, which leads to delays in the eventual execution of the plans. In the end, most administrative problems in IAA decision-making are overcome; bottlenecks tend to appear when it comes to the implementation by the municipal departments. They are often far removed from local problems, and the borough has to put much energy into communication with them. Moreover, the incentives to operate effectively and efficiently and the commitment and input among the actors involved might be increased.

Leadership Leadership has clearly been assumed by the elected chairman of the Hoogvliet borough board, who has been in charge from 1991 to 2002. He succeeded in bringing all relevant actors together to jointly develop and support the strategy. The 'adoptive' alderman (deputy mayor) conceived of her role as that of a governor, leaving sufficient manoeuvrability to the borough. That configuration seems to have worked quite satisfactorily until now. The IAA district manager and programme managers are first and foremost coordinators between the borough and the municipality, between the municipal departments involved in projects and between the programmes carried out in his/her district.

Societal support To have obtained societal support can be considered a decisive success factor in the Hoogvliet approach. The peripheral situation of Hoogvliet, outside the built-up area of Rotterdam, constitutes an important advantage in terms of social involvement in the problems. There is much solidarity here. All actors who might play a prominent part in the IAA understand the importance of consensus and of the firm and decisive taking in hand of the quality of living in Hoogvliet. The innovative approach adopted is that of timely communication with residents and strong citizen involvement in the decision making. A major portion of the housing stock is going to be replaced without giving rise to massive protests until now. The people fully participate in the process and can express their wishes for their future dwelling and living environment. More than anything else, this has been conducive to broad social support for the restructuring. Still, some tension has risen at locations adjacent to the demolition area and in areas to be demolished later, through lack of a definite timescale for this work.

Political support Given the serious social problems there is strong political support for the IAA approach on the national (GSB policy) as well as on the city level. Within the municipal strategy and the current policy programme the fight against social exclusion has a prominent place, although clear priorities have not been formulated; many things are considered of equal importance. The comprehensive approach has been embodied in the concept of the *adoptive alderman*, an innovative way of making 'divisional' politicians feel involved in the complex problems of a backward neighbourhood. Still, the adoptive alderman cannot be made responsible for sectors that do not belong to his political portfolio. Political support on the borough level is clear: the IAA programme is given political priority in all respects. It is the most important policy programme to which all other schemes are subordinated: the future of the borough is at stake!

Communication To create sufficient support for the drastic demolition plans, adequate communication is considered of the highest importance. The message broadcast is that demolition is a reason for celebration rather than fear, because it is a golden opportunity for improving the individual quality of life. To ensure trust, the message has been carried to the residents by a neutral party (a welfare NGO), and not by a direct stakeholder like the municipality, the borough or the housing corporations.

To raise Hoogvliet's poor image among outsiders (second communication objective) individual Hoogvliet residents have been encouraged to play ambassador for their own neighbourhood. The International Building Exhibition too is to contribute positively to Hoogvliet's image.

Evaluation Instead of the 'input-controlled' method of the early days, a 'result-oriented' approach has come in vogue. From the first evaluations it has become clear that a proper delimitation of the areas to be evaluated, the frequency of measuring, the way of formulating targets, external forces and sudden incidents all substantially influence the evaluation results. Although the IAA is an attempt at integrality, comprehensive evaluation processes and instruments are still lacking. All those involved (Europe, state, city) call for their own evaluation, given specific responsibilities. As a consequence of the ensuing spate of evaluations, much is measured, but hardly anything is done with the results. Little has been distilled from the evaluations that could bring forth better programmes and projects, and failures (if registered) are not clearly associated with (political) consequences. Given the huge number of projects to be implemented, setting distinct priorities seems advisable. Such priorities are now lacking, especially on the municipal level.

A clear conclusion from the results of the IAA cannot be drawn, because the four-year programme is only halfway through. Compared to the preliminary results in the other IAA boroughs, the Hoogvliet results look promising. Since the start of the GSB policy in 1995 and the municipal Integrated Area Approach (1998) positive developments have been achieved. The favourable economic tide has certainly lowered the number of unemployed, but weak points and threats, especially in the field of education, still abound.

Some final remarks Apparently, the municipal departments are not quite sure who is supposed to take the IAA in hand. On the municipal level, the IAA is just one of many policy programmes. It comes on top of the regular package, which most often has priority. Therefore, priority is not always given to the implementation of the IAA. Nor are there always adequate means available on the municipal level to put in manpower for it. The financial resources available for the IAA seem to be insufficiently used to enlist the human resources required for the IAA policy implementation.

What matters in the organisation of the Rotterdam IAA is to strike the right balance. There is much energetic renewal going on in Rotterdam, but sometimes the impression prevails that the policies are not adequately anchored. A long-term structural approach seems to be weighed down by a problem-oriented attitude responding to acute needs. A serious pitfall for the IAA is therefore the temporary nature of the measures. For a given period extra means come available. One challenge which confronts the city is to use temporary means in such a way that the measures to keep the boroughs attractive become incorporated in regular policy, and thus to prevent the IAA from becoming just a secondary concern. Finally, the right balance between a top-down and a bottom-up approach seems not yet to have been found. The borough complains about too much municipal control and interference with details, while on the other hand the municipality wishes to keep its hand in with strategic efforts aiming at the reinforcement of the city's prosperity and welfare in the long run.

Notes

1 Part of the text of this section is lent from van den Berg et al., 2000.
2 'Polder model' is a nickname for the Dutch habit of trying to achieve wide consensus before taking decisions. This model is considered the basis for the strong development of the Dutch economy since the mid-1980s.

Chapter 3

Restructuring Social Policies in Strasbourg

In 1996, the City Council of Strasbourg agreed on the implementation of the Masterplan for Social Intervention, which introduced a new approach to social policies, in which the client is central. The plan also initiated a district approach; a specific package of social services will be provided in each of the six territories of the French city. This case study describes and analyses the implementation of the Masterplan carried out in several stages in the period from 1996 to 2001. There will be special attention for Neuhof, a district with a strong concentration of social problems. The data of the metropolitan profile of Strasbourg are summarised in Table 3.1.

Table 3.1   Data of metropolitan profile of Strasbourg

Characteristics	Size
Population of the city (1999)	264,000
Population of the urban region (1999)	451,000
Growth of the urban population (city, %, 1990–99)	+6.5
Share of the population of foreign extraction (city, %, 1999)	14
Proportion of population of working age in employment (city, %, 1990)	45
Unemployment rates (city, %, 1999)	6.1
Proportion of employment in industry (city, %, 1982–90)	23.3
Proportion of employment in services (city, %, 1982–90)	76.6
Number of administrative tiers (including state and boroughs)	4
Borough Boards	No

Sources: European Commission, 2000, Vol. 1, p. 122; idem, Vol. 2, pp. 54, 110.

3.1   Social-economic Profile of the Strasbourg Region

Demography

Strasbourg, the seventh city of France, is located in the Alsace region, in the department of *Bas-Rhin*. It counts as a regional metropolis, and owes its growth to its geographical location on a European crossroad. That situation has favoured a centuries-long development of exchanges and commerce, without too much intervention from the capital (Berg, van den, et al., 1998). Strasbourg has its own cultural history, much influenced by the Germans, who occupied it during two periods of the nineteenth and twentieth centuries (from 1870 to 1918 and during World War II). At present, Strasbourg has 264,000 inhabitants. The *Communauté Urbaine de Strasbourg* (CUS) groups together 27 municipalities with a total population of 451,000. Strasbourg experienced its fastest demographic growth after 1968, when masses of immigrants started to flow in and natural growth increased as well.

The conurbation of Strasbourg is organised in three concentric rings. The innermost one is the enlarged centre, where a process of gentrification is taking place, concentrating young people and highly-qualified workers. The middle ring is formed of neighbourhoods that differ widely in social composition, from areas with mostly young households to areas where large families, workers and unemployed are overrepresented. This ring displays the worst social problems. The outer ring comprises peripheral municipalities characterised by strong demographic growth, which have preserved the traditional image of rural Alsace.

Economy

In the economy of Strasbourg the service sector is dominant; about 77 per cent of the economic activities are services. The presence of European and some international institutions is one of the main causes of that dominance. The financial activities concentrated in the centre of the city account for 5.4 per cent of the jobs. Thanks to foreign investments, the industrial sector has remained quite important for the regional economy. The prominent sectors are the metal, agro-industry, the chemical industry and pharmaceuticals. Construction and public works are other important sectors in Strasbourg's economy. In the last few years, the medical sector has also developed thanks to the implantation of international pharmaceuticals groups. Transport and logistics are concentrated in the port, with important container-networks to

Rotterdam and Antwerp. Strasbourg is a crossing point in the European road network and will also obtain good external accessibility by HST to and from Germany on the north-south axis, and within France on the line Paris-Strasbourg. The regional airport has connections with the main French and European cities. Internally, the city is well equipped with two new tramway lines that connect the different parts of Strasbourg.

The Administrative Framework of France and Strasbourg

There are four administrative levels in France.[1] The state is still the most powerful of them. The municipalities (*communes*) are the oldest administrative regime of France, corresponding to the parishes of the old regime, before 1789. The third administrative level is the department (*département*), organised mainly such that its inhabitants could go back and forth to the main administrative city of the department on horseback within a day. The number of departments has not changed notwithstanding technological progress. Each department raises a portion of its own financial resources. The regions are the latest local entities. They were first created in 1972, as a new administrative level between the state and the departments, but without much financial power. There are 22 regions, 95 departments and 36,664 municipalities in France.

The department is responsible for social, education and cultural activities, among other tasks. After the decentralisation law of 1986, the general council of the department is also competent in sociomedical matters. The region is in charge of economic and spatial planning, vocational training and some education aspects. The most important administrative body on the municipal level is the city council. It is elected every six years by the local population and is in charge of local administration, police, and municipal budget management. The local council elects the mayor from the council members. The most important power is the financial one, the right to vote the yearly budget and supervise its management. Other competencies are public local services (water and waste disposal management, urban transportation, primary education) and economic and social development.

As mentioned, Strasbourg is part of a *Communauté Urbaine*. In general this is a public body in which communities cooperate belonging to an urban region of at least 50,000 inhabitants. The cities which are part of the *Communauté* transfer tasks and responsibilities to the partnership, so that it can work as an administrative unit. It operates a revenue system that is comparable with that of municipalities. The administration of the CUS coincides nearly completely with that of the City of Strasbourg. It is almost the same organisation with the same politicians and civil servants having responsiblity. This situation is peculiar to Strasbourg: in the other French cities with a *Communauté Urbaine* there is a clear division between the two administrations. Since 1972 the services of the city of Strasbourg and of the CUS have been grouped together in one administrative system, which employs around 6,300 persons. Some competencies are compulsory and some voluntary. The main domains are land management, urban transport, water management, economic and education development. For historical reasons the CUS is also responsible for the development of social policies. In 1995, the *Direction Territoriale et de la Tranquillité Publique* was created, as a result of the decentralisation of local public action undertaken in France. The DATTP is in charge of the *Contrats de Ville*, contracts between several public actors to develop social and urban programmes for the most disadvantaged neighbourhoods. In Strasbourg, Neuhof is one of the areas that has benefited from this programme.

3.2   Social Problems in Strasbourg

The region of Alsace is one of the wealthiest of France. In general terms Strasbourg is a prosperous city, although it suffers from severe social problems, such as relatively many long-term unemployed, deteriorated neighbourhoods, crime, etc. The region of Alsace has a relatively low unemployment rate (5.3 per cent) compared to other French regions. However, in the city of Strasbourg the unemployment rate rises to 6.1 per cent. Young people are also much affected by the unemployment, which amounts to 20 per cent for persons under 25. This situation is a result of the economic decline the city suffered during the 1980s, which generated what is known as 'new poor', people suffering from long-term unemployment. For them, a minimum salary of integration (RMI) was created in 1988. About one-tenth of the city's population has a relatively low income. Within the *Bas-Rhin* department, 66 per cent of the persons receiving RMI live in Strasbourg, which indicates the degree to which social problems are concentrated within the city. In some neighbourhoods of the city, about 17 per cent of the population depend on the minimum income. As a result, spatial-segregation phenomena prevail in certain areas of the city. About 14 per cent of the population in Strasbourg are foreigners. The largest groups are Moroccans, Turks, Algerians, and Tunisians.

Social problems are related to the deterioration processes of some neighbourhoods which have the greatest concentration of social housing. They are characterised by a concentration of unemployed, foreigners and low-income groups. Loss of population has left many houses vacant and has led to a decrease in social diversity. In this case study we will give special attention to Neuhof, a neighbourhood that is seriously affected by social problems. About 100 years ago this area was set up as a modern garden city. Many four- and five-storey blocks were built here during the 1960s and 1970s. Nowadays the neighbourhood is sadly deteriorated and is a sore spot in the city. The neighbourhood has a population of immigrants and nomads, and a high proportion of its inhabitants depend on social income. One of the worst problems is the occurrence of much (petty) crime as well as drug trade and absue, and setting fire to cars, which has a negative impact on the safety perception of the inhabitants and the value of the houses.

3.3   The Masterplan for Social Intervention

Because of its specific historical situation, Strasbourg has a particular administrative situation. From 1870 to 1918 and from 1939 to 1945 Strasbourg was part of Germany, and some of its institutions date from that period. Under the German law, the city developed some specific social services earlier than other French cities, for instance mother and child care and assistance to homeless people. In France there are in general three groups of actors that intervene in social policies:

1   Private associations (*secteur associatif*). Historically, all kinds of nongovernmental organisations, from the church to small NGOs, have intervened in social policies. From 1908, there has been a special law that supports associations to provide social services. Nowadays these actors are subsidised by the state and local governments and for a relatively small part are financed by their members or the revenues from paid services to the population. In Strasbourg, these actors still play an important role in the 'social arena'.

2   Public authorities (*collectivité publique: état, région, département, commune*). From 1945, the state has taken care of the development of social policy. In the 1980s however, a process of decentralisation started and lower governments now have more responsibilities in social policies. The state still plays an important role in financing social services laid down in laws, for instance the RMI. The role of the region in social services is small. This governmental layer is responsible for providing vocational training and urban planning. The department has relatively many

responsibilities in the social field. Instances are mother and child care, preventive health care, funding of infrastructure for social services (such as care centres for the handicapped and elderly). According to French law, the municipalities do not have responsibilities in social policy. They are not obliged to provide services, but they can do so if they want, which is a matter of political choice. They can do so through the CCAS (Community Centres for Social Action). In the case of Strasbourg the city has traditionally taken care of social services, even before the *ordenances* of 1945 regarding mother and child protection. As from the 1980s the state and the *département* have collaborated in such policies as the RMI and social housing. In Strasbourg the City has kept up social services that in other cities have become the responsibility of the *département*. The *département* only subsidises the activities of the city.

3 Social assurances (*protection social*). As from 1986, a system of social assurances has been active. Financed through levies on wages, allowances can be paid to people who fall ill or become unemployed. Before 1986 such a social protection system had to be financed by the associative sector of the public authorities.

In Strasbourg there used to be several institutions that provided social services, which sometimes created fragmentation in the social help. The Masterplan for Social Intervention (*Le Schéma Directeur de l'Intervention Sociale)* aims to reorganise the organisational structures to achieve a more comprehensive approach to social policies, in which the client has a central position. The social services have to be improved in view of the clients becoming more autonomous. In that train of thought, in the new framework social programmes are to be carried out together with the clients and not independently of them. Two important factors at national level have stimulated the development of this local plan.

1 In France there is a decentralisation debate in progress on social and other policies. The idea is that the local level should have more autonomy in the provision and organisation of social services.

2 In 1998, a new French 'Law to Fight Social Exclusion' was issued. This was a general framework that recognised that even the most underprivileged person is a citizen and has autonomy and capacity to take his own decisions. The implication was that social services should not be only providers of financial means but are also expected to help people to come back into society.

These two developments needed to be implemented at the local level in Strasbourg. With the help of the Masterplan this is being attempted. The Masterplan aims to create a new relation between the users of social services and those who provide them, and to make these services more direct and client-friendly.

Strasbourg benefited from the fact that a large number of social services are concentrated within one city department, the Department of Social Actions (*la Direction de l'Action Sociale* (DAS)). That situation is quite unique for France. In most French cities, social services such as social work, mother and child protection, minimum integration wages (RMI), school health services, are dispersed among several actors.

The plan aims to increase the coherence of a system and an arena in which the actors used to operate quite independently from one another. There was too strong a compartmentalisation of social policies, which reduced their effectiveness and efficiency. The need is stressed for an adequate sequence of actions during the implementation of the Masterplan. Firstly, adequate social services focused on the clients have to be realised; secondly, regulations or laws might be changed to incorporate the new approach. A change of regulations or laws might thus occur as a result of the new approach, but must not be its objective.

Main Elements of the Masterplan

The core of the Masterplan is to restructure social organisations according to three dimensions:

- a territorial dimension: a kind of district approach; social services should be set up in the direct vicinity of the clients. They could be differentiated among different districts, according to specific needs;
- a thematic dimension: intervention by themes that are relevant to the competencies attributed or delegated to the DAS;
- a logistic dimension: complementary activities that have to support the social services carried out under the first two dimensions.

The reorganisation of social services is being implemented in stages, taking account of the old situation. In 1996 the Municipal Council agreed on the project. Four major steps have been distinguished.

1) Reorganisation of the DAS (June 1997) At the first stage, the administrative and organisational foundations were laid, which were necessary to implement the basic ideas of the Masterplan. They comprised in particular the four logistic services: human resources, finances, construction and communication, information and psychologist services. These logistic poles supply complementary services to the 'social actors'. The logistic services have to support the territorial and thematic poles, so that those two poles can focus on their core business.

2) Territorialisation (September 1998–99) At the second stage, according to available demographic data of Strasbourg, six territories are defined in which social services are to be delivered. There were already different territorial divisions for administrative, education, health and other purposes. For the social services the DAS wanted to create a division based on such socioeconomic criteria as housing, social composition, economic level, perception of inhabitants, etc. The idea was to delimit areas that show a certain coherence in socioeconomic structure, nature of social problems, etc. Often such territories are separated from others by transport infrastructure. The distinctions realised are based in part on those made by INSEE, the French statistical organisation. In total six territories have been defined: west, east, southwest, centre, north and south.

3) Stimulating cooperation between professionals (2000) The idea is that field workers have to learn to work together so that the client may have unified attention. Within the DAS there are a wide variety of employees, varying from social workers (working with clients to solve different social problems), social consultants (applying regulations on social aid), child care, psychologists, etc. They often worked independently from one another, carrying out their own procedures regarding clients and maintaining their own databases on clients. Clients thus might visit several DAS employees, who were not in touch for a coherent treatment of clients. According to the Masterplan, this is to be fundamentally changed. For each client one datafile will be kept and the DAS employees involved have to keep in contact to achieve a coherent approach to the client. A new procedure has been developed to that end, according to which a social intervener first makes an overall broad evaluation of the client's situation, before he or she is to be supported by specific employees of the DAS or associates. When needed, DAS employees also have to cooperate with those of associated organisations. Examples are the CCAS for clients without fixed abode, or the CAF (*Caisse d'Allocations Familiales*) for 'family support'.

4) Coherent actions and first evaluation (2001) At the current stage, the new approach is expected to be fully operational. This implies that the actors involved now have to operate more coherently. At the same time, the social observatory (the database on the territories) is expected to work well. This should permit the first evaluations of the new approach. Both the better knowledge of the social problems by the field workers and the better statistical information should lead to more efficient and effective social actions in Strasbourg.

Complementary programmes Three additional programmes have been implemented to complement the Masterplan, an infrastructure programme, a training programme and a database programme.

1 The first established that each territory should have its own health/social centre. These more or less standardised centres are designed to be multifunctional and to be used by different professionals together. They must be centres for social and health assistance for the local population. In each territory there is a main location and some annexes.

2 The second programme concerns the creation of a database with information about users and facilities of the social services in Strasbourg. To that end, new information and communication technology is used. A specific database for the social problems in the several districts of Strasbourg has been set up on CD-ROM. The goal is to provide a tool for partner analysis, which means that all institutions involved provide and use the information to develop a common action. The intention is that field professionals can also use it to improve their service to the clients. This database is called 'Social Observatory' and combines macro and micro information as well as qualitative and quantitative data. Partners in this Observatory are the CAF, the CUS, the city (DAS and CCAS), the department, and the state (through the Prefecture and the Education Department).

3 The third programme is the training for managers and workers in the field to prepare them for the new way of working of the DAS. Since 1997, the social agents involved have followed a number of professional courses, for instance professional reporting, management of conflicts, and elaboration of joint projects.

Thematic example of a changed approach under the Masterplan: The RMI The RMI is a minimum integration wage for those who have no income or not enough to live in good conditions (law of December 1988). The RMI is funded and managed by the state and the *Conseil Général* (*Département*). The Bank for Family Funds (*CAF*) is responsible for the financial settlement of these social allowances towards the users. With the Masterplan, the RMI service has become more integrated in a wider organisation. Traditionally the social worker was just an intermediary between the user and the service. Since the Masterplan was implemented, CAF employees have cooperated with social field workers to reintegrate their clients in society, through specific training programmes and other means. Relations between RMI people and other staff have become easier as a result of common meetings and the territorial approach. RMI workers have regular meetings with other workers (as social assistants) to discuss each case, which should improve the effectiveness of the help.

Territorial example: Strasbourg-South This territorial unit comprises the city districts *Canardière, Villas-Plaine des Bouchers, Stockfeld, Neuhof* and *Polygone*, and has about 37,000 inhabitants. This area has a concentration of severe social problems such as unemployment (about one-fifth) and an immigrant and nomad population (about 23 per cent of the population are of foreign origin) who live excluded from society. About seven-tenths of the houses in this territory were constructed during the 1950s and 1960s; the social housing is now badly deteriorated. Some of the dwellings are in such a bad condition that the best solution seems to be to demolish them. Important problems that affect the population are a lack of financial means and/or dependence on social allowances and problems with the administration (for instance how to reach the institutions and ask for help). Other matters that must be dealt with in this area are education, housing and child care. The government has intervened several times already in the Strasbourg-South area without much success. The problems require a comprehensive action that was not possible in the period before the Masterplan. This area is now the first to have a health/social centre (created after the Masterplan), which regroups social, medical-social and educational functions. About 24 professionals work in this centre. They are from different disciplines such as social assistance, psychology, gynaecology, mediators, people in charge of the RMI. The centre thus fits nicely the idea of the multidisciplinary approach promoted by the Masterplan.

There is also a large city project (*Grand Projets de Villes*, GPV) in progress in Strasbourg-South. This is a strategic urban development plan, initiated by the national government, and carried out in 50 urban areas in France. These areas are high priority areas because their socioeconomic problems are relatively great and substantial physical and social restructuring activities have to be carried out. Sometimes these programmes are undertaken in collaboration with the European Programme URBAN, which (at least in theory) aims to fight the worst socioeconomic problems in European urban districts by linking them to economic opportunities. One of the aims of the GPV is to cope with the problems comprehensively, stimulating cooperation between different governmental layers and different urban actors.

Under the GPV a new regeneration programme has been developed for the Neuhof quarter in the Territorial Unit South. In this quarter an URBAN programme is also being carried out. The GPV comprises three elements: to stimulate cultural and social inclusion; to improve living conditions; and to accomplish urban and economic transformation. Much attention is given to the physical restructuring of the urban area. One of the aims is to improve the image of the district, which is currently rather poor. Several partners participate in the GPV: the state, the department, the region, the city, construction companies for social housing, etc. Under the GPV programme, €0.9 million is available for a period of six years. The DAS also participates in the GPV thanks to the Masterplan, which enables different institutions concerned with social development to work together. The social aspects of the project have been defined with the help of DAS, who also maintains communication with the families in the area. Nine professionals from different disciplines work together with people from other city departments (such as health and child care) to find means to relocate families and to stimulate their social inclusion. There is now a single file for each family. This is something new because previously each discipline and each department had its own file. One of the ideas of the GPV programme is to exchange experiences in fighting social problems, thus breeding ideas for further development programmes.

Actors Involved

The Bank for Family Funds (Caisse d'Allocations Familiales, CAF) The CAF is a departmental bank/insurance institution which among other tasks, manages the monetary provision of social services for the city of Strasbourg. It has about 400 employees and provides services to 160,000 households. The CAF receives a total amount of €750 million yearly from the state to finance social activities. The CAF has three main action areas:

1 *Demography*: this was the main goal of the institution when it was created. During the post-war period, the state wanted to stimulate demographic growth and to that end supported families with economic help.

2   *Child care*: this is also related to the policy to increase the number of births, by providing good mother and child care for children from 0 to 6 years old. Seven-tenths of the costs of child care are paid by the CAF. Another service of the CAF in this category is the support for acquiring housing.
3   *Services for handicapped and socially isolated people*: this includes the management of the RMI.

The CAF contributes to the local social services by providing financial means. It finances projects in the social field that are proposed by the city. Apart from that, it also invests in equipment and provides examples of working methods through operational subsidies, that is to say, it acts as technical adviser for the development of programmes by the city. Lately under the Masterplan, the CAF has become more active as a partner in local social policy. It has extended its activities to care of adolescents, especially the funding of leisure activities. The CAF establishes contracts with the city in these matters. Other new areas of intervention are housing and infrastructure (equipment as the health/social centres at the Territorial Units) and support to associations.

Municipal centre for social action (Centre Communal d'Action Social, CCAS)
Community Centres for Social Action are public-private partnerships through which cities can carry out social policies together with their local partners. These services have to be centres for reflection, participation and cooperation, and thus instruments to improve the working of the local democracy. According to the 1992 law, the CCAS can have an important role in determining and analysing the social needs. For that goal, it can set up observation systems for social phenomena and systems to evaluate the implemented social policies. In 1997, a CCAS started operations in Strasbourg, with three missions:

• management of temporary housing of people with social problems;
• cooperation of the city with private organisations in the social arena;
• development of innovative, experimental projects in the social field.

3.4   Analysis of the Organising Capacity

Vision

The client is central to the new approach   The central vision behind the Masterplan is to make the client the focus of the social policies. The 1998

French law to fight social exclusion seems to be the main inspiration of this vision. The main underlying philosophy of this law is as stated that in principal every citizen has to be considered as an autonomous person capable of taking his own decisions. An important complementary element of this idea is that, though there are exceptions, every citizen in principle has to become self-sufficient, but retains the right to obtain support from social institutions under certain circumstances and certain preconditions. Those actors have the duty to help the client to become self-sufficient in time (*the empowering of individuals*).

The strategies that were developed on the base of the new vision on social policies in Strasbourg are laid down in the urban Masterplan. It says that existing organisations in the social arena have to be restructured to enable actors to cooperate to serve the clients better. The new approach is that social policies are in principle to be carried out *together* with the client. That demands a more active attitude from either party, the social workers as well as the clients.

Improve services first, change regulations later In France, laws and regulations play a dominant role. Often policy changes have to be laid down in a formal way before they can be carried out. That is evident from this case study. For the description of social policies in France, the introduction of new laws and regulations is especially important for changes in this field. The Masterplan, however, aims to change this dominance of the formal aspects of policy. The strategy of the Masterplan is to mobilise the existing services and to make them more efficient, but using the existing laws and regulations. The intention is that once some results are achieved, they can be used to change the laws. First a more comprehensive approach of social policies has to be realised in which the customer has a central position. This aim has to be the focus of the reorganisation of the 'social arena'. At a later stage the resulting changes could be formalised in one way or another. Thus 'form follows function'.

Strategic Networks: Cooperation between the Actors Involved

Cooperation between government levels The administrative structure of France is highly centralised. The national government has always been relatively dominant. National laws and regulations play a very important role in the French cities. Moreover, there are representatives of the state (*Préfet*) active at lower administrative levels (region, department), taking care of the adequate implementation of these national laws and regulations. However, nowadays a decentralisation trend is noticeable in France. Lower governmental levels get more policy freedom. And more and more the national representatives in lower governments seem to pass on local needs and wishes to higher governmental levels, instead of just carrying out national interests. Besides, as stated above, the national law of 1998 to fight social exclusion was a major inspiration for the Masterplan. In that respect, the national government has boosted the development of social policies in Strasbourg.

A development favouring intergovernmental cooperation is the GPV policy. Within its framework, there is a quite intensive cooperation between the governmental actors involved, from the municipal level to the state. They cooperate with one another to find appropriate ways to tackle the socioeconomic problems in the designated priority areas, and negotiate the financial contributions that are to be made by the actors involved. The results of these negotiations are laid down in urban contracts.

A problem that confronts the Masterplan is related to the special situation of Strasbourg in comparison with other French cities. As mentioned before, for historical reasons Strasbourg has taken responsibility for the provision of social services. This sometimes collides with the tasks of the department, which in the French system is the responsible government layer for most of the social services. To solve the problem of competencies a more flexible spatial division of tasks would be desirable, with a clearer definition of levels of intervention for each spatial area, taking into account the subsidiarity principle.

According to some discussion partners, it would be desirable for the *Communauté Urbaine de Strasbourg* to obtain more responsibilities in the social field. That would enable the municipalities within the territory of the CUS to work together without having to deal with the department level. An advantage would be the possibility of differentiating provision and definition of social services in rural and urban municipalities, since the more rural municipalities of the department *Bas-Rhin* outside the CUS have fewer social problems than the urban districts. Thus, according to the subsidiarity principle the CUS would be a more appropriate governmental level for social policies than the department. In fact, CUS municipalities already cooperate in matters of transport or employment, but – according to some discussion partners – more responsibilities for social policies would be desirable too.

Cooperation between social workers One of the key elements of the Masterplan strategy is the cooperation of the workers in the social field, so that the clients get more coherent and effective help. In the period before the restructuring of the social policies, social workers used to operate quite independently. Social workers were taught that their work was based on an individual relationship between client and worker, without taking into account the other institutions and society. According to the Masterplan, the field workers now need to change their work culture and mentality and adapt to the new desired approach. They need to be more proactive and help the client in a more coherent way, for which they might need the cooperation of other experts in the field. To achieve these changes, new ways of training and education are needed. Therefore an important complementary training and education programme has been set up for the professionals.

The new approach met with some opposition among the professionals who were not used to working together, and they took exception to a project that in a way had be 'imposed' on them by the administration. During the implementation stage there were even some strikes. Nowadays, the cooperation is improving. Teams of social workers discuss together individual files of clients and coordinate the different roles they have to play with respect to these clients.

Leadership

The realisation of the Masterplan has been the result of a strong political drive by the mayor of Strasbourg and the alderman for social action. It explains the decisiveness with which the Masterplan has been developed and is being implemented. A strong political force behind the changes seems to be a necessary precondition to set in motion such massive changes of social actions. For indeed the entire structure of the social arena is being changed, and from the social workers a change in mentality is expected. To implement such changes in a successful way without a strong leadership would be well-nigh impossible. This is especially true in France where hierarchical relations are still very much respected. The director of the DAS has played another important role in leading the actual implementation of the ideas of the Masterplan and motivating the employees by explaining why the proposed changes were so important.

Political Support

The development of the Masterplan was the result of political will on the part of the mayor, the alderman for social action, as well as the city council. Within the city council there was broad political support for the objectives and the implementation of the Masterplan.

When we analysed the Strasbourg case, the department, which takes a regional approach to policy, had a different political constitution from the city. Its officers seemed to be more inclined to give priority to problems on the rural level. The city of Strasbourg objects to this, stressing that social problems cumulate in particular on the urban level. According to urban actors the department allocates too few resources to the city to manage the social problems in an adequate way.

Societal Support

One of the difficulties confronting the city of Strasbourg is the decreasing interest and participation of citizens in public matters. This is considered an adverse tendency, especially in a period in which the city wants to stimulate social networks and to know much more about the needs of its inhabitants. Therefore within the framework of the Masterplan the idea has been considered to set up *inhabitant committees* in each territorial unit. These committees have to help to decrease the distance between the urban government and the inhabitants. They are to be started in 2001 and can have a twofold function: to inform the urban government about the needs of the inhabitants and the inhabitants about the governmental policies.

Strategy Development and Implementation

The implementation of social policies at territorial level allows problems to be identified faster, and facilitates the provision of services to the user. One inconvenience is that this approach is time-consuming because a lot of time is 'lost' in meetings to exchange ideas. This is considered to be partly a temporary inconvenience during the adaptation to the new way of working. Especially during the transition period, the new approach did cost a lot of time because of the numerous meetings that had to be held. Now obviously the main philosophy of the new approach is to make social policy more effective by regular discussions among the workers involved. The idea behind the main strategies of the Masterplan is that the advantages of better mutual communication will outweigh the time spent in the discussions and therefore not available for direct help to the clients.

The Masterplan expresses new ideas developed by the administration about the provision of social services. One prominent aim is to operate in a less bureaucratic way. Bureaucracy has always been and is still a major obstacle to improved social services in the city. It limits the possibilities of innovative creation of new programmes responding to user needs. The city administration is relatively large and rigid. Much time is needed to change the mentality and work culture. During the implementation of the Masterplan things have improved, but according to some discussion partners still not enough, because they feel that while ideas have changed, actions have trailed behind. In their viewpoint, the administration should be more flexible and less centralised. To achieve a new approach, workers should have more power of decision in their daily work. They admit that the idea of much more cooperation between them is crucial to building up a more coherent social system. What came out of the discussions is that the main problem lies primarily in the culture and mentality of the actors involved and less in the organisation structure.

Monitoring of Output and Outcome

Much attention has been given to the set-up of an adequate monitoring system. A number of associative and governmental actors cooperate in the so-called social observatory that was created in the framework of the Masterplan. It has to contribute to the new approach in the social policies. The idea is that anybody can provide information to this system and anybody can use its results. It is to help the social actors to cooperate better, by giving them the same access to the same high quality information data. In the observatory, linkages can be made between micro and macro data. With help of the observatory, social problems can be recognised earlier and customers can be served in a more coherent way. The observatory also has to serve as a powerful tool to evaluate the results of the new approach to social policy.

It is too early to judge the results of the Masterplan. At the moment of our analysis, the last stage of implementing the Masterplan had just started. At this stage also the first evaluations of the new approach are to be made. So we could observe only that the first intended changes that were necessary in the framework of the Masterplan have actually been achieved.

3.5   Conclusions

Masterplan: a New Approach that Seems to Meet Modern Social Demands

With its approach to social policy Strasbourg seems to be ahead of other French cities. This approach has changed drastically after developing and implementing the Masterplan for Social Intervention. The basic idea of the new approach is to put the client central to the implementation of social policies. The Masterplan, the focus of this case study, aims to restructure the social-policy field according to three dimensions: a territorial, a thematic and a logistic dimension. Special attention has been given to the territorial approach, which is to permit a more comprehensive approach in the direct vicinity of the clients. Stress has been put on the fact that the new approach should primarily imply a change of attitude of the actors involved, rather than an immediate change of laws or regulations. In particular the way social workers operate in the field, their mentality and their attitudes to clients had to be changed to achieve the envisaged goals. This idea has grown especially since the introduction of the French law of 1989 to fight social exclusion. Besides more client-oriented social policies, a prominent consequence of this law was the drive to make clients more independent and self-sufficient.

The ideas of the Masterplan can be considered as a modern approach to social policy. The first novelty is the focus on the customer. In the current society, it is almost impossible clearly to identify groups by distinguishing characteristics. Customers show a more individualised behaviour, thus demanding individualised responses. No standardised packages of social services can be provided any more, but tailor-made solutions, which have been agreed on by professionals from different disciplines. Secondly, the need is more and more felt to make every individual independent and self-sufficient. There is a growing awareness that to fight social exclusion effectively it makes more sense to strive for self-sufficiency of people than to go on giving them financial and social support. The best way is to stimulate clients to find adequate work, provide for themselves and become independent. This will also help them to become socially included. Thirdly, there is a growing need to deal with social problems in cities at the district level. That seems especially true of suburban areas in medium-size and large cities. Especially in France, many social problems occur in the so-called hard rings of cities, in urban districts that were erected during the 1950s and 1960s, and are often regarded as not the most attractive areas. These problems cannot be adequately dealt with any more from the metropolitan level: the distance to organisations at central level has become too large. Metropolitan organisations lack commitment with the districts located at a certain distance. And the inhabitants feel too large a distance between themselves and the administration. Therefore, cities would do well to find out what the appropriate scale is on which to deal with social problems, and then reduce the distance accordingly. That has indeed been done in Strasbourg, by making a division into six urban districts.

The CUS can be Considered an Adequate Level for Direction and Coordination of Social Policies

Although the district is considered to be on an adequate scale for the direct implementation of social services, obviously a higher level is necessary for the coordination and direction of the urban social policies. According to the subsidiarity principle, a higher government level is desirable when the size and the consequences of the proposed interventions exceed the geographical scale of the government concerned. If they do not exceed this scale, a lower government could be more appropriate for the policies concerned. In that respect, some consider the department too high a level for some social policies which were attributed by the French law to this public body. The *Communauté Urbaine* is considered to be a more appropriate level for dealing with social policies, since the areas within the territory of the CUS are often confronted with more or less similar social problems. When problems manifest themselves especially at the metropolitan dimension (and hardly outside that territory), solutions must take this dimension into account. The social problems of the metropolitan area differ from those of the more rural parts within the department. That is the major reason for discussion partners to look upon the department as a less appropriate level for handling these policies. Currently, the CUS is not competent in social policy but many would like it to be.

Relatively Bad Social Circumstances are a Major Incentive for Decisive Actions

The implementation of the new and modern approach to social policy seems to be strongly stimulated by the bad social circumstances in some districts of Strasbourg. Strasbourg is comparable in terms of size with the cities of Malmö and Utrecht. Our perception from field visits was that social problems in Strasbourg were serious compared with these northern cities. In this case study we have described the case of Neuhof, which has a poor image because of the concentration of socially excluded people. The larger houses in the Neuhof area have much decreased in value and many shops have closed, owing to image and security problems. Quite a few houses are in very bad shape and are going to be demolished. An extensive physical restructuring programme is to be carried out to raise the attractiveness of the district. All these relatively bad social circumstances in this and other districts of Strasbourg have stimulated the actors involved to speed up the restructuring programme of the 'social arena'. There was a broad conviction that only the new approach could help to fight the social exclusion problem effectively and efficiently. In the Neuhof district, there is hope that the combination of this physical programme and the new approach of social policies will help to reintegrate the inhabitants of this district in civil society and improve the appeal and image of the area.

Opportunities: Attractive Suburbs and Empowering of Individuals

In Strasbourg, as in Rotterdam and (on a smaller scale) in Utrecht, social measures are combined with physical restructuring measures. In the framework of the GPV, a relatively large number of deteriorated houses in Neuhof are to be demolished, and new more attractive houses are to be constructed there. One aim is to realise a more varied housing stock and supply of facilities in the district. Pleasant suburbs should help to diminish social exclusion phenomena. The opportunity-oriented approach of Strasbourg can be founded not only in the physical restructuring of deteriorated districts, but also in the policy of empowering individuals.

Note

1   This information is drawn from van den Berg et al., 1998.

Chapter 4

Organisational Reforms in Antwerp

4.1 Introduction

As a prominent harbour city as well as a town of industry and commerce, Antwerp is the motor of the Flemish economy. The value added and employment created here are to the benefit of many people within and around the city limits. But, like so many other towns, Antwerp is beset with serious social problems. The city is among the towns in Belgium with a concentration of the unemployed, those in need of social assistance, or illegal immigrants. Antwerp scores highly on poverty and social deprivation. 'That duality obscures Antwerp's real standing as a city with economic prospects and sufficient trump cards to grow and to cope with the social problems' (Stad Antwerpen, 2000).

The Antwerp authorities understand that a new, comprehensive and more coherent policy is a prime condition for coping better with the social problems. In that view, there is an urgent need for social-economic policy objectives and policy activity for both the short and the long term. That need can only be met through the cooperation of many organisations and agencies, including the national and Flemish governments. That is indeed well understood on both government levels. For several years the Flemish government has pursued a policy specifically oriented to urban and metropolitan social problems by means of the *Sociaal Impuls Fonds* (Social Impulse Fund, SIF). Initiatives and actions undertaken under that heading are the subjects of the Antwerp case study. Before going into the details of this SIF scheme, we will sketch in section 4.2 a profile of the Antwerp region. Section 4.3 sheds light on the social problems, which the SIF scheme sets out to alleviate. After the description of the SIF programme and the most prominent actors in section 4.4, section 4.5 elaborates the elements of organising capacity that have become apparent so far in the implementation of the SIF scheme. Section 4.6, finally, summarises and concludes. The data of the metropolitan profile of Antwerp are summarised in Table 4.1.

Table 4.1   Data of metropolitan profile of Antwerp

Characteristic	Antwerp
Population of the city (1995)	456,000
Population of the urban region (1995)	1,161,000
Growth of the urban population (city, %, 1991–1996)	-2.50
Share of the population of foreign extraction (city, %, 1997)	14
Proportion of population of working age in employment (city, %, 1991)	61
Unemployment rates (city, %, 2000)	12
Proportion of employment in industry (city, %, 1997)	24.9
Proportion of employment in services (city, %, 1997)	71.1
Number of administrative tiers (including state and boroughs)	5
Borough Boards	No

Sources: van den Berg, Braun and van der Meer, 1998, p. 38; European Commission, 2000, Vol. 1, p. 122; idem, Vol. 2, p. 54.

4.2   Social-economic Profile of the Antwerp Region

Demography

The city of Antwerp has 456,000 inhabitants. The 'functional' Antwerp city region (based on commuter relations) houses over 1.1 million, a little more than the nearly one million accommodated in the administrative region of Antwerp. In the early 1970s, the area which is now the city of Antwerp registered 550,000 inhabitants, which implies a reduction by 100,000. However, in the last decade of the twentieth century the decline slowed down considerably and by now the population volume seems more or less stabilised. So far, there have not been any signs of the new metropolitan growth ('reurbanisation') that seems to have been instigated in several European central towns by a renewed interest in urban living, an urban policy trying to restore the appeal of city life, and considerable natural growth among citizens of foreign extraction. Within the Antwerp region, it is the more 'rural' municipalities in the second ring east of the town, far from the harbour industry in the west, that show clear growth tendencies. The urbanisation features of the first ring around the city are very similar to those of the central city itself.

The impression is (there is little relevant quantitative information available) that single persons (46 per cent of all households), one-parent families, ethnic minorities (over 9 per cent), senior citizens (one-fifth are older than 65), lower-income groups and social benefit recipients dominate the urban population. That is confirmed by the lagging growth of purchasing power within Antwerp and the fact that the average income of the Antwerp population lies four percentage points below the Flemish average. Antwerp also trails behind other Flemish cities in income growth.

Economy and Employment

The multimodal transport junction Antwerp is prominently situated within the European core triangle made up by the Paris, London and Randstad regions. It is also well positioned in relation to the Ruhr area. As a European port, Antwerp comes second (after Rotterdam) in terms of tonnage, with general cargo and containers as its strongest points. By recent data (of the 1993–1996 period), the Antwerp regional economy is doing well. In growth of turnover (over 11 per cent) and value added (nearly 9 per cent), Antwerp ranks above Flanders. Remarkably, in those respects the city seems to score even better than its suburban municipalities. The growth figures for investments give more reason for concern: Antwerp is clearly trailing behind the Flemish average (3.9 versus 5.8 per cent). 'Lack of space and lack of public funds to attract business companies are apparently driving investors away from the cities towards regional urban areas' (Stad Antwerpen, 2000). Figures from the National Bank reveal that there is a sharp contrast between the positive growth of value added in the city of Antwerp during the 1990–1996 period and the decline in employment (-6.2 per cent) and investments (-22.4 per cent). The National Bank concludes that though the suburban municipalities have managed to compensate for the drop in employment and investment, the region of Antwerp still trails behind the average Flemish growth.

Antwerp functions as an employment centre for the region. Two-thirds of the people who work in Antwerp live outside the city. The employment ratio is 100, which means that in quantity, local employment equals the potential active population. However, its position as an employment centre is in jeopardy. Since 1985 Antwerp has suffered a net loss of 2,000 jobs, while 30,000 new jobs have on balance been created in the region. The loss of jobs in industry could not be fully compensated by the growth in services. Many jobs were lost in the port in particular: compared to 1985, the number of jobs dropped by one-fifth. On the other hand, the port achieves strong turnovers and much value added. In fact, the creation of jobs can no longer keep pace with the generation of prosperity. Industrial towns like Antwerp are in particular confronted with that divergence, 'the more so as the local industry is slow to renovate and assume its proper place in the new economy' (Stad Antwerpen, 2000).

The Antwerp economy is dominated by a few large companies. The enlarged scale of the production structure makes the city sensitive to the decisions of those companies, decisions that are often made outside Antwerp (and even outside Belgium). The formation of European and global conglomerates of internationally operating companies has rendered many European cities, including Antwerp, more dependent on decisions made abroad. Most of the large companies are found in manufacturing industry, which accounts for about one-quarter of total employment. Within industry, metal works and chemical companies are dominant (together accounting for three-fifths of total industrial employment).

The tertiary sector is good for three-quarters of all jobs, the greatest numbers being found in transport and storage (one-quarter), business and financial services (one-third) and trade (one-quarter). Compared to other large West European towns, the share of industry in local employment is high.

Employment is growing fastest in business services (20 per cent between 1993 and 1998), waste processing (16 per cent), and public government (12 per cent). In business services, part of the growth is due to making up for arrears. The strongest clusters within the Antwerp economy are still transport and distribution and the port-related industrial cluster. The diamond trade is traditionally a strong element of Antwerp exports. There appear to be promising prospects for cluster development in environmental technology, telematics and tourism. The growth of tourism is reflected in, among other things, the progress of hotels and catering, accounting for nearly 5 per cent of all employment. Compared to dominant industrial sectors such as chemicals (almost 6 per cent) and metal industry (8.4 per cent), the hotels and catering branch (at any rate in terms of employment) constitutes an economic sector to reckon with.

The port of Antwerp is still the motor of the economy but no longer the pre-eminent generator of jobs. Antwerp has made the switch to a modern service economy, but as such is still trailing behind its direct surroundings. One negative effect of the growing service sector is the lack of jobs for low- or unskilled workers and the ensuing persistent unemployment. Like other labour markets, that of Antwerp is characterised by the spatial paradox of a great demand for labour side by side with considerable unemployment. With seven jobseekers to each vacancy, entrepreneurs are still complaining that they cannot find suitable workers. In January 2000, 12 per cent of workers in the city of Antwerp were unemployed. In the suburban municipalities the percentage was a mere five, which brings regional unemployment to some 8 per cent.

Obstacles to further economic development are the lack of space for new activity, the greatly increased traffic congestion, and the poor cooperation with the suburbs in the functional Antwerp region. Yet another bottleneck is the weak financial position of the city, which prevents large-scale public investment in traffic infrastructure or development of the waterfront, for which there is a large need and there are good opportunities available.

The Central Station Area: an Economic Chance

Thanks to financial support from the federal government, one important project has been taken in hand, namely the construction of a tunnel for the Paris-Brussels-Amsterdam HST section, in which Antwerp Central Station is to be a point of call. That opens up prospects of revitalisation for the station area. However, this is mainly a concern for Antwerp itself, possibly supported by Flanders in the matter of infrastructure. The response to that opportunity seems to become decisive for the successful revitalisation of the backward neighbourhoods of northeast Antwerp, Borgerhout and the *Eilandje* (small island). Indeed, these neighbourhoods could profit in particular from the quality impulse of the HST. An important condition for success is good internal access to the station. There is no early solution on that score in sight (van den Berg and Pol, 1999). Such an involved intra-urban project requires a comprehensive approach in which the various functions (living, working, transportation, hotels and catering, leisure, culture, meeting) can be balanced for mutual reinforcement. The combined strength and knowledge of all the public and private parties involved can create an added value that could never be achieved by any one of the parties on their own. In view of the social problems the challenge is to seize this opportunity, which is not likely to be repeated in the future. It is a matter of profiting from the momentum, if necessary by resorting to creative financing methods (van den Berg and Pol, 1999).

Administration

Since the early 1970s, Belgium has gone through a process of federalisation, which was completed in 1995 by the first elections for the three regional parliaments. The government of Flanders then became for many purposes the prominent centre of address for the Antwerp administration.

The joining of seven suburbs with Antwerp in 1983 (which more than doubled its territory) has not improved the cooperation with the regional municipalities that were not included in the merger. Rather, intra-regional competition has sharpened, for one thing making the problem of scarce business sites harder to solve. For another, the present regional distribution of municipal revenues and expenses is unacceptable to Antwerp. There is a painful lack of balance between the rich suburbs which draw for services upon the relatively poor Antwerp, beset as it is with social, accessibility and environmental problems.

The Antwerp administration falls into two independent bodies: the city government, of which port management, spatial planning and various municipal services are prominent elements, and the *Openbaar Centrum voor Maatschappelijk Welzijn* (Public Centre for Societal Welfare, OCMW), which can be understood to represent the social and care sectors of municipal policy. That division, not found anywhere else in Europe except in France, is a legacy from Napoleonic times. After the mayor, the chairman of the OCMW holds a prominent public function within the local administration, comparable to that of deputy mayors. Until recently, local policy was primarily understood as rendering services and the municipal organisation was concerned more with implementation than with strategic planning and/or (long-term) policy formulation. However, the international context is changing fast. What with globalisation and the increasing importance of information technology, the competition among urban regions is becoming fiercer all the time. In Antwerp, as elsewhere, people are increasingly waking up to the need for a more entrepreneurial attitude, and in particular for more cooperation with private and public partners in the region (and beyond). Nowadays a change towards a more proactive, strategic and comprehensive approach of urban matters can be noticed.

4.3   Social Problems in Antwerp

For the *description* of social problems we concentrate on problems of unemployment and the spatial concentration of social problems in some neighbourhoods. Problems that considerably contribute to the quality of the social environment, such as inadequate education, criminality and feelings of insecurity, environmental problems, deteriorated housing, inadequate service levels, poverty and social exclusion, etc., will only be touched upon.

Antwerp suffers the consequences of growing prosperity and the rising information society. The gap between those who can and those who cannot share in the prosperity, is steadily widening. The social problems are most painfully evident in the high and persistent unemployment rate, the unequal spread of prosperity and the poor quality of housing. The city government at the time of writing (formally in function until the autumn of 2000, when new elections were held), has granted policy priority to these problems (one consideration being, no doubt, the political aspects, such as the rise of a right-wing nationalist party). The prime ambition is to reduce the psychological distance between authorities and citizens, get a better grip of the social problems, and improve the quality of the housing stock. The unemployment problems have been described as follows (Stad Antwerpen, 2000):

- there is a wide difference in unemployment rates between the city and the suburban municipalities; within Antwerp, unemployment is concentrated in a few neighbourhoods;
- unemployment is very persistent. Despite the favourable economic tide of recent years and the steady reduction of total Flemish unemployment, the same positive result has not been achieved in Antwerp. Obviously, local jobseekers do not meet the demands of the market;
- citizens belonging to an ethnic minority and low-skilled citizens are high-risk groups. In particular young people are excluded from the labour market.

These phenomena are not peculiar to Antwerp. Many major towns in Europe (notably the older industrial and port cities) are similarly beset. In Antwerp, one-quarter of the nearly 23,000 registered jobseekers (in early 2000) are under 25; half of them have no more than a certificate of elementary education, about one-fifth possess another type of certificate (foreign diploma, small business certificate, etc.). Unemployment among women is as high as among men, unlike in Flanders (including Antwerp), where three-fifths of the unemployed are female. So, compared to Flanders, Antwerp has a surfeit of male unemployed. Persons of foreign extraction in particular apparently fail to benefit from the growing economy, since, despite the many vacancies and the increasing tension in the labour market, unemployment among foreigners is slow to decline.

Young people make up the bulk of high-risk groups. Their rate of unemployment is twice or three times as high as that among older citizens. Moreover, nationality and age appear to be strongly correlated, which results in almost one-third of the young people of foreign origin being without a job. The demographic development suggests that this is the very group most likely to increase in number, which is one more reason to try and stem that process.

A great obstacle to participating in the Antwerp labour market appears to be the insufficient supply and high expense of day nurseries. That is a problem for single people with children especially (16 per cent of the unemployed). The positive difference between a social benefit and, for instance, a full-time job in the care sector hardly makes good the expense of nurseries. Lack of skill and linguistic backwardness are other obstacles, but 'they explain only half the story. Unequal treatment of people on account of their skin colour, race or name are other factors which explain the weak labour-market position of persons of foreign extraction' (Stad Antwerpen, 2000).

Underprivileged neighbourhoods In 1987, the city of Antwerp commissioned the University of Antwerp to carry out a first inquiry into the phenomenon of 'deprivation'. The specific situation and the social-economic profile of the socially underprivileged neighbourhood have been charted in the 'Atlas of Deprivation'. The outcome was that there are 25 poor neighbourhoods to be found in the ancient city quarters along the quays, stretching from the Zuid to the St Andries Quarter and on to the *Eilandje*. Stuivenberg and the ancient part of Borgerhout also count as poor neighbourhoods, as are, in the northern part of Antwerp, the environment of the Dam down to the Merksem Docks (Van Hove, 1987). Other inquiries into Antwerp's underprivileged neighbourhoods were undertaken in 1994 by the RISO (Lescrauwaet) and in 1996 by the Catholic University of Leuven (Kesteloot, 1996). By the ranking which the Flemish government had drawn up as a justification for the SIF programme and which was based on some indicators of social backwardness, 35 per cent of all Flemish underprivileged neighbourhoods are found in Antwerp.

Underprivileged neighbourhoods are defined as:

> ... those urban neighbourhoods that are often marked by external decay due to the convergence of economic depression, loss of employment, departure of tradesmen and the outflow of the more affluent citizens. The process is often attended by loss of social tissue, cultural experience and solidarity. Especially the simultaneous occurrence of certain factors causes a kind of social, economic, cultural and architectural tension that causes a neighbourhood to come under the definition of deprivation (Stad en OCMW Antwerpen, 1999, p. 7).

All these neighbourhoods house a high concentration of the lower income groups who are incapable of investing in their environment, and thus find their neighbourhood gradually falling into decay. This group comprises unemployed people, persons who are entitled to a disablement benefit and people who exist on a minimum wage or a small pension. Besides, there are those who are at a disadvantage in any case, namely, untrained or unskilled labourers and migrants. And finally, there are single individuals who have to survive without the support of a sound social structure. Deprived neighbourhoods are marked by poor housing, empty buildings, inadequate social services and a relatively poor quality living environment.

The conclusion must be that the cumulation and culmination in some underprivileged neighbourhoods of such urban problems as persistent unemployment, an increasingly lopsided distribution of prosperity and poor housing is not only socially unacceptable but also a threat to the future (economic) attractiveness of the city. In the regular constellation, the government seems to lack the equipment to fight the problems efficiently and effectively. On the foundation of a comprehensive (social) policy strategy, efforts must be made towards closer cooperation, the formation of networks of actors involved in social improvement activities, the mutual adjustment of measures, and a more market-oriented attitude, all this to achieve better results than have so far come within reach. To that end, short-term actions as well as more long-term structural changes are needed. The SIF scheme is intended to support such actions and changes.

4.4 The Social Impulse Programme and its Actors

The SIF Programme of Antwerp

The SIF scheme initiated the current comprehensive programme of social policy in Antwerp, including the adjustment of several organisations. By the Social Impulse Fund Decree of 14 May 1996, the Flemish Community set out to help cities and municipalities carry out a policy intended to:

• restore the living and environmental quality of the city and the backward neighbourhoods;
• raise prosperity and fight deprivation (Ministerie van de Vlaamse Gemeenschap, 2000).

A prominent object of the SIF is to help switch the present (urban) social policy to a more effective and efficient approach. On the basis of a contract concluded between the Flemish government and some Flemish cities, financial impulses are given for that purpose. The SIF has drawn attention to the backward neighbourhoods in Antwerp. It has also stimulated important organisational changes within the municipality of Antwerp. The bureaucratic organisation used to be predominantly oriented to the supply of services, and lacked what it takes to orchestrate and coordinate new social policies. The proper knowledge and functions were absent; new functions had to be created and new people recruited.

In 1996, a one-year SIF programme was carried out as a test. Next, a three-year programme ran from 1997–99; it was evaluated after completion. Total budget for the first SIF period was ¤136 million, of which ¤68 million went to OCMW. Early in 2000 a new three-year SIF-period started (2000–2002). The second SIF policy plan should have more substance and status. It has to place more distinct accents, attack real bottlenecks and thus make the city's attractions more visible (Ministerie van de Vlaamse Gemeenschap, 2000, p. 7).

For Antwerp, the general mission of the SIF was translated into four policy options:

- urban support: the attraction and image of the city have to be made visible again. The quality of life in the whole city needs raising;
- neighbourhood development: some neighbourhoods in Antwerp need extra support to regain their living qualities. In such underprivileged neighbourhoods, drastic intervention is urgently needed;
- basic services: the welfare of the Antwerp people is to be improved by the supply of basic services that correspond to their current needs and wants;
- integration: specific measures are needed to grant certain groups that are seriously hit by social exclusion an opportunity to integrate in the Antwerp community.

The above policy options are laid down in Table 4.2, together with a tentative ex-ante division of the available funds. From this table, the greater part of the

Table 4.2   The SIF policy options
The planned global distribution of financial means is indicated between brackets

	Improving living and work environment	Improving well-being
General policy	Urban base (9%)	Basic services (55%)
Specific policy	Neighbourhood development (27%)	Integration (7%)

Source: Sociaal Impulsfonds Antwerpen: Beleidsplan 1997–1999, 24 March 1997.

funds (55 per cent) would serve to expand basic services and 27 per cent for neighbourhood development. The extension of the basic services is notably a task of the OCMW. Employment services come under this heading and are given priority. A subdivision has been made into general policy (for the whole of Antwerp) and specific policy (for certain neighbourhoods and groups).

The policy options have been translated into seven strategic objectives (6+1):

1 to make the city more appealing to the middle classes without causing social displacement;
2 to raise the quality of life and attractiveness of the designated neighbourhoods;
3 to optimise the positions of high-risk unemployed groups on their relevant labour market;
4 to catch up educational backlogs in particular for adults and children;
5 to make local policy for children and young people more comprehensive;
6 to raise the welfare of backward groups and individuals;
7 to improve the comprehensiveness of social policy.

The seventh objective differs from the other six in that it can be perceived as a derived objective of the organising social policy: to take care of the coherence of policy. This final objective is concerned notably with the organising capacity of social policy.

> One of the prominent objects of criticism of the former social policy was the fragmentation among organisations and services with similar purposes. Too often, each 'actor' was operating from his own point of view, with his own priorities, his own objectives and work programme (Stad en OCMW Antwerpen, 1999, pp. 11, 12).

For more efficiency, the government decided to create specific consultation and work agencies to coordinate activities in certain policy domains. These will be dealt with in the next section.

The three-year SIF programme is built up as a fully fledged social strategy, including strategic objectives subdivided into one or more programmes. Each programme consists of one or more operational targets. For each operational target indicators, domains of action and actions are indicated. Each year the actions are summarised and the results monitored. An amount of money is allotted per operational target. In Scheme 4.1 an example of an operational target is given.

Scheme 4.1 Example SIF strategy in Antwerp

Strategic objective 3: to optimise the position of high risk unemployed on the labour market, given their capabilities

Programme 1: trajectory guidance
- Operational target: to guide 2,200 high risk unemployed of which 700 have to find a job.
  Funding available: 16 million (of which 10 million for OCMW and 6 million for the City).

Actions domains:
- Development instrument for trajectory guidance (1.3 million available);
- Implementation/optimisation trajectories (14.7 million available).

Actions:
- Setting up registration system;
- Making 'guidance' instrument operational;
- Setting up supply of trajectories and instruments;
- Job announcements in neighbourhoods involved;
- Neighbourhood based activities to prepare migrants for labour market;
- Intervention Fund Employment Projects;
- Job experience projects on schools;
- Coaching young migrants.

Indicators:
- Registration system;
- Number of guided persons per trajectory;
- Number of persons that found a market job.

Results year 1999:
- Implementation instrument 'guidance' including registration, monitoring and forecast systems;
- 2,200 persons involved of which 700 found a job.

The programmes are to be evaluated by indicators drawn up specially for the purpose. The evaluation of the first SIF programme has been carried out by SOMA *vzw* (the organisation to which the coordination and evaluation of the SIF are entrusted) jointly with the ECWS. The process and contents of the SIF have been analysed separately. The SIF programme is subject to five broad evaluation criteria:

1 innovativeness;
2 visibility: the results of the SIF policy must be actually perceivable;
3 sustainability: the impulses given by the SIF programme should make an impact on regular policy and thus acquire permanency;
4 cooperation and network building;
5 participation.

Public Actors Involved

The city administration Until a few years ago, the City of Antwerp occupied itself primarily with tasks in the public domain (laying out and keeping up public spaces) and the supply of municipal services. In the area of social and economic policy the municipality was hardly, if at all, active. The municipal services have recently been reorganised. Nine policy departments have been created (see Figure 4.1), with a central role allotted to the Department of Civil Affairs. This department comprises the '*Dienst Samenlevingsopbouw*' (Community-building Department, DSO), which is responsible for welfare and social policy. This unit develops and coordinates city initiatives concerned with neighbourhood development.

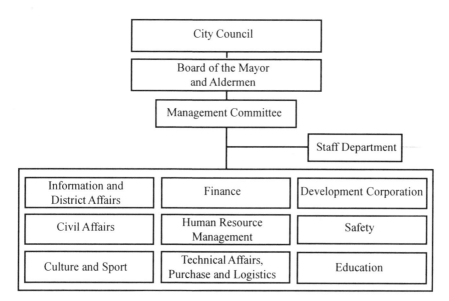

Figure 4.1   The nine departments of the City of Antwerp

Source: http://www.antwerpen.be/stadhuis/organisatie.htm.

Openbaar Centrum voor Maatschappelijk Werk (OCMW, Public Centre for Social Work) The OCMW has responsibilities in the area of welfare and health care. The OCMW is accountable to the city council, but functions independently. It carries out tasks imposed by the Federal and Flemish government. These tasks are clearly defined and cannot be delegated. The fight against deprivation is a prominent point of attention. OCMW tasks are, among others, distribution of social allowances, responsibility for care for young and elderly people, health care, mental health care, psychiatry, and care for disabled persons. The Antwerp OCMW administers nine hospitals and 19 care homes as well as social centres and provision for the handicapped. The OCMW employs some 9,000 people, a few less than the number employed in the city administration. About 15,000 citizens of Antwerp are 'clients' of the OCMW. The OCMW cannot possibly approach all high-risk groups, but needs the help of NGOs. Sometimes, municipal services carry out certain tasks, which the OCMW cannot undertake. For instance, while the OCMW provides shelter to drug addicts, the City takes care of drugs-prevention measures.

Quasi-public Actors Involved

Stedelijke Ontwikkelingsmaatschappij Antwerpen (SOMA vzw, Antwerp City Development Company) SOMA (a *vzw*, a non-profit association) coordinates and orchestrates the spending of some external funds, in particular those made available for the SIF scheme. In the coming period some additional funds will be joined to it, such as the Belgian major cities policy (Plan Piqué 2000–2004) and the European programmes (Objective 2 and Urban 2, if Antwerp is selected). The SOMA was already in existence before the SIF programme was introduced. Initially, it was an organisation primarily occupied with housing improvement, but has gone on to accommodate several 'units' concerned with strategy and (coordination of) social policy. The City of Antwerp had difficulty coordinating and orchestrating the SIF programme within the existing administrative structures. The functions needed to that end were lacking within the Antwerp administration, nor could they be easily created in the face of stringent community personnel recruitment policy and administrative procedures.

The City Council acts as principal and inspector of the SOMA through the City Board (specifically the Alderman of Social Affairs). The Council has the final approval. In legal terms, the *vzw* is separate from the city administration. The SOMA, like the CISO to be discussed later, serves as the legal vehicle to make the organisation of the social policy flexible. Important advantages of such vehicles are the easier recruitment of staff[1] (less stringent proceedings and freedom to attract scarce high-quality workers), and the more flexible operation (less stringent procedures for several activities). Besides, *vzw*s appear to be much less sensitive to political influence than the official city administration, and guarantee greater independence of evaluation and a more or less apolitical position to negotiate between different interests in order to put together the SIF programme.

Closeness to the city is considered important for the *vzw*s. They must not grow into independent entities. The city must have a chance to monitor and influence their performance. The intention is for the SOMA to function as a kind of nursery of new organisations capable of innovative operation. In principle, the new organisations will in time be incorporated into the city administration. The *vzw*s are considered necessary for innovativeness and development, while for services and administrative tasks the existing municipal departments are deemed more appropriate. The SOMA thus functions as a kind of think-tank for the city.

Although the SOMA is not yet optimally fulfilling the tasks of orchestrating and drawing-up business plans, in comparison to five years ago there has been much improvement. Most of the actors involved agree that the operations could be more effective and efficient. At the moment the question is under discussion whether the SOMA should not be brought closer to the city. The discussion is conducted notably by political circles, but also by the sitting bureaucracy, which looks somewhat askance at the position of the quasi-officers. Whether, when and to what extent the new organisation might be included in the regular administrative structure is still an open question.

Centrum voor Informatie en Samenlevingsopbouw (CISO vzw; Centres for Information and Community Development, vzw) To get to grips with Antwerp's social problems, the decision has been made to spread the services across the city and create neighbourhood offices in the so-called underprivileged neighbourhoods. These neighbourhood offices (CISO) address all the Antwerp population in specific areas and are also the driving force behind the implementation of the local welfare policy. The CISO works within the DSO, but they are legally separated. Like the SOMA, the CISO can attract new staff in a more flexible way.

CISO is a *vzw*, which accommodates public organisations that cannot find a place within the regular bureaucracy, but nevertheless need to be close to it. Some 160 persons are employed by the CISO. Several public organisations were set up within the SOMA and subsequently placed with the CISO to be closer to the city administration (see Figure 4.2). Examples are the units for housing and neighbourhood development. The satellite structures, which the *vzws* actually are, are considered necessary for a successful social policy. Admittedly, it is a second-best solution. Ideally, their tasks should be carried out within the existing bureaucratic structure, for that is the environment where organising capacity should ultimately be consolidated.

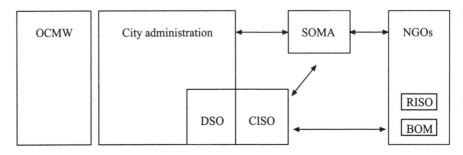

Figure 4.2   Relevant organisations for the SIF policy in Antwerp

Some Elements of the vzws

Employment unit Until some five years ago, the City of Antwerp did not much bother with employment policy. An NGO, Vitamin W, had assumed that task at the time. Vitamin W is a partnership of NGOs in Antwerp whose object is to reintegrate long-term unemployed persons into the labour market. This partnership acted to some extent as orchestrator of Antwerp employment policy.

Since then, an urban employment unit has been created with the aid of SIF money. Its task is to direct initiatives to create jobs and coach the unemployed. So, the orchestration of employment policy has been taken over by the City. The employment unit became operational early in 1998 and comes legally under the CISO, but is in practice under the DSO unit within the Civil Affairs department.

In pre-SIF times, a good employment policy was hardly possible on account of the strong fragmentation of the field. A tangle of bodies was active, mostly getting in one another's way. The employment unit has achieved some kind of order. The prominent partners of the local government in matters of unemployment policy are at present the Permanent Workgroup for High-Risk Groups, VDAB (labour market office), Vitamin W, the Chamber of Commerce and Industry, TISO (*Tewerkstellingsinitiatieven Stedelijk Onderwijs*: Employment Initiatives of Municipal Education), and TIVO (*Tewerkstellingsinitiatieven Vrij Onderwijs*: Employment Initiatives of Private Education). Vitamin W, quite dominant at first, is now assuming a role as a partner.

Before the employment unit was created, the only form of employment policy for the long-term unemployed was the offer of social employment. In the context of SIF that principle has been abandoned in favour of a more market-oriented approach. The orientation of the employment unit is pictured in Figure 4.3: first efforts are made to create jobs by a good match of supply and demand on the labour market, and only in the last resort are 'social' jobs created for the long-term unemployed. That is a clear break with the past, when the emphasis was on the bottom line of the schematic and the market was hardly if at all considered. From the evaluation, the results have surpassed the pre-set objectives. In 1998, the SIF yielded more than 2000 additional jobs, either directly (SIF staff and results of coaching trajectories and job creation) and indirectly (spin-off from infrastructural works) (Stad en OCMW, Antwerpen, 1999, p. 195).

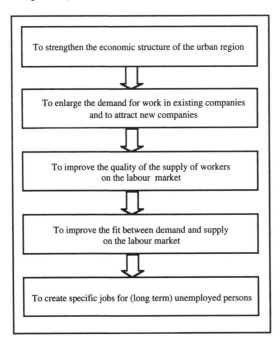

Figure 4.3   Ranking of employment instruments in Antwerp

Source: Rotterdam Employment Advisory Board in Stad Antwerpen, 2000, p. 30.

Planning unit The planning unit was started within the SOMA with some delay, by mid-1998. The initial intention was to start up this unit within the city administration, which already boasted a (small) planning department. That intention failing, the SOMA was resorted to. The planning unit is intended to be integrated within two years with the municipal development company. Its task will be to draw up spatial plans for the neighbourhoods eligible for the SIF programme. High-grade spatial elements such as buildings, streets and squares should make the relevant actors confident in the neighbourhood approach.

Several disciplines are represented in the planning unit, such as an architect, a spatial planner, a sociologist, an economist and a communications expert. The unit will monitor interventions in the public domain from the design down to the execution, including the communication with the citizens. Great importance is attached to communication. For maximum support, the activities undertaken for the neighbourhood approach should be adequately communicated to the city, the companies and the citizens.

The planning unit is also contributing to the realisation of a cluster for 'design and product development'. Twenty-five premises[2] have been bought up as a sign to the private sector of the city's confidence in the prospects of such a cluster. Actually, the city cannot legitimately conduct a land and building policy, which is why speculation in certain neighbourhoods cannot always be prevented. As a result, private actors can sometimes make a more than proportional profit from the construction of new infrastructure within the neighbourhood approach.

The City of Antwerp itself has only a small planning department employing about six people. For many years there was no spatial planning to speak of in the city. Nevertheless, there is some tension between the planning unit and this regular bureaucratic planning organisation, centring around the question who is to undertake which spatial task inside the city.

Nongovernmental Organisations (NGOs)

Regionaal Instituut voor Samenlevingsopbouw (RISO, Regional Institute for Community Development) The RISO occupies itself with neighbourhood activities and specific development projects. Founded in 1981 and initially funded mostly by the Flemish government, it now receives half of its expenditure from the Ministry of Social Welfare and the other half from SIF means. In practice the RISO does not receive more money than it did before the SIF programme was introduced, but the allocation is different. On certain conditions the SIF funds can be used for continuous tasks of the RISO which otherwise would be in jeopardy. The SIF project has consolidated the financial and practical bond with the City of Antwerp. Its work in the SIF context has gained the RISO 'recognition' in Antwerp and acceptance as a serious actor in the implementation of social policy.

The evaluation required for SIF undertakings has compelled the RISO to work more systematically and according to plan, but also caused some practical problems. The RISO was, for instance, required to make an innovation indicator, an unknown concept that remained unexplained. The request to perform a 0-measurement of existent and nonexistent neighbourhood activity was likewise seen as an impossible task without further explanation. Nettled by such commissions and to gain an insight into results achieved, the RISO undertook to develop its own – bottom-up – indicators. The RISO also asked its implementing bodies to develop such indicators. Thus stirred, the private actors were enabled to contemplate anew the goals of neighbourhood activities, and possibilities of renewing them. What it comes down to is how to strike a balance between the (mostly broad) measurement of results (top-down approach) and the quality of individual achievement (bottom-up approach).

Buurt-Ontwikkelings-Maatschappij (BOM), (Neighbourhood Development Company) On the initiative of the RISO, research was undertaken in the 1985–88 period into the deprived neighbourhoods of Antwerp. A report was published, titled the Deprivation Atlas of the city, which inspired the idea to create an organisation for dedicated neighbourhood development. In consultation with the citizens, the '*Buurt-Ontwikkelings-Maatschappij*' (BOM for short) was founded. The city government, the OCMW, the regional development company (GOM), the Flemish office for job mediation and professional education (VDAB), the RISO, the King Boudewijn Foundation and the University Office Antwerp (UIA) were involved as partners. At first, the City of Antwerp was not active in neighbourhood development, which was not an article of its policy.

A great external incentive for the BOM was a subsidy from the European Union. On the strength of subsidies from the Third Poverty Programme of the EC (1989–94), the BOM started its attack on social deprivation, first in north Antwerp. The BOM operates from an economic philosophy, quite a revolutionary approach, since, so far, the social and economic policies had been two different worlds. The BOM has played a prominent role in policy making in that respect, and is therefore regarded as a kind of think-tank in matters of neighbourhood development. It employs about 130 persons. The

BOM mostly plays the initiating role of developer of neighbourhood projects. Some new BOM projects are a recreational survival route near the forts (supposed to become self-supporting), a cyberspace meeting place, and neighbourhood promotion through billboards and advertising on trams. BOM plans to end its activities after the second SIF programme, on the assumption that, by then, the neighbourhoods would have no more need of such incentives.

In the first years of neighbourhood development especially, the municipality played a secondary role. In the course of the process it assumed an ever-increasing role, however. Neighbourhood development was for some time coordinated through the SOMA, and has now been transferred to the city (to DSO). New initiatives are taken by the municipality, which is assuming leadership in neighbourhood development.

Bedrijfscentrum Noord Oost Antwerpen (NOA, Business centre Northeast Antwerp) The NOA business centre for new entrepreneurs opened its doors on 1 January 1995. It was a BOM initiative funded by the European Urban Pilot programme. To develop a business centre in a deprived neighbourhood was considered a great innovation. The economic effects were supposed to benefit the direct neighbourhood. The Flemish government and the GOM contributed to the financing. The City of Antwerp made an abandoned school building available for conversion to accommodation for 30 small businesses. Once a business plan had been drawn up, private companies were found willing to participate financially (among others, Mercator Verzekeringen, HAS Spaarbank, and De Hefboom). They did so not so much for the envisaged return as because of the standing of the project ('social enterprise') and to develop and consolidate a good relationship with the municipality. Managing directors of those companies are on the NOA Board of Governors. They take the 'social side' of enterprise very seriously. The new entrepreneurs are offered accommodation and administrative support at relatively low prices. There is no selection procedure; in principle, settlement is open to any business. Meanwhile, a great variety of companies have settled here, such as media coaching and business communication, a publisher, informatics consultancy, a company for expert research into labour market and business science, a bicycle messenger service and an industrial paint and plaster company. The centre also boasts a café, which fulfils a prominent function as a meeting place for the neighbourhood.

The business centre tries for an 'open' attitude, which means that service is also given to companies in the neighbourhood who are not established within the centre itself. Moreover, growing companies are assisted to find other accommodation in the neighbourhood or the town, so that there is a sufficient turnover of activities. NOA was considered an innovative project, based on a new vision of the city. For the first time a neighbourhood project paid attention to the possibility of drawing profit from new economic sectors. The NOA has been profitable for two years now. The NOA is also involved in a project of ethnic enterprises, which helps entrepreneurs of foreign origin to run their own companies in a more professional way (for instance by providing training courses). Jointly with Belgacom and other actors, NOA has founded a Telecentre, which employs between 50 and 70 persons who could not be placed through the labour market.

4.5 Analysis of the Organising Capacity

In the analysis of the organising capacity, the activities related to the SIF policy are confronted with the theoretical framework. The intention is to analyse the same elements of organising capacity for each case. However, depending on the specific context and project circumstances, other elements might be highlighted in the differing cases. In the case of Antwerp particular attention is given to institutional aspects. Regarding social policy the city had to start almost from scratch. Before the SIF project the city had hardly developed any social policy; delivery of social services was carried out by NGOs. For the City of Antwerp it was therefore necessary first to set up adequate institutions for social policies. As a result organisational changes were the most noticeable results of the first SIF period, rather than tangible results regarding the contents of the social policies. To judge the results of this first period it is therefore logical to focus in particular on organisational elements, such as vision and strategy in particular *regarding organisational changes*, administrative structure, strategic networks, leadership and communication, and not on material elements like on the results of the social policy (output and outcome).

Vision

The starting point in Antwerp was the idea that the existing organisation was not capable of changing social policies to meet current demands. Thus, first of all, organisational changes were considered necessary, before new ideas on social policies could be developed. In the period before the SIF programme, the City of Antwerp did not have a well-articulated vision on social policy.

The Flemish subsidy programme, however, emitted a strong impulse towards drawing up a comprehensive vision for that field of policy. This has been developed over time, after the organisational reforms took place. As the SIF scheme was implemented, social policy evolved from an inward to an outward orientation; instead of just trying to alleviate the pain of deprivation, explicit endeavours are now being made to attack social problems in a structural way, for instance, by relating to the economic opportunities of city neighbourhoods. The idea is to focus on a limited number of districts in which there is a concentration of social problems. However, the question remains how this social vision is to be embedded in an overall urban or regional long-term vision including spatial, economic, transport and other elements and interrelations crucial for future urban development.

The Antwerp government now pays far more attention to the contents of social policy than before the SIF programme. At the time of the scheme's initiation, the city government was unable to indicate clearly what direction the social policy should take. The changed attitude in that respect is one of the most important results of the SIF. The municipality is much more inclined than before to think about new directions of development. The municipality's social-economic report *Antwerpen, scheve stad in sterke positie* ('Antwerp, Biased City in a Strong Position') is a good case in point. That such a strategic social-economic memorandum should be written by the city would formerly have been unthinkable. It marks a considerable step forward. A comprehensive, sufficiently supported, strategic plan for the city is still lacking, however.

Another important external catalyst for formulating ideas on social policies was the availability of European subsidies. For instance, the BOM partnership initiative was accelerated by financial funds from the European Community. European programmes (such as the Urban Pilot Project and the Community Initiative Urban) seem to have accelerated important changes as a consequence of conditions set by European institutions. The existing administration appeared not always properly equipped to meet these conditions. For instance, the UPP management and implementation were entrusted to the BOM. The setting up of a neighbourhood business centre (NOA) by BOM was stimulated by UPP funds. The Community Initiative Urban required a neighbourhood-based integrated socioeconomic approach.

A thorough conversion of the strictly hierarchical and bureaucratic municipal administration has been initiated, to pave the way for the next step: towards strategic planning. Antwerp has decided to take as its example the successful Barcelona model (in particular Barcelona Activa), which has demonstrated how a flexible organisation and relative autonomy (escaping a little from the bureaucratic straightjacket) can open the way to entrepreneurial cooperation with investors, entrepreneurs, public bodies, etc. This Catalan organisation is responsible for the realisation of the economic and employment policies of the city of Barcelona.

> The mission of Barcelona Activa is to put Barcelona on the map as an investment- and enterprise-minded town. Its customers are entrepreneurs, investors, educational organisations, jobseekers and public authorities. To please those customers, the unit has a flexible structure and can proceed with a measure of autonomy (Stad Antwerpen, 2000, p. 67).

In Antwerp, a comparable commission has been given to *Stadsplan,* which has not yet been approved by the City Council. '*Stadsplan*'s mission is to prepare large, significant projects that are likely to upset the urban spatial-economic structure, for policy acceptance and operation' (idem).

In Stad Antwerpen, 2000, the organisational conversion is presented under the heading 'From City Administration to Urban Policy Guidance'. According to the editors of this report, the role most fitting to the local government is to organise the active involvement of all relevant parties and to monitor the policy coherence. In other words, the city administration should be the orchestrator. That implies a new approach to urban management, with the government as one proactive policy partner among others, the partner that is primarily responsible for strategy building and the orchestration of policy processes. To achieve this, not only would the existing administration have to undergo a radical change of culture, but strategists of various disciplines would have to be enlisted next to that of implementers.

Administrative Structure and Culture

The SIF programme stirred the city government to think about the desirable orientation of its social policy, and the changes needed to that end. The desired changes proved difficult to accomplish within the existing rigid bureaucratic structures. The staff employed by the city were experienced in implementing, but lacked strategists. Indeed, they lacked the equipment – that is, the knowledge and the functions – needed to orchestrate and coordinate the SIF programme. Creative thinking was required to set up new agencies capable of decisive and result-oriented action.

As a result of that thinking, two existing semi-public organisations (CISO and SOMA, both so-called *vzws*, not-for-profit associations) were used by the municipality outside the formal administrative structure to enable it to assume a directing and coordinating role in a more flexible way. The sitting bureaucracy tends to look upon these new bodies as threats to their own functioning. As soon as the new organisations have evolved sufficiently to function sustainably within the municipality, they should preferably be integrated in the regular system (see Figure 4.4). The *vzws* should be regarded primarily as a breeding ground for new policy and the hatching of new ideas. The important thing is that the SIF Impulse has stirred up the bureaucracy. The new flexible organisations just outside the established bureaucracy are inciting the city administration to flexibility and dynamics. Such an evolution needs time to consolidate, however. Meanwhile, the *vzws* are there to ensure efficient and decisive action, and to strengthen the organising capacity of Antwerp.

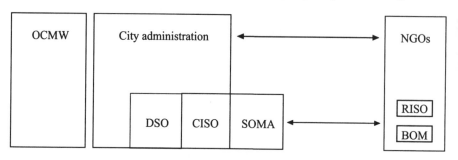

Figure 4.4   The envisaged institutional situation in the social policy field

The question whether or not to integrate the *vzws* in the city administration is something of a dilemma. Integration has the advantages of a transparent structure and an undisputed distribution of competencies. A great disadvantage would be the loss of flexibility. Notably the trade unions and the OCMW, who disapprove of the present fragmentation, plead the integration of the *vzws* in the regular bureaucracy. They regard their present status as a violation of the competencies of the city administration, which to their mind should not cede the policy of care and employment to the market. Politically too, the current approach, how valuable it appeared until now, is considered a second-best solution; the setting up of new or the expansion of existing *vzws* seems not to be appreciated.

An important topic is: what role will and can be assumed by the City Administration? During the last decade the Antwerp administration gradually is changing from a bureaucratic, rather inflexible and reactive organisation, merely oriented to the delivery of public services and to the implementation of public works, to a more proactive organisation, where strategic and comprehensive thinking and acting and a more cooperative and entrepreneurial spirit is developing, meeting the requirements of what can be indicated as 'modern urban management'. The recent reorganisation of the administration is a step in this direction. However, despite the emerging changes the impression is that there is still a way to go.

Strategic Networks (Interaction of Actors)

Before the SIF programme, fragmentation thwarted the pursuit of a coherent social policy. A tangle of mostly publicly funded nongovernmental organisations were sometimes working at cross-purposes and left gaps in social policy. From the evaluation, the neighbourhood activities seem hardly coherent, while substantial parts of the field remain untended. One ambition of the SIF programme is to counter fragmentation by stimulating network building among the actors involved in the making and implementation of policy.

In the evaluation (Ministerie van de Vlaamse Gemeenschap, 2000, p. 33 ff.), networks are cautiously suggested. 'There is a strong tendency towards cooperation and network formation, for instance within OCMW and between OCMW and the city. That cooperation should indeed be structurally anchored.' The wording indicates that there are *intentions* of more cooperation, but that the practical results have been disappointing yet.

Before 1996/97 public actors and NGOs hardly if at all cooperated in the area of social policy. There has been much improvement on that score, but most interaction of actors is on the level of implementation, and far less on the management level.

The public body OCMW is an important actor in the social field. With a few exceptions (such as night shelters for the homeless), the OCMW does not wish to cooperate with NGOs. Some people think that the OCMW could have done several things better than the NGOs, but these would not have fitted in the pre-set task load. The OCMW management regrets that in the frame of SIF some of its proper tasks are allotted to RISO. Between the OCMW (public) and the RISO (NGO) differences in culture have prevented almost any cooperation on the management level. However, on the implementation level associates of the two organisations are working together quite happily.

Another example of a problematic partnership can be found in the field of education. Education has a century-old structure that is difficult to change. The Education Council, where the different blocks (public and special education) are represented, does exist; however, this is a compromise pact between separate blocks rather than an instrument of promoting cooperation. Here too on the working level some results have been accomplished

The basis of the BOM-initiative is a partnership of major public actors, some NGOs (among which are organisations with an economic or a social scope) and a university. The seven partners are represented in the board of BOM. Together they decide about the activities of BOM. The experience of BOM is 'that partnership does not work as a matter of course' (Van Hove and Nieuwinckel, 1996). The experience with BOM is that a partnership needs a formal status, such as a convenant. Informal statements or 'gentlemen's agreements' are too weak as a reliable working basis. Next, a partnership needs to be managed continuously: the partners have to be encouraged to do their job properly within the limits of the covenant. Given the shared responsibilities another problem to solve is: who takes the lead in the management and the development of the partnership? The experience in Antwerp points to the local administration having the strongest relation with the complex field of social problems. But the daily management should not automatically be entrusted to the city as well, because the experience is that the city as a partner also needs to be activated to play its partner role properly. The conclusion within BOM is that partnerships have to grow and a lot of energy is needed to guide and maintain this growth process. Forming the right coalition of partners proves to be a decisive success factor, next to the right ideas, sufficient means and communication with the target groups.

Private banks and insurance companies are involved in the financing of NOA (the neighbourhood small business centre). These companies appear to appreciate their participation, despite the relatively low yields on their investment. Societal interest, improving their image and good relations with the city seem to compensate for this. This public-private 'network' could only be created thanks to a businesslike approach in the form of a business plan.

Leadership

Before the SIF programme was set up, new social and economic policy was mostly initiated by NGOs. With the exception of the activities of the public OCMW (such as distribution of social allowances, responsibility for care for young and elderly people, health care, mental health care, psychiatry, care for disabled persons) there was hardly any municipal activity in that field. BOM assumed the leading role in neighbourhood development, Vitamin W in employment policy, RISO in community development. However, an orchestrator of the total social policy was lacking.

To carry out the more outward-oriented social policy set in motion by the SIF programme the many actors involved in the implementation of the policy needed good navigation to be effective and efficient. The changes initiated in the organisation and the contents of social policy have been directed mostly by the Alderman of Social Affairs. He assumed the political leadership role and appears to play this role very convincingly, probably also thanks to his long experience within the municipal board. He entrusted to SOMA the coordination of external means, which were to be the catalyst of the new social policy. Decisions about important options of social policy are and must be for the city government to take, in close cooperation with the public body that is fully engaged in social services, the OCMW. The city government is the appropriate body to act as overall director, since adequate democratic legitimacy has to be guaranteed. Flexible and innovative independent organisations can rightfully be brought in to coordinate and monitor the implementation of policy measures.

Political leadership is crucial for the results of a programme. Our impression is that, given the close relation within SIF with domains other than the social one, the leadership role of the other aldermen involved is not quite clear. Current leadership seems to be person-related, which makes it rather vulnerable. Given the importance of the programme it is advisable that the programme is adopted by the entire city board and that the aldermen involved play their leadership role more explicitly.

Next to political leadership that is considered as very supportive for the current activities in the framework of SIF, there is the leadership of the SIF programme itself and the leadership of subprogrammes and organisations involved. It is our impression that most persons invited to take up these roles have been selected not only for their personal expertise or competence, but also for leadership and networking qualities. Persons capable of motivating others have been involved. The role of the programme leader especially seems to be appreciated by most of the interview partners. The new three-year programme that started in 2000 had a different leader. His role is somewhat different from that of his predecessor, now that institutional structures have been set up and many other things are set in motion. In the second stage the concrete results of the individual programmes will become more important. Another challenge is to link the new institutions (*vzws*) to the regular municipal organisation without losing pace. Finally, it seems important to put more emphasis on the coherence (and the synergies) between the many still rather separate subprogrammes. Until now the SIF programme has been rather complex and not very transparent, given the many actors and actions. To make things more transparent and to communicate the activities and achievements to the public is another task. Political leaders have to play an eminent role in this respect.

Political and Societal Support

Communication is important to gain support for a successful execution of policies. Lack of substantial political and/or societal support is a failure factor for any plan, programme or project. The impression is that it is exactly on the point of communication the SIF programme could use some improvement. This concerns political as well as societal support. Political support is more than the formal approval of a programme by the city council. To gain societal support responsible politicians should clearly show their involvement. This involvement should preferably receive wide media attention to show the importance of the programme for the city. An important point is to make clear for which serious urban problem the programme will offer an adequate answer. Political support should be very convincing. The support of higher layers (the Federal and Flemish government, or even better the European Commission) is also very important. Moreover, a programme like SIF should be supported by the entire city board. The impression is that support is now primarily given by the alderman of social affairs. To create a more powerful basis for the programme full support by all the members of the Antwerp city board seems to be desirable.

As regards societal support, the 'customers' of the social policy should support the activities within the framework of SIF. Here too some remarks have to be made. In the evaluation report of the first SIF scheme the visibility of the efforts is taken as a major element. It is rightly stated that the value as perceived by the citizens will increase if visibility is taken care of; in other words, you believe what you see. Until now important visible realisations are only limited, which hampers societal as well as effective political support. The expectation is that during the second SIF round there will be more concrete evidence to convince citizens of the positive impact of the programme.

Next, the way citizens become involved in the activities is very important. The participation procedure has not met with great success: 'We observe that the citizens are not entirely happy with the participation rounds' (Stad en OCMW Antwerpen, 1999). And if citizen participation is not running well, citizens are apt to consider the entire process as problematic. Perhaps the approach should gradually change its emphasis from 'product-oriented' to 'market-oriented'. During the interviews too, the impression was given that the citizens have to be more properly involved. The RISO, which has expertise in this field, has been invited to think about a more appropriate way of citizen participation.

4.6 Conclusions

Major lessons to be drawn from the Antwerp case are the importance of organisational reforms and leadership and a changed attitude within the social policy field to support specific neighbourhoods in an outward-directed, opportunity-oriented way. In this sense the Antwerp case is about setting the right preconditions for social strategies rather than about the implementation and evaluation of a single strategy or project.

The Organisation of the SIF Policy

Institutional reforms An important lesson of the Antwerp case seems to be that the administrative structure can form a major barrier for an innovative, opportunity-oriented policy. The functions needed to execute the new social policy in Antwerp were lacking, as were people with the right capacities. It turned out that it was hardly possible to create the necessary functions within the existing administrative structure. The SIF fund of the Flemish government was an important incentive for institutional reforms in the social policy field in the urban region of Antwerp. By creating a kind of organisational 'bypass' new incentives and dynamics have arisen in the social policy field. New functions are now integrated in specific units (*cellen*) within non-profit associations (*vzws*). Major advantages of these *vzws* are the flexible way they attract employees and the flexible way they operate. In the social policy field there is now a gradual change from being almost entirely simply the execution of existing rules towards developing innovative policy ideas. A major disadvantage is the 'organisational distance' between the new units and the regular administrative structure. This is a source of tension between the actors involved. As a consequence, there seems to be decreasing support for the continuation of these *vzws* outside the existing administrative structure. In the long term, when they have been developed into adequately operating units, it will be desirable to integrate these units fully within the regular administrative structure. A necessary precondition for this is, however, that the culture and the application procedures of the city administration have also become more flexible (less rigid) and innovative (more proactive).

Leadership   Another important lesson of this case is the crucial role of leadership for the organising capacity in the social policy field. To initiate a new institutional and material approach the leadership of the alderman of social affairs and the SOMA has been crucial. They have functioned as catalysts for creating new ideas in the social policy field. The dependence on only a few persons makes the new approach vulnerable. Only a few persons have a total overview of the social policy field and the entire SIF project. It is therefore of utmost importance (besides gradually changing leading actors and finding new adequate actors) to broaden the support for the new approach to more actors and to communicate in an adequate way the importance of the new social policy.

The Contents of the SIF Policy

Concentrating efforts and means in specific neighbourhoods   A great advantage of the SIF is that it permits quite heavy flows of money to be channelled to a problem neighbourhood and spent on projects there, whereas in the past the available means had to be distributed proportionally and across neighbourhoods and sectors. The possibility of concentrating financial means and policy efforts in specific problem neighbourhoods in integrated projects can be considered a breakthrough. Before the SIF era such a possibility was hardly thinkable. This was partly due to the former mainly reactive approach. There was hardly insight in the specific needs in the social policy and in the spatial distribution of the most serious problems. Only after carefully analysing the social problems in the different urban districts was a more area-based approach possible. This analysis was started with the 'Deprivation Atlas' and some follow-up studies. The next step however to allocate more means and efforts in those districts that have the largest needs is considered to be quite revolutionary. In terms of the research framework it can be stated that the policy implementation is now more based on a developed vision (though embeddedness in a comprehensive city wide vision is still missing), while in the past the implementation has been more pragmatic, without sufficient insight in which districts or target groups really needed support.

From an inward to an outward directed social policy   The approach in the social policy field in the Antwerp region is gradually changing from being problem-oriented towards being opportunity-oriented. The BOM (the Neighbourhood Development Company) has played a major role in this respect by creating new economic opportunities in specific problem neighbourhoods.

The approach has also been changed fundamentally within the employment policy. In the new approach, fighting unemployment means in the first instance creating opportunities in the normal labour market. Only in the last instance are jobs being created outside this market. This is a fundamental break with the past in which only the creation of jobs was the aim (without sufficiently considering the demands of the market). One of the most tangible results of the SIF programme is the creation of more than 2,000 extra jobs. To measure the effectiveness of this employment policy is tricky, however, for many people owe their new jobs to the prosperous economy. One criticism of the new social policy is that the approach has become too economically biased, neglecting those people who can no longer acquire a position on the labour market and need another kind of help.

General Conclusions and Recommendations

The SIF programme is considered highly ambitious. In view of the serious social problems in Antwerp, great store is set by the programme's success. One of the principal objectives is to enhance the decisiveness and effectiveness of organisations involved in social policy. To break out of the straightjacket of existing organisations, new flexible agencies have been created to serve as nurseries for new ideas in social policy. Compared with the old administrative situation much has been changed. Especially the new outward and opportunity oriented approach is important. But obviously the road to the envisaged situation is long and beset with obstacles, and the results will be slow to appear. The wording of the evaluations performed so far testify that:

* *The SIF cannot yet boast great tangible realisations* (Stad en OCMW Antwerpen, 1999, p. 194). From the evaluation, the preparatory activities will not become visible to the neighbourhood inhabitants before 2000. So far, the SIF programme has been appraised primarily on the programme level. Such evaluations were very broad and in the eyes of some people not highly significant, since certain successes on the implementation level remained obscure. Evaluation of the operational objectives and actions is still in progress.
* *In particular encourage coordination and coherence of policy* ... In other words, this coordination and coherence have not been as good as expected. Much more effort is required to achieve a more comprehensive approach within the social policy field.

- *Lack of openness of the policy has not been overcome* ... Due also to the lack of coordination and coherence of the policy, the field of social policy is too fragmented. Only a few people seem to have an overview of the social policy field. However, for most of the persons working in the field of social policy there is still a clear lack in openness.

Some recommendations It will be of the utmost importance to realise that a lot remains to be done to achieve satisfactory results in the new social policy approach. In the second SIF period more tangible results have to be achieved, to enlarge the political as well as the societal support for the new approach. Political backing from other government layers will be vital in obtaining the financial support required in order to assure the continuation of the social programmes in the future. Political support within the city will be important to be able to continue with the new institutions in the social field. Without sufficient tangible results it can be expected that there will be more resistance to the new institutions. Also the citizens of Antwerp have to see tangible results of the new policies. When they do not see sufficient improvements with respect to social problems, they might lose confidence in the new approach and/or in the city administration. Under normal democratic rules a lack of societal support will ultimately be translated into lack of political support.

The SOMA seems to be the most appropriate actor to encourage further coordination and coherence of policy. The SOMA wishes to coordinate more external funds for the execution of social policies. This organisation can become an important director for the coordination of social policies, of which external funds form important catalysts. A precondition to achieve this is that the SOMA builds sufficient credibility by clear tangible results of the new initiated policies.

Currently, there is a discussion about whether and when organisations within the SOMA should be integrated within the regular city administration. It can be stated that this is a trade-off between striving for a flexible and innovative approach and to further institutionalisation. On the one hand there are high expectations concerning the output and outcome of the achievements of the new organisations. On the other hand, there is a growing concern regarding the setting up of public tasks outside the existing city administration. It is important in this respect to realise that the new external organisations were set up because they were considered to be necessary to achieve a flexible and innovative approach in social policies. This ultimately has to lead to a better ability to counter social problems in the urban region of Antwerp. To show tangible results in this field is therefore necessary, to prove the necessity of this second-best organisational structure. It is second-best because they are considered to be public tasks, and – in an ideal situation – they should be tackled by the regular public institutions. There is thus a need to change these regular institutions in order to make them capable of carrying out these tasks. Ultimately it is desirable to integrate the new institutions (the units within the SOMA) within the regular city administration. This implies, however, that in the meantime the new flexible and innovative approach must have been adopted by the public institutions. It is realistic to suppose that this will not happen overnight.

Notes

1   The SOMA now has a staff of some 35 persons.
2   These premises are located in the environment of the Offerandestraat.

Chapter 5

Integration and Employment Programme in Malmö-Hyllie

5.1 Introduction

Malmö is Sweden's third city and a major commercial centre. It forms part of the Öresund region, comprising the urban regions of Copenhagen, Malmö and Lund. This 'Euro region' belongs to the most dynamic regions in Europe, with leading companies in the fields of medical science, biotechnology, information technology and the media. The knowledge cluster, which comprises four universities (Copenhagen, Roskilde, Lund and Malmö), is an especially valuable asset. Malmö used to be a city of fishermen and farmers but rapidly became a vital commercial centre. The beginning of the twentieth century marked the industrialisation of the city. For 100 years, Malmö was one of Sweden's leading industrial cities. However, in the past decades Malmö, like many other traditional European industrial centres, has faced serious problems that have made this city one of the less wealthy in Sweden. Compared to the national Swedish figures Malmö suffers high unemployment rates, low education levels, and the highest concentration of immigrants in the country. Together these problems threaten Malmö's social structure. The municipality has recognised this and in recent years has made many efforts to overcome this situation. The concern has extended to the national government, which has launched a special programme, the *Metropolitan Initiative*, intended to help the most disadvantaged regions in the country, among which is Malmö.

This chapter will analyse the implementation of this *Metropolitan Initiative* in Malmö. More concretely, some projects implemented in one of its most underprivileged neighbourhoods, Hyllie, will be described and analysed. These projects were carried out in particular in the recently opened Work and Development Centre of Hyllie (WDCH). The data of the metropolitan profile of Malmö are summarised in Table 5.1.

Table 5.1   Data of metropolitan profile of Malmö

Characteristic	Malmö
Population of the city (1996)	247,000
Population of the urban region (1996)	618,000
Growth of the urban population (city, %, 1991–2001)	+1.1
Share of the population of foreign extraction (city, %, 1998)	11
Proportion of population of working age in employment (city, %, 1997)	61
Unemployment rates (city, %, 1997)	11.0
Proportion of employment in industry (city, %, 1999)	21.0
Proportion of employment in services (city, %, 1999)	76.0
Number of administrative tiers (including state and boroughs)	3
Borough Boards	Yes

Sources: van den Berg, Braun and van der Meer, 1998, p. 381; *City of Helsinki Urban Facts*, 1999, pp. 30 and 31; Nordstat, 1999, pp. 106, 110, 113 and 115.

5.2   Socioeconomic Profile of the City of Malmö

Location

Malmö is located in the southwestern part of Sweden in the Scania region. Air, sea and land communications are the best developed of Sweden; 70 per cent of Swedish exports pass through Scania. As well as the local airport Sturrup there is Copenhagen Airport, which can be reached by train in less than 30 minutes. Malmö is served by the high-speed train X2000 which provides fast connections to Stockholm and Gothenburg. The municipalities within the Scania region are connected by a dense network of commuter trains. The City Tunnel, a 6 km-long railway tunnel under central Malmö is expected to be open by the year 2005. It will connect the city centre with the Öresund link and serve as the Underground for regional trains. The fixed link has considerably improved the spatial situation of Malmö as Sweden's gateway to Europe.

Demography

After the population growth of the industrialisation period, from the 1970s onwards Malmö began to lose population, with people moving to suburbs and 'satellite towns' (geographically detached from the core city). However, since the 1980s the city has been growing again. Nowadays Malmö has around 250,000 inhabitants and the region 620,000 (1996). Malmö is not the pre-eminent employment centre of the region; the region's share in employment is not higher than its share of population. The Malmö region is a typical multicore region, including the university city of Lund, which recently has been growing fast (100,000 in 1996).

In the last five years (from 1995 until the time of writing) Malmö has experienced an increase of 3,500 people a year. This increase is the result of a surplus of people moving to the city, mainly young adults and foreign immigrants. More than two-fifths of the people moving to Malmö are in the 20–29 age group. Apart from the concentration of young adults, the other influx is constituted of immigrants. The proportion of immigrants has been rather constant in the last 10 years and is related to the influx of refugees into Sweden. There is also secondary immigration of relatives of immigrants who had arrived earlier. From 1993 to 1997, the number of newly-arrived immigrants in these two categories was 13,000. Gradually the number of Swedish nationals of foreign extraction is increasing as foreign nationals take on Swedish nationality. This group presents a high birthrate, and in the past five years has been growing by some 3,000 people a year. Altogether 70,000 residents (one in four) have foreign roots, of which 28,000 are foreign nationals. The largest groups of immigrants are from former Yugoslavia, Denmark, Poland, Iraq, Iran, Turkey, Finland, Hungary and Somalia.

Economy

As mentioned before, Malmö owed its economic development to industrialisation. To illustrate the importance of industry: in the 1950s the employment rate among men was 90 per cent, with over 50 per cent in industry alone. That accounted for a major expansion of the city during the 1950s and 1960s when the population grew by almost 4,000 a year. Around 1960 industry showed the first signs of losing its dominant position. First the textile industries declined, and later the manufacturing and construction. In the 1990s economic recession once more brought heavy job losses in industry, for instance in the newly-established SAAB factory. In total, some 12,000 jobs were lost in manufacturing and construction industries. The crisis also meant a break in the long-term trend of job growth in the public and social sectors. The number of jobs in the industrial sector dropped from 26,000 to 18,000 between 1990 and 1995 owing to economic crises confronting the city. The economic performance of the city could be qualified as poor (Nilsson, 1998).

In recent years, from 1998, the trend appears to have been more positive than previously. In 1999 the proportion of people with a job increased from 60 to 62 per cent of the potential labour force (persons between the ages of 15 and 65). The current trend indicates that new businesses have an interest in locating in the city. Big companies such as Mercedes Benz and McDonald's will locate their Swedish headquarters, and the latter also a new bakery, in the area. Moreover, some IT companies are establishing offices in Malmö to profit from the expected economic development of the Öresund region. According to the County Labour Board, the greatest job growth (8.2 per cent by 2000) is expected in the financial and business service sectors. Thanks to the opening of the fixed link between Denmark (Copenhagen) and Sweden (Malmö) the expectation on both sides of the Öresund is that the newly-formed region (about 2.3 million inhabitants) will create new opportunities for economic growth, although it is not yet possible to estimate the effects.

Nowadays there are 9,000 companies in Malmö, of which 1,100 are wholesale businesses and 800 manufacturers; 74 per cent of these companies are of medium or small size, with fewer than 10 employees. In the region there are many food and packaging-related companies, but the region is especially known for its health-related companies. More than three-fifths of the Scandinavian pharmaceutical industry is based there. Malmö lacks the presence of really large business companies. The trade and communication sector and the private-service companies account for half of the employment in Malmö, and together with health care and welfare display the highest rate of employment (see Table 5.2).

Table 5.2   Distribution of employment in Malmö

Trade and communications	25%
Private service companies	23%
Health care and welfare	17%
Industry	15%
Education	6%
Construction	6%
Public Administration	5%
Others	3%

Administrative Organisation of Malmö

Local autonomy is the cornerstone of the Swedish administrative system. The Swedish constitution decrees that the 289 municipalities and 23 county council districts have taxation authority and that the right to make decisions lies with the elected representatives. The county administration authorities are primarily responsible for health care. Municipalities are independent, well-developed organisations. Each municipality is responsible for such services as social welfare, child care, geriatric care, compulsory school and upper secondary school education, environmental and health protection, emergency services, and city planning.

The city's highest policy-making authority is the City Council with 61 elected members. It decides about such matters as municipal tax, which is €30.05 per taxable €100 for 1999. The City Council elects the Municipal Executive Committee, which leads and coordinates the work of the municipality. The opposition can also participate in the Executive Committee, and usually the different parties must collaborate to accomplish the distribution of seats in the committee. There are seven delegates and a number of deputies. There are 12 municipal committees with specific responsibilities in their sectors: Chief Guardian, Community Services, Cultural Affairs, Education, Elections, Emergency, Environment, Health and Medical Advisory Board, Leisure, Public Audits, Public Works and Town Planning.

On January 1999, a Joint County Council for the southern Swedish County of Scania was formed (combining two former counties). Malmö's health care system, including the University Hospital MAS with 1,200 beds, was transferred to this authority. There are thus three layers of government that take on the different matters affecting the city of Malmö and the Scania region. There is no kind of functional regional authority on the metropolitan level. An association of local authorities is the forum in which the development of the Malmö region is discussed (Nilsson, 1998). The opening of the fixed link with Copenhagen has complicated the organisational framework on the regional level. The idea is to develop a functional transnational metropolitan region united by an integrated system of public transport. An Öresund Committee has been formed for the purpose. This Committee is to achieve greater cooperation in communications, infrastructure, traffic, business, research, education and culture. The Committee is made up of leading politicians from counties, county councils and municipalities from both sides, as well as national representatives.

In 1996 a major democratic reform divided Malmö into ten city districts. Each city district appointed its own City District Council in charge of municipal services, comprising child care, compulsory school education, recreation, local culture and libraries.

Thanks to the taxation authority only 8 per cent of the cities' income depends on the state. In the case of Malmö, the city traditionally had a good financial situation thanks to the taxation of people and companies. However, nowadays with a less favourable economic situation and more deprived groups in society, the city cannot raise enough income through this system. Most of the people, although they work in Malmö, live in the suburbs. Therefore, the foundation for taxation appears to be deficient. In 1994, the City of Malmö had a deficit of €125 million.

5.3   Social Problems in Malmö

The City of Malmö

In the early 1990s, Malmö experienced a massive decline from which it has still not fully recovered. Unemployment is still one of the city's greatest problems. In 1998 an average of 13,500 persons were unemployed, among which were high proportions of immigrants and young people with low skills. In 1998, 66 per cent of the people born abroad were without work and 18 per cent were openly unemployed. As mentioned before, this is the result of the economic crisis that the city – and Sweden as a whole – experienced in the early 1990s. Even prior to the economic crisis of the 1990s Malmö had the lowest employment rate of the country, a situation comparable to that of other industrial European cities that have undergone a process of de-industrialisation. After the crisis of the 1990s, the gap between the national and the local rate increased. In 1999 unemployment in Malmö was 12.2 per cent, twice the national level. Both men and women are expected to work in Sweden. Otherwise families earn too little to pay their living costs.

Unemployment is not the only problem in Malmö. The city has a relatively large number of people dependent on social allowances and with relatively low education. In schools in the city centre about 50 per cent of the pupils have a foreign background. The education facilities within the city centre are not always perceived as being of high quality. For some, lack of confidence in the quality of the schools is a reason to move out of the city centre when they can afford it. Furthermore, houses in the hard ring of Malmö particularly (urban extensions directly surrounding the historical centre) do not always meet the requirements of people who can afford better. Most of the houses were built in the 1950s and 1960s (the so-called 'Million Programme'[1]) to satisfy demand from the fast-growing population needed by industry. Nowadays, people with low incomes and poor education live in the areas where most of this massive, rather dull apartment housing is concentrated. The most affluent and well-educated tend to settle in satellite municipalities (the so-called soft ring of the city). There is indeed spatial segregation within the urban region. Moreover, non-native inhabitants tend to flock to the eastern part of the city. Ninety per cent of the immigrants live there. Currently, about 70 per cent of the social allowances of Malmö city go to immigrants. There is relatively high unemployment among non-native inhabitants.

More immigrants to be expected with the European extension The expectation is that the entrance of new member states to the European Union will provoke new migration flows within Europe. More people might also want to migrate to Sweden. For Malmö, it is therefore very important to be prepared for more people wanting to live and work in the city. It will be crucial to develop good methods to stimulate integration of the new inhabitants in the Swedish society. Moreover, to adopt these people into the existing system also demands a changed attitude.

The Hyllie District

Hyllie is one of the 10 city districts and one of the four that participate in the Metropolitan Initiative taken by the national government to improve employment and living conditions in the most underprivileged areas of Sweden. The district of Hyllie has about 30,000 inhabitants. It is a typical 1950s area; the majority of its housing units were constructed during the 'Million Programme' housing initiative. The idea was to create a vast quantity of new houses to meet the large demand. However, less attention was paid to the quality of the living area. Neighbourhoods such as Hyllie lack any identity or attraction, although the quality of the houses itself is relatively good. Peculiar to these town quarters are the relatively scarce (commercial and other) facilities and services. For most of them (shops, restaurants, pubs) people have to go to the inner city or out-of-town shopping centres.

The social structure of Hyllie varies among the different neighbourhoods. The district encompasses three of the socially weakest neighbourhoods in Malmö. One of them, Holma, contains some of the worst social problems of the district (see Table 5.3). In this case study we will describe some of the activities undertaken by the district Hyllie in the Holma neighbourhood as part of the Metropolitan Initiative.

In these neighbourhoods there is social segregation. The people living in these areas lack sufficient fundamental living conditions such as health, social and community ties and participation in society. Unemployment, high dependency on income support and concentration of non-Swedish population are some of the problems this district faces (see Table 5.3). The difficulty of getting into the labour market is a feature common to large groups in these areas, especially immigrants. A major problem is the lack of knowledge of the Swedish language. There are roughly two groups of immigrants: those that have had a relatively high education and those that are illiterate. The latter often come from countries at war; often the women are illiterate. Not only for those with a low education level and no knowledge of the Swedish language, but also for those refugees who are highly educated and had work experience in their former country, integration in the Swedish society or finding an appropriate job proves to be difficult.

Table 5.3   Socioeconomic structure of the Hyllie district and its most disadvantaged neighbourhoods compared with Malmö, 2000

	Population (age 20–64)	Employment rate	Population with foreign background	Dependency on income support
Holma	3,377	38%	45%	58%
Bellevuegarden	3,904	47%	32%	41%
Kroksback	4,683	50%	34%	43%
Malmö	*254,904*	*61%*	*18%*	*28%*

Source: 'Breaking the Cycle of Segregation', document handed out by the Malmö City Administration Office, November 2000.

The unemployment rate of non-Nordic citizens in Hyllie is 13 per cent, twice as high as the rate of the native Swedish population living in the same district, which is more than 6 per cent. The children and adolescents are also affected by this segregation because in these neighbourhoods they have few opportunities to speak Swedish and to make contact with the Swedish society.

Traditional social policies have not been able to overcome the hard core of the new social problems.

To bring about positive and lasting social changes in Hyllie and Holma, new approaches to the problems mentioned were urgently needed. The opportunity to find them came with the Metropolitan Initiative implemented in Malmö. In the following section this programme will be described, with a special focus on its implementation in the Hyllie district.

5.4   The Metropolitan Initiative in Malmö: the Case of Hyllie

First Urban Policy Initiative at National Level

At the end of the 1990s the Swedish government established a metropolitan policy objective for the most socially disadvantaged metropolitan areas in Sweden. It was a kind of follow-up to the so-called Bloomberg Programme (called after the responsible minister), by which employment measures within urban areas were financed. That was the first time the national government had supported work programmes directly targeted to cities. The idea of the Metropolitan Initiative is jointly (residents, NGOs, municipalities, regions and county councils and the state) to create growth in vulnerable metropolitan areas. This policy has for its main goals to stop social, economic and ethnic segregation in metropolitan regions and to contribute to the creation of new employment. To achieve this, long-term and coordinated measures are required. A Commission on Metropolitan Areas, including state secretaries of seven ministries and the Prime Minister's Office, chaired by the state secretary to the Minister of Metropolitan Affairs, has been appointed to develop and coordinate this national policy. The state has allocated nearly €225 million for a three-year period (1999–2002). Part of these funds have been set aside for preschool projects (€17 million yearly), language development at schools (€5.7 million yearly), sports and recreation (€2.3 million yearly) and adult integration and language instruction (€2.3 million yearly). The rest of the resources are to be used to finance measures which the state and the municipality will decide on in the local development agreements. Most of the resources should be used to increase self-sufficiency, however. The municipalities are responsible for the development of these measures, in accordance with the central government. Seven municipalities have been chosen to develop the measures and receive a central government fund.

Malmö's Objectives

Malmö participates in the Metropolitan Initiative through four of its 10 city districts. The city has defined several objectives according to those of the Metropolitan Initiative and according to its own needs. The actions taken are seen in a long-term perspective, and are intended to result in time in improved conditions for the most disadvantaged groups of Malmö.

Six programme objectives have been identified in Malmö (Document of the City Administration Office, 2000):

*   *Cooperation for jobs, education and self sufficiency*: to help the unemployed people in the segregated neighbourhoods to get jobs in the market sector by offering special assistance in the job-seeking process.
*   *Integration into working life*: to increase the contact of foreign background citizens with the Swedish labour market. The municipality wants to increase immigrant representation in its offices, as well as implement training courses to adapt the skills of the immigrant labour force to the demands of the municipality.
*   *To raise the level of education*: the general level of education in Malmö is low, which may inhibit opportunities to benefit from growth in the labour market. Therefore, to solve employment problems, education is a key element. Education and training should be provided for those whose skills are not viable in the labour market, combined with internships and counselling.
*   *Dependency on income support to be reduced*: the low proportion of employed people is the main reason that Malmö has the highest rate of income dependency in the country. The four city districts that are participating in the Metropolitan Initiative account for 80 per cent of the municipality's expenditures on public assistance. The municipality has prioritised those initiatives that focus on long-term dependents on income support who do not qualify for employment. The Jobs and Development Centres initiative is one of the most important. It will be discussed later when the Hyllie case is presented.
*   *Better living conditions, increased security and social participation*: the objectives are to reduce the socioeconomic segregation in housing, to improve the (perceived) attraction of all neighbourhoods in the municipality, to increase citizen participation in the democratic process, to improve the public health in areas where the average life-expectancy is shorter than the average for the municipality as a whole, and to increase the (perceived) social security of the urban environment.

- *To improve prospects for children in environments characterised by unemployment and exclusion*: the objectives are for all preschool children to be given adequate language skills in Swedish before entering the first grade; for children and adolescents in the affected neighbourhoods to be given the opportunity to develop good Swedish language skills; and for all schools, regardless of neighbourhood, to provide adequate support in primary school to ensure that pupils achieve passing grades.

The Metropolitan Initiative in Hyllie

Through the MI Hyllie receives €5.1 million for a period of three years to be spent on various projects aimed at achieving the objectives. Nine programme areas have been defined, each with its own concrete objectives. Each area receives an amount of money that can be spent according to its own planning. These programme areas cover such aspects as employability, education, integration, culture, public health, local development initiatives and crime prevention. For the interest of this research, we shall focus on two of these programme areas that are concerned with employment and education and local development initiatives.

The employment and education programme area The interim objectives of this area are related to the increase of the employment rate for men and women in the district, the reduction of income support dependency, the raising of the education level and the improvement of Swedish-language proficiency. The target groups are young people and unemployed persons of foreign background, whose language skills are low. To achieve the objectives a 'Local Work and Development Centre'[2] was created in January 2000. It started its activities in March 2000 and was fully staffed after the summer of 2000. The centre has 35 staff members, of which 22 work on employment measures and 10 on democracy matters. The centre received about €335,000 for the year 2001. Two state offices and one urban office, the Employment Service, the Social Insurance Office and the Hyllie City District Administration, cooperate to bring the target groups back to work or education. The Centre is based on a *central directive* agreed between the City of Malmö, the County Labour Board and the Social Insurance Office. A *local steering committee* is charged with overseeing guidelines and following up the operations. Representatives of the Employment Service, the Social Insurance Office and the Hyllie City District Administration form this steering committee.

Unemployed participants The Employment Agency sends people with a long-term unemployment history to the WDCH. Usually they are people who receive social allowances. They are obliged to follow a programme at the centre. The sanction can be the loss of their social allowance. Seventy per cent of the clients are immigrants (mostly refugees) and many of them have good education but low self-confidence and/or a lack of motivation to obtain an appropriate job. Next, there are native Swedes who, apart from being unemployed, suffer from such problems as drug or alcohol addiction. In the centre these people can start a training process with, among other elements, individual counselling or more complete education.

The Swedish Social Insurance system can be counterproductive in the sense that people get used to receiving economic support without being encouraged to try for self-sufficiency. Nowadays the labour market offers many jobs and therefore it is important to use the abilities that these people have. The Centre has adopted an innovative approach to the organisation of projects for the unemployed. The centre offers individual attention and emphasises 'rebuilding' the motivation of the participants in their capability to work. There is for instance a workroom in which handicraft activities can be pursued. The collaboration between the participating (public) organisations is also something positive, because cases that used to be considered untreatable can now be treated in this Centre.

Language courses Another important activity developed in this centre is the language courses for people who are not skilled enough to enter the official Swedish-language instruction programme. Nontraditional teaching methods are used to reach the most vulnerable groups, such as illiterate women. A relatively large proportion of non-native inhabitants is illiterate. Some are refugees from war areas, like Afghanistan, Iraq, and former Yugoslavia, where education systems could no longer operate. Teaching these illiterate persons Swedish (by Swedish teachers) has generated many problems and in many cases it has been a complete failure. With the help of the new funds from the Metropolitan Initiative, projects have been set up to teach illiterates to read and write in their own language. The idea is that they will learn Swedish much faster when they are no longer illiterate. It has turned out that there are teachers among the non-native inhabitants who can help with the language lessons to non-Nordic people in their own language. This innovative way of teaching the Swedish language was in the first instance not accepted by the Education Board. They had insufficient confidence in this new method and were not prepared to allocate financial funds for it. The funds from the

Metropolitan Initiative were therefore very welcome to realise this new approach that appears to be rather successful.

Other projects developed in the centre are social care for children whose parents are unemployed and the possibility of accessing a database with job offers in Malmö. In general this centre's innovation is the custumer-oriented attention that is given to the clients, which makes use of their own capabilities.

Programme for local development initiatives The second major programme undertaken by the city district of Hyllie under the Metropolitan Initiative is the one for local development initiatives. The interim goal is to develop local democracy, giving more people support and assistance to solve social problems on their own and as part of the community. The main target group for these activities is people with a foreign background. This group is very difficult to reach for the public workers and a new approach to them was needed. Four 'integration secretaries' have been selected and appointed representing the four largest ethnic groups that live in the area (from Afghanistan, former Yugoslavia, Iran and Arabia/Lebanon). First, these 'integrators' contact 'their' people directly, visiting them at home or sending personal letters. The objective is to create networks of people with the same ethnic background. The second step is to try and help people to create their own associations, for instance by selecting 'leader' types. Another important element is cooperation with schools and the creation of networks with the Swedish society, bringing them in contact with politicians and other personalities. Finally, they help people to present their ideas on how to improve their situation, which assures a bottom-up approach.

This approach has been successful because of the new way of working. The integrators are active in social network-building and they try to create *societies* among the different nationalities living in the neighbourhood. A problem might be that integration into Swedish society, a prime objective of the Metropolitan Initiative, comes second to the ethnic integration. However, the intention is to build up contacts between the ethnic societies and Swedish society later on. To achieve their aims, the integrators cooperate with schools and NGOs.

Several activities have been organised with the intention of activating the participation of the immigrants in the local society. People flocked to these activities when the integration secretaries started to work. For instance on a 'People Health Day', organised with their help, more than 350 immigrants went to such an event for the first time. The same was true of the 'Summer International Day' or parents' meetings at school. Another important focus is the immigrant children and their education. The school system does not work for immigrant children, mostly because of language problems. To solve that difficulty, some schools in the area have contracted schoolteacher assistants of foreign background to help the children. This has met with obstacles because these assistant teachers are not formally recognised in Sweden, although they were professional teachers in their own countries. More collaboration with the Education Department is needed, something that has been difficult to achieve until now.

There are also problems related to cultural differences between immigrant and Swedish society, and to the confrontation between the integration secretaries and the District Council, which has a more conventional concept of integration.

Every three months new projects are started In the framework of the local development programme the district inhabitants can present their own ideas for projects. Four times a year ideas for new projects, directed at fighting social exclusion, can be submitted in the Hyllie district. The three councils of the Hyllie district together advise on the desirability of implementing these projects, but they seem to be quite conservative in their judgements. Ultimately, however, the programme manager of the Hyllie Work and Development Centre and the head of the city district administration decide on their actual implementation.

Actors Involved

The Metropolitan Initiative is a public programme. This means that only actors from the public sector have been directly involved in the definition of the goals and the implementation of projects. The national government participates only by providing resources. The municipality is responsible for the general coordination of the programme, which is achieved through a manager, who coordinates the implementation in the four city districts. Each of these districts has its own coordination unit. In the case of Hyllie, an Employment and Integration Unit was established in 1999 to take on this responsibility. The unit is responsible for programme efforts related to the Local Jobs and Development Centres and for the democratic and resident participation projects. Other public partners involved in the Metropolitan Initiative are the Social Insurance Office, the Employment Agency and the Public Health Council (for matters related to public health).

MKB[3] The housing company MKB is a very important partner in the overall effort. It runs tenant-management programmes and initially provides premises at no cost for various kinds of meeting places. MKB also tries to stimulate the inhabitants to upgrade their houses and surrounding areas (gardens and parks) by giving special facilities for that purpose and sometimes granting lower rents. The housing companies understand how important it is that residents are happy and can develop their interests where they live, making them less likely to move. This has made the neighbourhoods more stable and there are now almost no vacant flats.

5.5   Analysis of the Organising Capacity

Vision

A revolutionary change in the national vision For Sweden the Metropolitan Initiative is quite a revolution. In the past the national government supported peripheral regions especially. In Sweden, there has been an 'equity-efficiency' discussion about what kind of areas need additional support from the national government. Although rural areas still get support, the accent has recently shifted towards urban areas. The occurrence of social problems and the potential economic opportunities have been important considerations for the change of policy. Social integration is now one of the main policy priorities on the national as well as the urban level. The metropolitan programme is more or less comparable with the Dutch Major City Policy (see the Rotterdam case). The Swedish government gives financial support to cities with metropolitan problems. The idea is to realise a comprehensive approach to these problems. Different organisations in the field are therefore stimulated to cooperate.

No comprehensive vision and strategy on the local level A strategic comprehensive vision on the development of the city or region of Malmö does not exist. The implication is that social strategies are not embedded in a wider metropolitan context, but are developed more or less in isolation (from, for instance, physical policy, education policy, economic policy). The Metropolitan Initiative is considered a first step to an integrated partnership approach in metropolitan areas, focused on the new ethnic dimension and the social problems connected with it. The City of Malmö itself had to develop a specific policy programme for the Metropolitan Initiative. It chose to support four districts that (according to statistical databases) face the most severe social problems. It was realised that Malmö did not have much experience with the social integration problems of non-native people. Thus much had to be learned from experiences elsewhere or through experiments or pilot projects. There was also the conviction that to find out what social policies were needed was not an easy task. As one of the discussion partners stated: 'It is much easier to build a bridge than to take the appropriate social measures.'

Social vision developed on the district level The Hyllie district has a clear vision of what are the goals to achieve through the Metropolitan Initiative. These are mainly concerned with employment, education and integration of immigrants (Status Report, 2000), and have been translated into concrete interim objectives for each programme area defined. The idea is that people will be more socially included when they have a regular position in society through a job. To enable people to get an appropriate job is central to the programme, and education measures are directed to that aim. Participants in the programme have to learn the Swedish language or specific skills in order to get adequate work. The vision developed in Hyllie is in accordance with the one established by the MI. That vision was quite unrestrictive, allowing each city to come up with the most appropriate projects in each case. The WDCH has the main responsibility for the development of the goals related to employment and education. At the beginning of its creation this caused some problems with other organisations such as the Employment Agency, who saw it as a threat to their own role. The centre has established very concrete goals (for instance, that 40 per cent of the clients are expected to obtain employment) which put some stress on their employees.

Ambitions and integrality The level of ambition might cause some doubt. To aim at an employment rate of 80 per cent (men and women) of the active population does not seem very realistic, given the wide differences between the Swedish and foreign ways of living. The ideas to upgrade the standard of living of the Hyllie-district do not include physical elements. Although the quality of the houses and the maintenance of surroundings are quite good, the residential districts are monotonous and rather dull environments that lack adequate services (shopping for instance) or meeting places. We did not see shops run by foreigners, which might contribute to meeting opportunities. Such deficiencies are not conductive to community development, nor to integration.

Strategic Networks Cooperation between the Actors Involved

Rigid public sector The Swedish public sector is extensive and rigid. In Malmö, about 13,000 people (13 per cent) of the 100,000 employed people work in the public sector. The collective sector is so large as to induce a passive attitude in the private sector in societal matters. The private sector expects the public sector to solve most problems. Because of the weight of the public sector they hesitate to cooperate in (quasi-) public policy fields. Besides, the public sector is quite inward-directed. Perhaps from a kind of self-preservation, they do not cooperate much with other relevant actors in the field. There is, for instance, hardly any cooperation with business companies with respect to the job market. Only about three-tenths of the vacancies in the business sector are handled through the (national) employment office. The rest is not dealt with through public institutions. Better cooperation with business companies is hoped for, so that vacancies can be mapped out better and jobseekers are better informed what education route to follow.

From the discussions the impression is that the public system works relatively slowly and bureaucratically. For instance, to get financial support for plans to fight social exclusion, each year these plans have to go through the entire public chain from district, through local and municipal, to the national council. In principle, it was required to assess in advance the needs of the local population, and subsequently to draw up plans that could be brought in for financial support. To remove the insecurity of ultimately obtaining the required funds, the procedure at district level has been reversed. To prevent disappointment, financial support now must be secured before the population is asked to state their needs and to come up with projects to cope with these needs.

Cooperation of organisations in the social field In Malmö the labour market and the social allowances offices hardly used to work together. They operate quite bureaucratically and inwardly-directed, focusing only on their own obligations. However, the Metropolitan Initiative programme has had a positive impact on that organisational barrier to a comprehensive approach of the unemployment problem. The national organisations involved (social security and employment offices) as well as the urban organisations (social welfare office) now work together for the first time through an employment programme. In this respect, the incentive of (temporary) extra finance, supplied through the Metropolitan Initiative, has turned out to be a sound lubricator to change attitudes and willingness to cooperate.

However, a kind of competition seems to have arisen between a regular institution (labour market office) and the Hyllie Work and Development Centre. Some potential problems of competence and loss of credibility are imminent. For instance, the employment office might lose part of its credibility when the Hyllie centre proves to be more effective in finding people jobs.

Education system works quite independently While in some countries schools have been given an important position in neighbourhood policies aiming at better integration of socially-excluded people, in Malmö (and this probably holds for the rest of Sweden) there is hardly any cooperation between the education system and social organisations. Yet their cooperation is needed to fight social exclusion phenomena. Currently, schools try to solve problems on their own and are mostly not inclined to cooperate with other actors. Only a few school directors are willing to cooperate with social institutions. According to our discussion partners more cooperation with the schools seems imperative for integrating non-native people into society. To that end both pre- and after-school activities are desirable, such as additional Swedish language lessons for non-native people. For children from three years old onward especially, language lessons are essential to prevent them lagging behind at school at a later stage. It was also difficult to involve the Education Department in the financing of the new scheme of language classes for illiterate immigrants. The Education Department wanted them to join the regular classes offered by them, although this has proved unsuccessful over the years. Finally the immigrant classes were implemented with money from the Metropolitan Initiative and the collaboration of the Folk University.

Leadership: Important for Success

The success of the programme and the project depends in an important part on the personnel capacities and way of working of the key persons. The programme manager of the Hyllie Work and Development Centre plays a very stimulating role. Together with the head of the city district administration, she decides on the implementation of specific projects. In particular, the programme manager is considered to play a positive role in this. She is considered a modern civil servant, stimulating new ideas and ways of working. She is experienced in the social field. She operates rather in the background and so gives her employees space to elaborate their own ideas. She has much trust in the abilities of her employees and directs them only when it is considered necessary. In particular, the involvement of non-Swedish 'integrators' and listening to and successfully following the advice of these dedicated people has made an impression. The results of this approach to integration are promising.

The integration secretaries, or integrators, employed at the centre are important to the immigrants as leaders, since they have been able to involve them in the activities of the centre. However, this can be dangerous since the efficiency of the programmes could be affected if they disappear. Realising this, the programme manager has suggested that choosing new leaders from the different groups and associations created should prevent person-related solutions.

Communication

In the Hyllie Work and Development Centre, much value is attached to the democratic involvement of the local inhabitants. Inhabitants with foreign backgrounds are employed to help their compatriots and other non-Nordic people to integrate better into the Swedish society. These integrators try to get in touch with the local population to hear what their wants and needs are. They work in this respect as a kind of broker. They mediate between the local people and the official organisations regarding needs and projects. Subsequently, they try to develop projects that are helpful towards integration in cooperation with these inhabitants.

The WDCH is also working on a newspaper to disseminate the activities and results of the centre, in order to involve more people from the neighbourhood. The creation of meeting places has also been a way to (re)establish communication with the inhabitants, to better reach their real needs and demands.

Political Support for the Programme

Social Democrats (Labour) are in favour of the employment programme set up in Hyllie. The fact that the national and the local government have the same political colour may have helped to achieve the political support needed on the local level. At district level, there is a good relationship between the District Council and the manager of the WDCH, which has allowed many small projects submitted by residents to be accepted. As always, the question that remains is whether a change in political colour at local level would imply less support for the programme.

Societal Support for the Programme

The city district and the local MKB have set up three councils[4] in Hyllie, which have to give their advice on the desirability of newly-submitted projects in the field of employment and integration. Some of our discussion partners pointed out that these councils do not represent the neighbourhood population very well, as they are composed only of Swedish natives. A more acceptable distribution between native and non-native population would improve the credibility and democratic degree of this institution.

A positive development is the creation of meeting places (dwellings in apartment blocks that are available for community activities) all over the district. These places were created (with the help of MKB, the housing company) with the intention of extending the points of contact between immigrants, Swedish and the public institutions. There are now 17 meeting places in the district, which have served to shatter much of the passivity of the inhabitants.

Policy Development and Implementation

Some non-native people turn out to be excellent employees for a variety of organisations. Some of them had good positions in their homelands. However, Swedish companies still seem to be very hesitant about employing non-native people. They seem to have too little experience with non-Nordic employees and focus more on their possible disadvantages (lack of knowledge of Swedish language, culture, and habits) than on potential advantages (well-skilled people, good mentality, broad knowledge of international affairs, etc.). Another great disadvantage is the lack of flexibility of the Swedish job market. Companies are quite reluctant to offer people fixed-term jobs. During our conversations this problem appeared to be rather serious. Even people with good qualifications have difficulties simply because they are foreign. The position that the business sector is not really interested in engaging employees of foreign descent, despite increasing tensions on the labour market, raises the question of whether a nationwide communication campaign could help to change this somewhat discriminating attitude.

Swedish public institutions (e.g. national and urban government) are aware that they have to set a good example by employing non-native people. The WDCH has a relatively large number of non-native employees; 45 per cent of the staff has a foreign background. The employees in the centre are, for a large part, non-native, to reflect the composition of the local population in Hyllie.

Swedish language lessons It is obligatory for foreign people to learn Swedish (to be eligible for social allowances), but the results are disappointing. To teach illiterate foreigners the Swedish language is a rather hopeless undertaking for native Swedes, who cannot communicate with their students. The first impressions of the new kind of language lessons for non-native people are positive. It seems that the new method is more effective, and might be more cost-effective, than the traditional lessons. Moreover, acquiring better knowledge of the language gives the adults more self-confidence, which is a precondition for integration and plucking up the courage to apply for a job. Until now, the education system has paid more attention to the wide knowledge differences among the non-native people. On the one side there is a group of well-educated people; on the other there is a group of illiterates. It would be more efficient to take these differences into account, and to supply more customer-oriented programmes.

Output, Outcome and Evaluations

The WDCH started in March 2000, so it is too early to say anything about the outcome of the programme. The local universities (Faculties of Sociology) have been enlisted to evaluate the Metropolitan Initiative. The method chosen by the researchers and approved by the principals (the city) is to register how inhabitants perceive their districts because of changing relationships. In that way they try to find out whether people have come to like their neighbourhood better now that social networks between the inhabitants have been set up or stimulated. By interviewing people every six months the researchers hope to identify changes that might be stimulated through the programme, and in particular by the activities of the Hyllie Work and Development Centre. For their evaluation they strongly depend on reports drawn up by (mostly foreign) project leaders. Until now this system does not seem to have fulfilled the expectations of the researchers.

Another problem noticed is the relatively short timespan in which the evaluation has to take place. Politicians want to see results within one to three years. However, some changes, for instance improved language lessons, are apt to generate results only in the longer term. The discussion partners indicated that it would be good to evaluate some changes at longer timespans, for instance in 10 years time.

In the programme very detailed objectives are stated (for instance, two-fifths of the registered clients are expected to obtain employment; an equal percentage to be placed in educational programmes/individual development programmes; one-fifth are expected to need further study and planning services). Hopefully this will help to evaluate the results of the project properly. When participants find a job it is written down on a board in the entrance hall to motivate others who can see that there is quite a good chance of success. So far 180 persons, 44 per cent of those who participated in the programme, have secured a job. Thus, in the short period that the centre has been active, the stated aim has been achieved. On the one hand, this could mean that there were good incentives to reach the stated objectives. On the other hand, it must be admitted that the economic context has been positive; the demand for employees is relatively high.

5.6   Conclusions

The Metropolitan Initiative meant a switch of Swedish state attention from the rural areas to the most disadvantaged urban areas. For the first time the Swedish government launched an explicit urban policy to break the vicious cycle of segregation. The city of Malmö, and within Malmö the city district of Hyllie, have been able to profit from that opportunity. A new way of working for the improvement of the social conditions was made possible.

Dominance and Rigidity of the Public Sector

The Metropolitan Initiative was created and implemented by the public sector. The national government and at the local level the cities and the districts have been responsible for its implementation. Other actors, such as the private sector or the third sector, have not been formally involved. The third or voluntary sector could have been used as a resource, but such organisations have no decision-making power with respect to, for instance, approval of the projects to be developed. The private sector has been contacted only on a very informal level; perhaps more communication with it would be advisable, especially since preparing people for the labour market is a major objective. In the objectives of the MI both at national and local level there is no reference to the private sector as a potential partner. Moreover, the private sector has not shown any inclination to cooperate in this programme. Nor do companies seem inclined to employ non-native people, for fear of the cultural differences and the effort they believe they would have to put into training.

Cooperation also fails with such public organisations as the Education Department. This lack has threatened the success of some of the projects implemented by the WDCH such as the language course for illiterate immigrants. The Education Department seems unwilling to change its methods or to cooperate with other institutions. Better involvement of this department would be necessary, especially if we consider that some structural changes in the education system may be needed to reach the underprivileged groups and offer them a proper education.

Focus of Project on the Relation between Work and Democracy

Central elements of the social programme in Hyllie are the expected relation between work and social integration and the democratic content. By finding work, people should become more socially included, able to establish contacts with Swedish society, and improve their living conditions. However, finding a job is not enough, nor is it the answer for all the clients. Therefore, it is also important to improve the social participation of the underprivileged groups. Through the programmes that have been developed the immigrants have started to create their own communities and have improved their communication with the local authorities. However, full integration will never be achieved by some non-natives. For them the idea is to strive for a minimum standard of living. For many the main concern is that their children get a good education in the Swedish language and culture, and that they will become well integrated into Swedish society. Instruments to that effect are language lessons and courses in specific skills for work. One recommendation is that schools should become more involved in the local programmes aimed at fighting social exclusion.

Innovative Elements: the Integrators and Language Courses

An innovative element in the programme is to map out the needs of non-native people through the so-called *integrators,* the non-Nordic employees of the WDCH who function as *brokers* between the locals and the centre. In this way the centre works bottom-up, in a *grassroots* perspective. After carefully finding out what the inhabitants think is needed, new projects are developed. The meeting places also have become an important part of the integration process, as they can be used as places of reunion where immigrants can develop networks with Swedish inhabitants also. The impression, however, is precisely that the meeting function is not supported by, for instance, shops or pub-like meeting facilities in the neighbourhoods. This could hamper community development.

One of the main advantages of the WDCH is that it works in a quite innovative, flexible way. Its workers develop new methods based partly on ideas of the local population, which help to stimulate social inclusion. It will be very important to prevent the centre from becoming bureaucratic, like many regular public institutions in Sweden. One way to achieve this is by formulating clear objectives and goals, which have to be incentives for this organisation to operate continuously in an efficient and effective way. The relatively detailed objectives that were formulated in the policy reports have to be considered positive in this respect, although the level of ambition does not always seem very realistic. This can lead to pressure on the social workers or dissatisfaction with the final results, given the concrete objectives to fulfil.

Leadership as an Important Condition for Success

The development of the Metropolitan Initiative in the city district of Hyllie has been possible thanks to the leadership of the manager of the WDCH. In fact, the other districts where similar centres have been established have been less successful in accomplishing the goals of the MI, according to our information. In those districts the traditional way of working was followed, leaving less opportunity for local democracy and participation to develop. As mentioned before, the leadership of the integration secretaries has also been an important factor in the success of the integration initiative in Hyllie.

   Although the programme started only recently and still has two years to go, the first impression is that the implementation of the Metropolitan Initiative in the Holma neighbourhood in Hyllie is on the right track. Some of the goals as stated in the programme have already been attained. Although the integration of immigrants into Swedish society will need much more time, the initiative has helped to change the pattern of isolation from which most of the inhabitants of Hyllie were suffering.

Notes

1   During the 1960s housing shortage was a major problem. A national housing plan was launched in 1964 to create one million new apartments in 10 years. Two-thirds were multiple dwelling units (Nilsson, 1998).

2   Such centres have also been organised in the other three city districts involved in the Metropolitan Initiative. The same institutions participate in those centres, although it seems their approaches have been less innovative and successful than the one established in Hyllie.

3   Source: 'Revised Programme for 2001 Hyllie City District Council Metropolitan Initiative', City of Malmö, 2000.

4   Standing Committee, Social and Community Health Committee and Social Welfare Committee.

Chapter 6

New Ways to Employment in Stockholm-Norrmalm

6.1 Introduction

Like other Scandinavian regions, at the beginning of the 1990s the Stockholm region was in an economic crisis. One result was a sharp increase in the number of unemployed people and, related to that, the number of people who were threatened with social exclusion. A European programme that subsidised local territorial employment pacts gave Stockholm an opportunity to set up innovative projects to fight unemployment. In the period between 1998 and 2000 more than 20 projects were carried out in four districts of Stockholm. Two of them, 'Aim your Future towards Employment' (August 1998–June 1999), and 'New Ways to Work' (October 1999–February 2000), carried out in the Norrmalm district, were chosen as the focus of this case study.

In the section 6.2 of this chapter we will describe the social-economic profile of the Stockholm region, thus the context of this case study. Then, section 6.3 discusses social problems in Stockholm. Here specific attention will be given to the Norrmalm district. The Stockholm Territorial Employment Programme will be described in the section 6.4. Here the two projects mentioned above will be presented. Section 6.5 analyses the organising capacity elements of this case study. Finally, in section 6.6 some conclusions are drawn. The data of the metropolitan profile of Stockholm are summarised in Table 6.1.

6.2 Social-economic Profile of the Stockholm Region

Demography

Stockholm is the largest city of Sweden, with 762,000 inhabitants. It is part of the Stockholm Metropolitan Area, with 1,762 million inhabitants, which, together with the Göteborg and Malmö regions, compose the Swedish urban system. Sweden is characterised by its late urbanisation, in the mid-nineteenth

Table 6.1   Data of metropolitan profile of Stockholm

Characteristic	Stockholm
Population of the city (1996)	762,000
Population of the urban region (1996)	1,762,000
Growth of the urban population (city, %, 1981–96)	11.0
Share of the population of foreign extraction (city, %, 1998)	10
Proportion of population of working age in employment (city, %, 1996)	76
Unemployment rates (city, %, 1997)	6.5
Proportion of employment in industry (city, %, 1991–96)	14.6
Proportion of employment in services (city, %, 1991–96)	85.2
Number of administrative tiers (including state and boroughs)	3
Borough Boards	Yes

Sources: van den Berg et al., 1998, p. 381; Nordstat, 1999, pp. 106, 110 and 115; European Commission, 2000, Vol. 1, p. 123; idem, Vol. 2, p. 234.

century. In that period urbanisation began to develop as a result of the expansion of the manufacturing sector, which attracted new employees with their families to urban areas. The period of expansion of Stockholm began in the 1950s and from then into the 1970s the population increased by almost 40 per cent. The city's expansion took the form of new city districts that developed around the newly-extended subway. These new centres developed their own local labour markets, housing and services. From 1970 to 1985 the population of Stockholm dropped by 80,000, while the periphery of the region grew by 181,000. A clear suburbanisation trend was noticeable between the city centre and the surrounding region. Nevertheless, employment in the centre rose by 14 per cent. Consequently, commuting also increased, and the employment possibilities in the suburban centres increased rapidly. During this period Stockholm became a metropolitan area, known as Greater Stockholm.

The population of Stockholm is relatively young; about 40 per cent is between 20 and 44 years of age, although in the inner city there is a tendency towards a concentration of elderly people. Approximately 10 per cent of the population are foreigners, most of them coming from Finland (one quarter), although recently other groups have also become relatively important (among others Turks, Poles, and Somalis).

Economy

Stockholm is the natural centre of the region and the central administration, with the ministries, courts, etc., as well as the parliament and the royal family located there. Stockholm also concentrates a relatively large part of the economic activities of the country. Slightly over one-fifth of the country's workplaces are in the region, while the total production value is as much as one-quarter of Sweden's production value (Nordstat, 1999).

For the economy of the Stockholm region, business-related services, ICT and public administration activities are quite important. In 1999, 45 per cent of Stockholm's city population was employed in trade, communication and financial activities. The service sector (from personal services to social welfare) employs almost 30 per cent of the population (see Table 6.2). By contrast, industry is seriously under-represented in the Stockholm region. In terms of added value, financial activities, media and business services are the largest activities in the Stockholm region. Another fast growing sector is the tourist industry, which generates almost 65,000 annual jobs.

Table 6.2   Stockholm's labour market 1999 (persons 16–64 years)

Employment (%)	Stockholm	Whole country
Agriculture and forestry	0.2	2.5
Manufacturing and energy production	8.6	19.5
Construction	3.2	5.5
Trade and communications	20.0	19.4
Financial activities	25.3	12.5
Education and research	8.5	8.5
Medical care and social welfare	15.1	19.0
Personal and cultural services	12.7	7.9
Public administration	6.1	5.1
Employed in all (absolute number)	376,900	4,066,000

Source: Statistics Stockholm (USK).

The Administrative Framework of Stockholm

There are three governmental layers in Sweden. Besides the national level, there are the municipal and regional levels, the latter comprising county council districts, which have a long historical tradition. Both the municipality and the county council districts have taxation authority and their representatives are elected democratically. However, they have different tasks: the county councils have responsibility in the regional social policy and planning, as well as the coordination of state, county council and municipal services. They act as a sort of metropolitan government when the borders of the council correspond with the borders of the region, which is the case in Stockholm.

Municipal autonomy is one of the cornerstones of Swedish policy. In the Swedish constitution it is written that municipalities and county council districts have taxation authority and that the right to make decisions lies with elected representatives. Municipality leadership rests with the City Council and the City Executive Board. The first is the supreme decision-making body and counts 101 members, elected democratically in elections held every fourth year in conjunction with the county council. It is the City Council that has the ultimate responsibility for ensuring that the standards of municipal services are equal throughout the city, that laws and municipal by-laws are observed and that the tax revenue is used to best effect.

The City Executive Board consists of 13 members who represent the parties in the City Council. Representation is in proportion to the number of seats held by the political parties in the City Council. The City Executive Board drafts or delivers its opinion on all matters before they are decided on by the City Council. The City Executive Board is also responsible for implementing the resolutions. Other relevant institutions on the municipal level are the Council of Mayors and the City's Executive Office. The parties that have the political majority in the City Council appoint the members of the Council of Mayors. The mayor and seven vice-mayors, who are full-time, professional politicians, are elected by the City Council every four years. Each of the City's divisions is headed by a member of the Council of Mayors. The City Executive Board Secretariat carries out assignments on behalf of the City Council and the City Executive Board, as well as their committees, drafting committees and advisory committees. The City of Stockholm's Executive Office has the responsibility for the direction, follow-up and development of the city's activities. It is in this office that the initiative to develop a TEP in Stockholm was taken.

The city is primarily responsible for business sector development, culture and social activities. All these activities are developed in eight divisions (see Figure 6.1). In 1997 and 1998, Stockholm was divided into 24 district councils[1] with the same responsibility and authority as the city's other committees and boards. One of the specialist committees is the Social Service Committee. The difference is that the district councils work within their respective

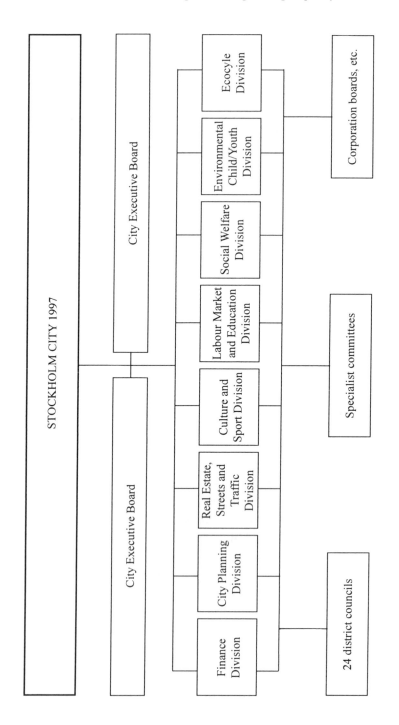

Figure 6.1   Stockholm's administrative organisation in 1997

Source: How Stockholm is Governed, 1997.

geographic areas and are responsible for their activities. The City Council has also assigned district councils the task of drafting local trade, local employability measures and industry programmes. Until 1997, the city administration was divided into eight divisions, among which was one for labour market and education matters (see Figure 6.1). In 1999 the city's administrative structure was reorganised, which affected the districts (which were reduced to 18) and the Labour Market and Education Division. This division disappeared and education matters are now the responsibility of the Schools Division, while labour market policy is not treated specifically by any of the present divisions.

The municipality is responsible for issues such as taxes and common budget. The major portion of the city resources – three-quarters – is passed on to the districts, all receiving different amounts depending on the number of inhabitants, age, living conditions, etc. On average, nearly three-fifths of municipal revenues come from municipal taxes. In the case of Stockholm, the tax revenues accounted for 64 per cent, while the state grants contributed only 11 per cent to the city's income (in 2000). These state subsidies have from 1993 been general revenues, which gives the municipality freedom of decision. The city's expenditure for 2000 shows that the district council activities receive, as mentioned before, much of the city's revenues. About 14 per cent of the expenses of the city are allocated to activities oriented to employability and education measures, which gives an idea of the important role that the fight against unemployment plays in this city. The money that the municipality gave to subsidise the Territorial Employment Pact (TEP) projects came from that amount.

6.3 Social Problems in Stockholm

In this section we will describe the situation of Stockholm in terms of its social problems. We will focus mainly on unemployment because this is one of the main concerns of the Stockholm municipality and the focus of the programme analysed in this case study, the Territorial Employment Pact. We will also describe the situation in the district of Norrmalm, as this is the neighbourhood where the projects analysed were implemented.

Stockholm

During the expansion years of the post-war period Sweden developed a broad welfare estate with a relatively good provision of social services. To a

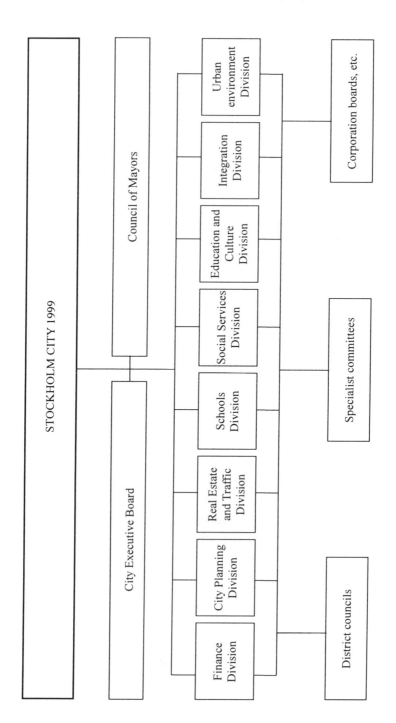

Figure 6.2   Stockholm's administrative organisation

Source: How Stockholm is Governed, 1999.

considerable extent the Swedish welfare state has been decentralised, and the municipality is the main body responsible for services such as care for children and the elderly, social assistance, and education.

Stockholm, and Sweden as a whole, were characterised by an expansion of its economy during the 1960s and 1970s, which translated into high employment, wealth and the access of every citizen to education, health care, etc. Immigrants have been present in Stockholm since the post-war period when the city and Sweden were experiencing a great economic development. Immigrants had the same rights as Swedish people. Equality and integration are the cornerstones of the Swedish and Stockholm social policy. The immigrant groups in Stockholm are diverse, both economically and culturally, ranging from Finns (18.2 per cent in 2000) – who came mainly in the period after World War II – to Somalis who came as refugees in the early 1990s, and now are the second largest group after the Finns, accounting for 8.5 per cent of the total foreign population (Statistics Stockholm USK).

However, during the 1990s a recession set in, and the economic conditions in Stockholm – and also in other Swedish municipalities – deteriorated dramatically. This resulted in a 4.7 per cent decrease in GDP between 1991 and 1993. In Stockholm the share of employed people decreased from 82.9 per cent in 1990 to 71.0 per cent in 1995. Rising unemployment had a negative effect on the tax revenues of the municipality, and to cope with it the municipality had to economise on municipal investments. These were cut back by 12 per cent between 1991 and 1993. The cutbacks affected all kinds of activities, but especially those that depended largely on municipal funding such as child care, education and care for the elderly.

From 1998 onwards the situation changed. The developments in the labour market in Stockholm were positive and the unemployment began to diminish. The development of the knowledge-intensive business sector (ICT/Telecom companies and research institutes) has been the main engine of this recovery. Unemployment in Stockholm fell to 5.3 per cent in 1997 and this also implied a decrease of the number of unemployed with social assistance (see Figure 6.3). Nowadays, unemployment in the Stockholm region is quite modest; 3.6 per cent in 2000, substantially under the national average of 6.8 per cent. In fact, nowadays there seems to be a lack of skilled people able to fulfil the kind of jobs required by the new information-related companies. About 70 per cent of all business companies suffer from the so-called bottleneck problem (Report TEP, 2000).

With the recovery of the city economy, some side-effects have developed. For instance, housing prices in the central regions of Stockholm have increased

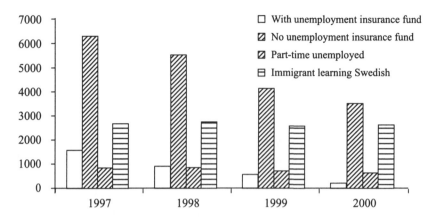

Figure 6.3   Households on social assistance due to unemployment in Stockholm, May 1997–2000

Source: Interviews, Stockholm.

dramatically. In the 1960s, many immigrants and lower-income households lived in inner-city Stockholm but, owing to renovation and higher rents, inner-city housing has become increasingly less accessible to lower-income groups (Murdie and Borgegard, 1998). This has reinforced a trend towards spatial segregation that could lead to social exclusion. Another relevant phenomenon is that people who lack the required skills are unemployed. In January 2000 about 45,000 long-term unemployed were described as jobseekers and about 8,000 households lived on social security due to unemployment. Immigrants, especially those coming from developing countries, are also affected by this type of unemployment. It means that much effort must be directed towards improving employability among the unemployed, not only through education but also by stimulating the opportunities offered by the present economic situation. As will be shown in the next section, the project analysed in this report, the TEP, is a response to a very specific situation of unemployment – long-term unemployment, a problem that requires innovative approaches.

Norrmalm

The district of Norrmalm has approximately 60,000 inhabitants and is considered one of the wealthiest districts of Stockholm. Norrmalm is one of the most important commercial areas of the city and many people visit the district's plentiful restaurants, shops, theatres and cinemas every day. There are about 17,000 businesses registered in Norrmalm. Most of them are one-man or small service enterprises with 0–20 employees. Some 90,000 people have their place of work in the area. Thus, it is usual for businesses in the area to recruit staff from other residential districts. The unemployment rate in Norrmalm is lower than the average for the municipality.

However, this situation is recent. When Stockholm was affected by the Swedish economic recession in the early 1990s, the city districts also suffered a decrease in their quality of life. In the case of Norrmalm, the employment rate decreased from 86.1 in 1990 to 75.3 per cent in 1995. Unemployment rose (4.65 per cent in 1997), as did the number of households depending on social assistance owing to unemployment.

Nowadays only about 1,000 (2.5 per cent) of Norrmalm's inhabitants do not have jobs in the regular labour market. As in the case of Stockholm as a whole, this small percentage is made up of the persistent long-term unemployed, who are subject to marginalisation. Therefore, in Norrmalm there was a lively interest in measures to support this group of people and encourage them to become self-supporting by finding appropriate jobs. That is why the Norrmalm district joined the TEP.

6.4   The Stockholm Territorial Employment Pact

The Territorial Employment Pact (TEP) in Stockholm is one of the 89 TEPs of the European Union. These Pacts were initiated as a way to apply the European Employment Strategy on the local level. The purpose of the TEP is to create more permanent jobs and to prevent long-term unemployment through the cooperation of various players in partnership. From the extraordinary meeting of the European Council in Luxembourg on 20 and 21 November 1997 the following goals of the TEP programme can be derived:

- improving employability;
- developing entrepreneurship;
- encouraging adaptability;
- equal opportunities.

As in the other European Pacts, the concept of the Stockholm TEP is to mobilise all the players in the city's districts in order to combat unemployment, as well as to strengthen the employment effects of European Structural Fund contributions.

In Stockholm, development grants were received from EU Objective 3 and Objective 4 Structural Funds to develop the TEP. Almost half of the technical assistance for the Pact has been financed by the European Commission and the national government, and the remaining part by the City of Stockholm's Labour Market and Education Committee. The initiative to apply for the TEP came from the City Council Executive Office. The City of Stockholm's Integration and Labour Division was the first responsible for organising the project. Preliminary work on the Territorial Employment Pact commenced in May 1997 at municipal level and was extended to the four district councils through that year. That decentralisation reflects the motives of the City of Stockholm's district council reform. At that time the City Council gave high priority to developing projects to promote employment and fight unemployment in Stockholm.

The programme was aimed at creating new job opportunities in the districts involved. The envisaged goal was to reduce unemployment by half from 1997 to 2000. That target was further specified by stating that:

- every unemployed person under the age of 25 had to be offered a job, training, work practice or other employability measure before reaching 100 days of unemployment;
- every unemployed adult should be offered a job, training, retraining, work practice or other employability measure before reaching six months of unemployment;
- 100 per cent of the unemployed should have individual action-plans prepared for them jointly by themselves and the public authorities concerned.

The goals mentioned above were further translated into concrete measures:

- improving existing methods for training and retraining;
- supporting lessons in speaking the Swedish language;
- supporting the establishment of firms and social firms;
- stimulating practical partnerships between enterprises;
- finding new sources of employment in sectors such as tourism, IT, health services, and education.

Finance of the plans The total costs of the TEP programme in Stockholm were €5.3 million, of which €2.1 million was financed from the EU Structural Funds and €3.1 million from national and local budgets. About one-tenth of the total costs were used to finance the Pact Administration. For the implementation of the TEP programme four districts were chosen in which 21 projects could be carried out. The four districts chosen for the implementation of the TEP programme clearly had different characters. They differed in social demography, the number of unemployed people and the number of located businesses, among other aspects. The intention was to see how more or less similar projects worked out in differing districts. The reason that Norrmalm was chosen as the focus of this study was a practical one. Unlike in the other districts, in this one projects are still going on.

A brief description of the projects carried out in the Norrmalm district is given below.

1 Local Enterprise Centres in Norrmalm

The Local Enterprise Centres were intended to guide small entrepreneurs in the developing of their enterprises. Local Enterprise Centres had to help entrepreneurs with their contacts with local authorities, with EU issues, network-building, etc. Apart from Norrmalm, the district of Vantör participated in this project. In those two districts, Local Enterprise Centres were created. The aim was for these centres to complement the work of SNK (the development company of Stockholm) at district level. Though there was much enthusiasm about the idea of cooperating in entrepreneur issues, this project was considered not very successful. One explanation might be its relatively short duration ($1^1/_2$ years). Another is the lack of confidence in the project among the entrepreneurs. The total costs of the project were €113,000, of which €50,000 was put up by EU Structural Funds.

2 Fresh start for former entrepreneurs

The project for former entrepreneurs invited a group of ex-entrepreneurs to start again. They were long-term unemployed who had had their own business, and were currently receiving income support or unemployment benefits. The participants were given the opportunity to start anew through in-depth guidance, business advice, seminars and information. They were also advised on how to develop new career opportunities. The City Job Centre provided the support they needed for reorientation. All 15 participants completed the course and seven of them applied for grants to set up in business immediately, while three others intended to start in the first half of 1999. The rest did not accomplish the goals of the project. The project costs were €141,000, of which €63,000 was financed by EU Structural Funds.

3   The First Step out of Unemployment

This project focused on long-term unemployed women, which turned out to be a difficult target group to work with. The objective – to bring single parents with low skills back to work – was not accomplished in most of the cases. There were 12 participants and the total costs of the project were €109,000, of which €49,000 was provided by EU Structural Funds.

4   Cooperation of Long-term Unemployed Persons

This was a project aiming at cooperative education, training and development. The partners were the Norrmalm District Council, the City Job Centre and the Cooperative Development Agency. There were 12 participants, the total costs of the project were €208,000, of which €93,000 was financed by EU Structural Funds.

5   'Aim Your Future towards Employment' (Employment Project I)

The target group of this project were long-term unemployed on social assistance. The purpose of the project was to create an environment that provides individuals with the scope and opportunity to change from a life based on income support to one with a job. Participants could learn to take their own initiatives and become responsible for their own development. They were, together with others, involved in daily activities aimed at creating routines and group dynamics giving them a feeling of power, energy and self-esteem and an identity other than that of 'jobless social benefit recipient'. During the project, the participants were given opportunities for personal development through guidance, project work, vocational orientation for contacts on the labour market, as well as help to gain practical experience. The project allowed participants successively to develop their competence on the basis of individual action plans. The participants were 20 long-term unemployed people who had income support and specific problems that prevented them from finding or keeping a job.

The project was carried out during 10 months, from August 1998 to May 1999. The idea of the project was developed by Millennium, a private company that designs and carries out projects to accompany unemployed people to get them back to work in the regular labour market. Millennium found the participants for the projects from the Social Welfare Department in Norrmalm. The participation was voluntary or semi-voluntary; people received extra money if they participated in the project. The course was developed in several steps. The first step was oriented to stimulating team work by establishing common tasks. The second step was to initiate looking for a job, and then establish an individual plan according to each participant's aspiration (from starting a new business to working in a specific economic sector). All this was done with a lot of team work and individual discussion. The intention was not to teach people specific skills, but point out to them their opportunities in society and to discover what prevented them finding a job. Their low self-esteem and lack of motivation seemed to be worse than their lack of skills. The results of the project were that 12 people found a job in the regular labour market, four started a business, and two enrolled in specific vocational training. The total costs of the project were €289,000, of which €130,000 was financed by EU Structural Funds.

6 'New Pathways to Work' (Employment Project II)

The intention was to develop a project similar to 'Aim Your Future towards Employment' but shorter, with a more concentrated and different selection. The purpose was for participants to increase their personal empowerment and initiatives, and to develop networks. All participants were to have found a solution for their predicament after five months. The managers initiated and supported a functional group dynamic in which the participants aided and helped one another. Strong emphasis was also laid on participants' ability to present themselves to potential employers. Partners in this project were the Norrmalm District Administration (Social Welfare Office) and the Employment Agency.

The second project was implemented during 19 weeks, from October 1999 to February 2000. The intention was to make this course shorter, to see whether the same objectives as in the first one could be accomplished in less time. The number of participants was 10. In this new project they implemented a theoretical model of personal change. This model established four steps toward personal change, namely: motivation (willingness), resources /abilities, vision, and how to start. Each participant had to discover for himself what could be achieved by a changed attitude, and from that starting point try to find an adequate job. The results are that eight persons are in work after finishing the project. That may be due in part to the good economic conditions in Stockholm, but the first aim of the course was to remove some personal barriers that prevented people from getting a job even at a time of high demand.

Actors involved in the employment projects In the first period of the TEP projects (from 1998 to 1999) both public actors (such as the city of Stockholm, the County Council, and the Public Social Insurance Office) and private ones (like the Swedish Association of Enterprises, and Sweden 2000) participated in the Central Steering Group. Each district has a local steering group, which, together with the project leader of each project was also represented in the Central Steering Group (see Table 6.3).

Table 6.3   Actors involved in the Stockholm TEP at city and district level

Central steering group – Stockholm's TEP	Local steering group – District Council Norrmalm
City of Stockholm	Norrmalm City District Council
County and local labour boards	City labour office
County Council	City Public Social Insurance Office
County Administrative Board	Leader of local private enterprises
Public Social Insurance Office	organisation
Business Companies	
Sweden 2000 (NGO)	
Swedbank	
The Swedish Association of Ethnic Entrepreneurs	

Source: Action Plan 1998–99.

New projects to be launched The current plan of the project partners is to start a new period of territorial employment projects. Whether they will succeed is still uncertain, in view of the political shift in the City Council. The present conservative majority does not support a direct financial contribution of the city to local employment projects. After the reorganisation of the municipal bodies, that followed the elections of 1998, the responsibility of the TEP was transferred from the City Council Executive Office to the Social Services department. The reduction of the responsibility to a lower position of the administrative hierarchy reflects the decreasing political support for the programme (Action Plan TEP, 2000).

The project partners have suggested some changes from the old TEP programme:

- *A more generous participation of the private sector in the TEP.* This is considered necessary to define the participation of the private sector more clearly, and to make its presence in the Steering Group stronger than before. It is also a way to ensure the support of the new conservative majority, which tends to prefer private sector initiatives.
- *Implementing the programme in all the city districts.* To that end, good communication and coordination from the steering group will be required. It will be the TEP leader's important task to convince the local government, for one thing in terms of future financing of the project. An aspect in favour of these projects is that they aim to reduce the number of people dependent on social income, thus saving money for the municipality.
- *Focusing on other target groups.* More attention will be given to the employability of handicapped young people and to stimulating entrepreneurship among people with psychiatric problems.
- *Combining the TEP project with another European project, EQUAL.* The EU initiative EQUAL is intended to function as a transnational laboratory for new methods to be used in the regular policies and programmes. A partnership with a Baltic city is foreseen to develop and exchange expertise about the TEP projects.

There are also plans to strengthen the ties with some actors of the TEP, mainly with the private sector and the Education Department. Furthermore, the Organisation for Small and Medium Enterprises (SMEs) and the private job agencies have to be represented in the steering group. The private job agencies are to be more actively involved in the projects, because they know the demands of the labour market. The aim is to stimulate, advise, and educate SMEs that want to develop and survive.

6.5   Analysis of the Organising Capacity

Vision

The visions that ultimately led to the employment pact carried out in the Norrmalm district of Stockholm were developed by a top-down approach at various government levels (EU, city and district; see Figure 6.4). Firstly, at European level a programme was set up to fight unemployment in European urban areas. The programme was meant to subsidise locally-developed employment projects, and had sprung from the awareness that unemployment was one of the main threats to the cohesion ideal of the European Union. Welfare differences within regions had become more severe than those between regions, and the best way to deal with them was to try to reduce (long-term) unemployment. This awareness led to the formulation of the four EU goals of the TEPs: to improve employability; to develop entrepreneurship; to encourage adaptability; and to create equal opportunities.

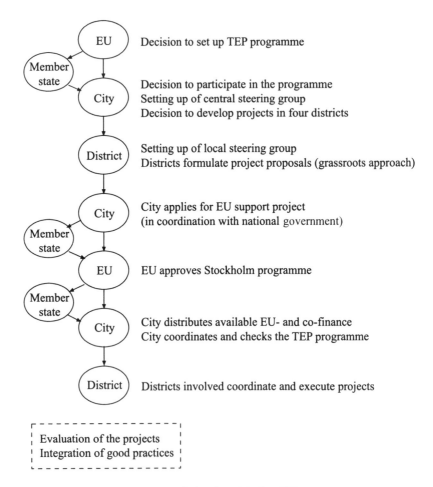

Figure 6.4   Decision process of the Stockholm TEP

The EU programme was the main catalyst to set up an employment programme in the City of Stockholm. But the city itself had to further adapt the programme for its own territory. The vision explicitly expressed in the

City Action Plan 1998–99 is that: *All people should have the possibility to support themselves through gainful employment.* This can be considered a summary of the four EU goals in one statement. At city level four districts were chosen, which had to tailor the programme to their specific circumstances. These districts differed from one another with respect to such things as socioeconomic structure, availability of facilities, demography and unemployment rates. Consequently, it became possible to see how more or less similar projects would work out in different circumstances.

Regarding the employment projects in Stockholm, there was an opportunity-based approach at three levels:

1 the EU initiative, which co-finances local employment projects. This formed the main catalyst for setting up the Territorial Employment Pact in Stockholm (TEP);
2 the opportunities of the participants themselves. The skills and abilities of the participants in the employment projects were the base for finding adequate work. Positive thinking has been crucial; the project workers believed in the possibility of finding an adequate job or education for every participant;
3 the opportunities of the relatively large number of vacancies in the very recent period. Many employers are seeking employees. This offers opportunities for more people to enter the labour market (even, for instance, for handicapped people, a target group for the new period), and thus contributes to the EU-goal to achieve equal opportunities for every citizen and to the above-mentioned city vision.

Strategic Networks – Cooperation between the Actors Involved

To the actors involved in the employment policies in Stockholm, the EU programme on TEPs was a major incentive to cooperate. In fact, this programme *prescribes* such better cooperation. The statement is thus warranted that the scope of the EU programme is much broader than just simply the co-financing of local policies. It also forms a major catalyst for setting up innovative policies, stimulating urban networks to learn from one another's experiences,[2] and thus stimulating strategic networks at local level. Whether these networks will outlast the European programmes depends on specific local circumstances, for instance on actors' cooperativeness, the local (financial) incentives for cooperation and the organisational structure and culture.

Strategic networks at local level are set up for different aspects of the social policies involved. They are set up to develop an adequate vision on the approach to the problems (the steering groups at city level as well as at district level), and to implement the policies (in particular at district level, see also Figure 6.4). The roles of the municipality in this programme were to coordinate and supervise through the steering group, composed of representatives of various municipal institutions. Other more active actors in the project were the Employment Agency and the Social Welfare Office of Norrmalm. Thanks to this project they have come together and are cooperating to exchange information, among other things.

The steering groups at city as well as district level are relatively formalised bodies. They have been set up to give every actor involved an opportunity *in principle to direct and decide* on the policy choices. However, the policy *proposals* are made by relatively small groups. After the political approval of the programme, these proposals are made by the project coordinators, the involved civil servants of the employment departments and private organisations involved in the implementation of the policies. These 'proposal networks' have a more informal character, depending on the willingness to participate and the interests and capacities of the people involved.

The steering groups are set up for the duration of the projects, that is, for a relatively short period. However in particular the initiated informal networks can be expected to last longer. These networks, initiated or at least stimulated by the EU, can also become active in follow-up programmes regarding employment policies or other social policies.

Until some years ago there was hardly any cooperation in the field of employment policies. The TEP project stimulated the actors involved to cooperate better among themselves and with businesses in Stockholm. The intention is further to improve the links with the business sector when new employment projects come to be worked out and implemented.

For the future, a more integrated approach between the different district departments (especially the Social Welfare Department and the Employment Department) involved in Norrmalm is considered desirable. In the first place to avoid the clients getting different messages from the two institutions and in the second place, to improve the effectiveness of the programmes. Another question is the participation of the private sector in the projects. The actors involved in the TEP projects have got in touch with some job agencies for guidance about minimum requirements to work and about the existing demand. These job agencies are expected to become more involved in the steering groups of the employment projects.

Adequate Leadership at Various Levels Important for Success

At city as well as district level there were two clear incentives to develop innovative employment projects: namely the availability of the EU funds, and the relatively high unemployment rates at the start of the project. It is important to realise that the second incentive deals with the problem proper, and the first incentive is only the (financial) facilitator to cope with it. The formal leaders of the TEP projects were the project coordinators at city level and at the district levels. They seem to have greatly stimulated the development and implementation of the TEP programme and the related projects.

At implementation level we have seen that the employees of the Millennium organisation played a stimulating role. They can be considered informal leaders of the projects we have focused on in this case study. They were motivated by the visible results of the projects: the individual successes of the participants. To see people's self-esteem increasing and to watch them become more motivated and have the satisfaction of getting a 'real' job in society were powerful incentives for these project workers.

For the follow-up of the project, the incentive of the EU-finance will remain important. However, partly thanks to the success of the project, but especially owing to changing economic circumstances, the second incentive (the relatively high unemployment) has lost its urgency. Norrmalm has now less than 2.3 per cent overall unemployed. Thus, the proper problem of unemployment has been almost solved, and other problems have now to be dealt with in the social policy field. To stimulate people to continue to carry out projects that help to reduce social exclusion, the formulation of new goals is crucial. The emphasis should now be on how to fill persistent vacancies.

Political Support for the Unemployment Projects

The unemployment problem within the EU has high political priority at European level. Hence the broad support for a European programme that stimulates local employment projects. To carry these projects out at local level sufficient financial funds have to be found for the required co-financing of the European programme.

In Stockholm, on the level of the city, there was also a broad support for co-financing the European employment projects. For one thing, unemployment was considered a major problem in the city; the unemployment rates were relatively high at the start of the TEP project. For another, at that time there was a left-wing city government that supported the employment programme.

It fitted clearly into the politics of the city majority between 1995 and 1998. Therefore, at that time there was no problem finding sufficient financial funds at urban level for the European employment programme.

In the meantime, some things have changed. First, the unemployment rates have decreased substantially. Secondly, the municipal elections in 1998 resulted in a changed majority in the city council. The new conservative majority does not consider the financing of the employment projects a priority, and is loath to co-finance them from urban funds. To them, economic and employment policies are national tasks and should thus be financed by the national government.

There is a tension between the tasks of the national government and the urban government. The national government carries out an employment policy for *job-ready people*. The city, on the contrary, cares for the other people, the ones that need intensive help to become job ready. The latter group was larger than that of the job-ready people. There is a risk that when the city no longer carries out employment policies there will not be sufficient attention paid to people who need additional individual help to get a job.

Policy Development and Implementation

Though the vision on the territorial employment pact was developed with a top-down approach (starting from the EU, via the city level to the district levels), the policy was developed through a bottom-up approach. This was described in the Action Plan 1998–99 (p. 3). Here, a four-step model was presented. In the first step the local steering group (at district level) draws up an inventory of the specific needs in the district, and develops tailor-made projects and actions to fight unemployment. Secondly, the central steering group (at city level), with help of EU support, coordinates and finances the proposed projects. During the third step direct actions and projects are implemented and evaluated and the lessons disseminated. In the last step, the good practices learned from the projects carried out are integrated into more sustainable projects. The grassroot approach has been considered essential for the success of the project: developing projects that directly fit the needs *and* the opportunities of the unemployed people.

The implemented employment projects have helped to change the vision of social workers about their clients. The crucial point is to see them as people with opportunities rather than people with problems. There was a clear divergence between the views of Millennium and of the social workers on how to approach long-term unemployed people. A consequence of this divergence was the difficult selection of participants. Millennium recruited participants through temporary social workers who came to work during the summer period. The suspicion arose that the regular social workers did not have sufficient confidence in their clients and their capacity to participate in employment projects. Perhaps they considered the long-term unemployed people unable to hold a normal job, and focused on giving them social assistance, thus perpetuating the idea that these people could never become self-supporting. Another possible explanation is the competition that was felt between Millennium and the Social Welfare Department.

Output of the Employment Projects

At district level, specific tailor-made projects were to be set up. Actors working at district level had to come up with creative ideas for innovative projects that could help to fight unemployment. In the Norrmalm district a relatively large number of projects were carried out, and some of them were quite successful. To develop ideas for these projects, special brainstorm sessions with actors involved were held. We formed the impression that some relatively successful project ideas were developed in Norrmalm. Four-fifths of the former long-term unemployed participants found work in the course of the projects. The analysed projects were relatively small however; the first project had 20 participants, the second only 10. Nevertheless, it appeared to us that a district that is relatively prosperous and faces relatively few social problems seemed to have developed successful projects under the Stockholm TEP. We think that this success owed more to the vision, creativity and organising capacity of the people involved in the programme development in this district than to the seriousness of the social problems.

The Social Welfare Department deals with people who suffer from other problems in addition to unemployment. This department's approach to unemployment has changed. The successes of the employment projects have probably contributed to this. The traditional approach of the department had proved to be not very effective. The social workers had to do all the work, even the administrative work, and this prevented them focusing on each case in detail. Currently a so-called 'individual approach' is being implemented to cope with the features of unemployment in the district. In the new approach, the administrative tasks of the cases are given to the Administrative Department, so the social workers can concentrate on their clients and on how to make them self-supporting rather than how to give them money.

Outcome: Has the Number of Socially-excluded People been Reduced?

After a period of relatively high unemployment in Norrmalm (4.1 per cent, about 1,750 overall unemployed in September 1997 in a district of 60,000 inhabitants) and a bad economic situation, by September 2000 this figure was reduced to 1,050 overall unemployed (2.3 per cent). Only 78 unemployed remained on social assistance; these are called the 'hard-core unemployed' because they often have a variety of problems, such as alcoholism, lack of skills, psychological problems, etc. To tackle that phenomenon a more individual approach is needed, focusing on each person individually, trying to find their capabilities and opportunities and not to focus only on their problems.

We think that the projects have certainly helped to get some relatively problematic long-term unemployed people into work. Without these projects they would probably still have been jobless, despite the good economic situation. Thus the projects seem to have been a good step forward in the fight against social exclusion. Evidently with a positive and personal approach even the more problematic jobseekers can be helped. One positive consequence is that this approach is now being adopted by the regular administrative services.

6.6   Conclusions

Employment Projects within the Information Economy: Opportunity-based

The present society increasingly demands an individual approach to unemployed people. In an economy that faces increasing competition at various levels, it becomes more important to find a good match between the demand and supply side of the labour market. The innovative aspect of the employment projects analysed in this case study is that they do not merely offer education, but follow a customised, tailor-made approach to the participants. The approach is a combination of individual attention and team activities. Participants learn to be more disciplined and to build up sufficient self-esteem to find an appropriate job in society. The idea is to make people more self-supporting. This was to be achieved by positive thinking; stressing the opportunities of the participants rather than their problems. The grassroots perspective was important (bottom-up approach) in that respect, for there was a need for tailor-made projects to fit the long-term unemployed participants. Furthermore, there was also room for 'after-sales activities'. Thanks to the individual or personalised approach, support was available even after the project ended.

Public and Private Tasks

One of the lessons of the TEP is that it is important to analyse thoroughly which tasks are public and which can be done by private actors. Not all the tasks regarding social policies in general and employment policies in particular have to be done by public organisations. Sometimes private actors can do this as well, or even better.

There are some tasks that remain public ones. For instance, the decision about which people have a right to social allowances is best taken by a governmental organisation. Since it is the government that distributes these funds, it is also the most appropriate body to decide on their allocation. But some tasks which are now carried out by public organisations could also be done as well or even better by private actors. A good example, emerging from this case study, is the implementation of employment projects. Because it was carried out by a private organisation that could focus on individual opportunities, an innovative approach could be achieved.

Projects were Important to Break through Fixed Patterns

There was a need to set up innovative projects, outside the regular services, to achieve a different approach to long-term unemployed people. This became clear, for example, when participants had to be found for the TEP projects. That was a task for the Social Welfare Department who had to select adequate candidates from among their clients. However, the regular people working in this department could not find sufficient candidates to participate. They seemed to have the idea that most of their clients – long-term unemployed people – were unable to work in a 'normal job'. They simply lacked the confidence in these people's potential. Holiday workers in the social department in the end came forward with participants for the project. They seemed to have had a more flexible attitude to the possibilities of the department's clients.

The success of the project – the relatively large number of people who indeed found a job on the market – showed the necessity of a breakthrough in the approach to long-term unemployed people. The project was thus useful to break the vicious circle of long-term unemployed who were dependent on social income and followed courses because they had to (otherwise they would lose their income), and not because they had confidence in finding a job. The innovation in the approach of Millennium is that they could offer individualised attention to each client, focusing on what they wanted to do and their capabilities. After this success, hopefully the regular services will also change their attitude to a more opportunity-based and individual approach.

There are some key factors for the success of the TEP programme:

- *The bottom-up approach.* This gave a good insight into the need of the people with social problems and made an individual approach possible.
- *Cooperation between the actors involved.* Before the programme, the actors involved in the employment programmes hardly cooperated with one another. The actual cooperation was considered positive even before it raised the actual effectiveness of the projects.
- *The focus on unemployment related to job opportunities.* People prefer to have 'market-conforming jobs' to 'created subsidised jobs', as it gives them more self-esteem and confidence in their own potential. From the interviews with the participants, the importance of the approach of this project is the personalised attention and the focus on enhancing the participant's capacities.
- *The help of the EU.* The technical assistance money was essential. There was a need for good *process* leaders to function as catalysts for the programme. In view of the success of some projects and the satisfaction of the participants, continued subsidising of similar projects by the EU seems desirable.

Notes

1   In 1999, it was decided to reduce them to 18 to improve the municipal services, and to reduce administrative expenses.
2   Stockholm is involved in a network of cities that are implementing TEP projects. This network, Metronet, is a collaboration of public/private sector partnerships located in eight metropolitan cities in five EU member states: Copenhagen, Malmö, Hamburg, Bremen, Berlin, Vienna, London and Stockholm.

Chapter 7

Preventing Social Exclusion and Segregation in Helsinki

7.1 Introduction

From 1997 onwards, the city of Helsinki has developed several actions to fight social exclusion and segregation. The first step was to identify the presence of these problems caused and/or aggravated by the economic recession of the early 1990s and elaborate an innovative strategy involving all city departments and local resources, both private and public. This strategy to fight social exclusion and segregation in Helsinki will be described and analysed in this chapter. In the section 7.2 the socioeconomic profile of the Helsinki region will be described. Social problems in Helsinki will be discussed in section 7.3. Section 7.4 describes the Strategy against Social Exclusion and Segregation. Some individual projects within this strategy are discussed in section 7.5. In section 7.6 the strategy is analysed with the help of the theoretical framework of organising capacity of social policies. Section 7.7 concludes. The data of the profile of Helsinki are summarised in Table 7.1.

7.2 Social-economic Profile of the Helsinki Region[1]

Introduction

The city of Helsinki is located in the northeastern part of Europe. With a population of 546,000 it is by far the largest city in Finland. Three geographical entities can be discerned in the Helsinki area: the city of Helsinki, the metropolitan area of Helsinki (comprising the adjacent municipalities of Helsinki, Espoo and Vantaa), and finally the region of Helsinki, with eight more municipalities. In terms of financial and political power, the municipalities are the most important unit, as they have a high grade of autonomy and generous financial means. The Constitution guarantees municipalities the right to self-government and to levy taxes. Two-thirds of public expenditure in Finland is expenditure by local authorities. Local income

Table 7.1 Data of metropolitan profile of Helsinki

Characteristic	Helsinki
Population of the city (1999)	546,000
Population of the urban region (1999)	1,172,000
Growth of the urban population (city, %, 1980–96)	+10.2
Share of the population of foreign extraction (city, %, 1998)	5
Proportion of population of working age in employment (city, %, 1996)	55
Unemployment rates (city, %, 1997)	10.5
Proportion of employment in industry (city, %, 1990–95)	14.4
Proportion of employment in services (city, %, 1990–95)	83.8
Number of administrative tiers (including state and boroughs)	4
Borough Boards	No

Sources: Nordstat, 1999, pp.106, 110 and 115; EC, 2000, Vol. 1, p. 122; idem, Vol. 2, p. 90.

taxes amount to 16.5 per cent of the personal tax burden, a very high figure in a European perspective. Some 62 per cent of the budget of the city of Helsinki comes from local taxes (Holstila, 1998). The dependency on the central government is low: only 3 per cent of Helsinki's budget comes from national government funds. This situation has advantages (the influence of higher tiers of government on urban policy development and implementation is limited) but there are drawbacks too, like lack of cooperation between local units within the metropolitan region and intraregional competition as a result of the fact that municipalities have to raise their own income, for instance by trying to attract higher income people and business investment.

The four municipalities within the Metropolitan Area – Helsinki, Espoo, Vantaa and Kauniainen – cooperate within an administrative body called Helsinki Metropolitan Area Council. This cooperation is limited to waste management, public transport, air quality management and spatial planning (European Commission, 2000). On a higher spatial level there is no governmental body responsible for the region as a whole. The regional council consists of members of the cities that constitute the region. In 1984 Helsinki was divided into seven major districts, 33 districts and 118 subdistricts, but these districts are mainly used for statistical purposes; they do not possess specific competences or tasks.

Population

Helsinki is the centre of the Helsinki region, which is a region with a population of almost 1.2 million people (see Table 7.2). Finland as a whole has only slightly more than five million inhabitants, which implies that more than one-fifth of the Finnish population lives in the Helsinki region. The population of the region is increasing. In the last few years, there has been a yearly migration surplus of some 10,000. For the years to come, the population is expected to grow further. From 1995 to 2015, growth is expected to be 24 per cent, which makes Helsinki the second growth region (in terms of population) in Europe, after Lisbon (City of Helsinki Information Management Centre, 1996). Metropolitan growth is mainly an effect of Finnish people migrating from the rural areas to the urban concentrations. The immigration of foreigners is growing slowly. The share of foreign people in the Helsinki population has increased from about 1 per cent in 1990 to 5 per cent at the time of writing.

Table 7.2   Population in Helsinki and Helsinki region (1998 and 1999)

City of Helsinki	539,000	546,000
Metropolitan area	920,000	934,000
Helsinki region	1,154,000	1,172,000

Source: The City of Helsinki Urban Facts, 1998a, 2000.

Economic Development

The city of Helsinki was founded in the middle of the sixteenth century, for trade purposes. Up to the nineteenth century however, the city remained insignificant. In that century, the city began to develop more rapidly. By the turn of the century, the city of Helsinki had grown into an important centre of services, commerce and administration. The industrialisation of the economy took off after the first world war, and was accompanied by a rapid growth in commerce and services. After World War II, this process continued, although employment in the services sector grew much faster than in manufacturing. By the end of the 1980s, nearly half the jobs in the region were in finance, insurance, business services and public services.

During the last decade, the economic development of the Helsinki region has been characterised by large dynamics. Up to the late 1980s, the Helsinki region prospered. Income levels were rising steadily, and the unemployment rate was very low, at only 3 per cent. In the early 1990s, the situation worsened dramatically. The main reason for this was the collapse of the Soviet Union, at that time a very important trading partner. Exports to the Soviet Union stagnated, while at the same time almost all of Europe was hit by a recession. In the period 1992/93, Finland's gross domestic product (GDP) dropped by 10 per cent, and the unemployment rate rose to 18 per cent. From 1994 on, the economic situation has improved. Growth rates of GDP rank above the European average. GDP growth rates have been around 6 per cent per annum lately, regional growth in the Helsinki region even somewhat higher, and the unemployment rate shows a clear downward trend. For Finland as a whole, the unemployment rate is 10.2 per cent, which is still relatively high from a European Union perspective (see Table 7.3).

Table 7.3   Unemployment rate in per cent in EU countries (1996)

Austria	3.1
Belgium	6.0
Denmark	6.9
Finland	10.6
France	7.9
Germany	6.5
Greece	6.6
Ireland	8.2
Italy	6.5
Netherlands	4.7
Portugal	3.2
Spain	11.0
Sweden	6.3
United Kingdom	6.4

Source: Urban Audit, EU, Regional Policy, 2000.

The Helsinki region scores better, with 7.2 per cent unemployment. However, the fairly high number of long-term unemployed is a special problem in Helsinki. It has proved difficult to bring these people permanently back to active working life.

The severe economic crisis of the early 1990s did not bring only misery. It was an important stimulus for the actors in the region to join forces and combat the crisis; momentum was created to achieve really fruitful cooperation.

As a result, in 1994, the key actors in the region – administration on different levels and the business community – developed an integral and broadly shared vision, and drew up a clear strategy. Key elements of this strategy were to develop Helsinki as a Nordic region of interaction, with a focus on sustainable, knowledge-based development. Many plans were developed to give substance to this strategy. Examples are the setting up of science parks, the Art and Design city, and the Innopoli cluster west of Helsinki, the European City of Culture 2000 project, but also many initiatives aimed at cooperation between business and research institutes were taken.

Economic Structure

The Helsinki region is the main economic centre of Finland. With one-fifth of the Finnish population it provides 514,000 jobs (one-quarter of all Finnish jobs), one-third of GDP and almost half of all R&D activity (European Commission, 2000). The municipality of Helsinki alone counts more than 40,000 enterprises. In Table 7.4, the distribution of jobs among different sectors is depicted, for Helsinki, the metropolitan area, the Helsinki region and Finland as a whole. The Helsinki region's economy is strongly dominated by services; some 80 per cent of employment falls into that category. There has been a boom in ICT business development in the Helsinki region. The growth of turnover in this sector has been 177 per cent between 1993 and 1998, while in all other branches growth was 52 per cent for this five-year period (City of Helsinki Urban Facts, 1999). Manufacturing is much less important, in particular compared to Finland's average. The high share of public services stems from the fact that almost all Finnish national public bodies are located in Helsinki.

Despite its declining share in the economy, manufacturing is still important for Helsinki. Within the manufacturing sector, food products, paper, machinery and electrical and optical equipment are the most important branches. The industry is particularly concentrated in Vantaa, the neighbouring city of Helsinki in the north east.

Espoo, the western neighbour of Helsinki (and Finland's fourth city), is the most prosperous city within the region. Headquarters of the communication industry (like Nokia) are located here, as are knowledge institutions. A catalyst for Espoo's strong growth was the relocation of the Helsinki University of Technology from Helsinki to Espoo. Espoo is also appreciated by well-to-do people for its high quality living conditions. There is an unmistakable sense of rivalry between Espoo and Helsinki.

Table 7.4   **Jobs by industry in Helsinki, metropolitan area, region and Finland, 1996, in percentages and absolute totals**

	Helsinki	Metropolitan Area	Helsinki region	Finland
Manufacturing	10.9	13.1	14.6	21.6
Construction	3.5	3.7	4.1	4.9
Trade, hotels, restaurants	17.7	19.8	19.5	14.5
Transport and communications	9.3	9.5	9.0	7.5
Finance, real estate and business services	20.2	19.0	17.7	11.1
Public and other services	36.7	32.7	32.4	31.1
Other, and unknown	1.7	2.2	2.6	9.3
Total	100%	100%	100%	100%
Total (absolute)	297,932	445,819	513,585	1,932,752

Source: City of Helsinki Urban Facts, 1998c.

The Helsinki economy is knowledge-intensive. Research and development are very important activities: they are considered the key to national and regional development, competitiveness and economic success. Research intensity (which can be measured in several ways) has increased in Finland throughout the 1990s. The region of Helsinki is by far the most important locus for R&D (research and development) activity in Finland: over 50 per cent of Finnish R&D expenditure is spent in the Helsinki region. Private involvement in R&D is high: the business sector accounts for some 62 per cent of R&D investments (City of Helsinki, 1998a). The knowledge intensity of the Helsinki economy can also be illustrated by the high educational level of its population. Some 50 per cent of Finland's academics live in the Helsinki region.

However, the growth of ICT activities is such that there is a need for qualified personnel. At the same time there is a large group of less educated long-term unemployed. This mismatch on the labour market, a well known phenomenon in many cities, appears to be new for Helsinki. It is considered one of the social problems and will be dealt with in the next section.

7.3   Social Problems in Helsinki

In the early 1990s Helsinki was a socially balanced city with small differences in the socioeconomic level among its inhabitants and its districts. The economic growth of the city seemed endless until that period, and that allowed the extension of a welfare model with good provision of social services and high income redistribution. However, in the early 1990s a serious economic recession hit the country and, in extension, Helsinki. Due to this, phenomena almost unknown for the city became common. Massive unemployment brought new, until then not familiar social problems with it, related to education, age, gender and housing. The problem was aggravated by a tendency to accumulation in certain urban areas. Moreover, in the last 10 years immigration has increased from 1 to 5 per cent of the population which also has a considerable impact. However, these figures are not comparable to those of some larger cities in some European countries (United Kingdom, Germany, France, Benelux) with percentages up to 30 or 40 per cent of ethnic minority people.

The fear is that all these phenomena could lead to social segregation. It is not yet possible to talk about slums in Helsinki but if problems are not solved in time, social deprivation and consequent problems will become more and more difficult to master in some neighbourhoods (*Helsinki Quarterly*, 1996). Therefore preventing rather than combating social exclusion has become a policy objective of the Helsinki government.

The development in jobs and national product is crucial to a city like Helsinki, whose income is based on local tax revenues. During Finland's and Helsinki's economic super-boom in the late 1980s, many new jobs were created in financing, company services, real-estate brokerage and other service businesses. As mentioned before, the structural changes in the global economy hit Helsinki very violently. The most affected sectors initially were manufacturing and construction. As the economy deteriorated, unemployment gradually extended to white-collar workers in the service sector and financing. As a consequence, job losses and increased unemployment reduced the municipality's assets and increased the expenses of its social services (Kattelus, 1996).

The worst of the recession lasted from 1994 to 1997. In 1994 the unemployment rate reached 18 per cent. Unemployment in 1997 in Helsinki was higher among men (14.6 per cent) than among women (11.2 per cent) (Urban Facts, 2000). Another risk group during the recession years was young people, among whom unemployment increased up to 30 per cent in 1994.

However, this group has showed a favourable evolution and in 1997 the unemployment rate for this group accounted for 9.8 of the total (people younger than 24). Another phenomenon that the city has confronted from the recession years is long-term unemployment. The number of long-term jobless is large, 43 per cent of the unemployed are long-term, and many have outdated education and skills. The prolonged lack of employment marginalises people not only from working life but also from many other functions of normal life. Connected problems are alcohol and drugs abuse, homelessness and mental problems.

These problems were aggravated by a tendency of concentration in some neighbourhoods. Although in the first years of recession it seemed that unemployment spread fairly evenly in all parts of the city, from 1994 onwards, a trend of neighbourhood differentiation has been observed. In 1994 the standard deviation of district rates of unemployment was 3.8, whereas in 1996 it was 4.3, which means that differences between districts have grown. A key issue for Helsinki is whether the process will cause increasing socioeconomic differences between districts or will remain a simple pattern of preference (Tuominen, 1997).

More recently it appears that the acute problems that hit the city have been solved. Unemployment especially showed an important decrease at the same time as Helsinki's economy recovered. In 1999 the unemployment rate was about 10 per cent, and this rate has been maintained. Also the difference among districts has not increased any more in terms of income and in 1999 the number of long-term unemployed decreased in all districts. The dependency on income benefit started decreasing in 1997. From 1998 the number of households receiving social benefit had decreased by 12 per cent in Helsinki (Partnership Working Group, 2000).

However, some problems still persist. In 1998 there were six districts in northeastern and eastern Helsinki where the long-term jobless amounted to 40 per cent and it is said that the 10 per cent rate of unemployment corresponds to long-term unemployed. Also it is said that local differences in income continue to grow, although incomes have started growing again in all city districts. However, growth has been stronger in those areas that showed no decrease of average income between 1991 and 1995. In those districts where average income was falling in 1995, it had not risen back to the 1991 level by 1997 (Partnership Working Group, 2000).

Another problem that faces the city is the increase of immigration, due to the city's internationalisation. Although immigration is seen as a positive phenomenon, it is a fact that foreign immigrants have a worse situation than the Finnish population with regard to unemployment and danger of social exclusion (due, for instance, to linguistic and cultural integration problems). In 1999 the proportion of foreigners in Helsinki was 4.7 per cent of the population. The majority of immigrants come from Russia, Estonia, Somalia and Vietnam. Among them, the unemployment rate varied between 10.4 and 67.3 in 1998 depending on their nationality. In 1999 the unemployment rate among immigrants was 33.7 per cent against 9.0 per cent among Finns (Partnership Working Group, 2000).

In conclusion, although fears expressed during the recession years that social exclusion would occur on a larger scale have not come true, there is the perception that action should be taken to prevent the worsening of existing problems. Therefore, much effort has been oriented to introducing innovative solutions in the fight against social exclusion and segregation. The Strategy against Social Exclusion and Segregation is a response to this situation.

7.4   Strategy against Social Exclusion and Segregation

Introduction

In 1997 the Committee on Social Exclusion and Segregation was created to identify the problems and establish the strategies. The Committee concluded that 'the economic recession, mass unemployment and the manifold increase in the number of foreign nationals have created a new situation with threats caused by social segregation and an accumulation of social problems in certain areas' (Helsinki City Office, 1997). The Committee advised that special attention should be given to the following issues:

- focus on employment as a basic tool against social exclusion;
- support the creation of partnerships between different sectors of city administration, as well as with NGOs and private citizens (as neighbourhood associations);
- special attention to the prevention of social exclusion in children and young people;
- bring new information technologies to all residents, as well as use them to find new solutions for social exclusion;
- creation of networks within the city administration regarding the fight against social exclusion and segregation. In this way, no new department needed to be created but all existing ones had to include this fight in their own divisional objectives.

Based on the outcome of the report of the Committee in 1998 10 objectives and measures were defined. In the same year the *Strategy against Social Exclusion and Segregation*[2] was approved as a special project by the City Council. The objectives of the Strategy are:

1 the prevention and alleviation of social exclusion and segregation must be one of the priorities of all departments of the City Administration;
2 the planning of services and the environmental quality shall be especially conscious to ensure the service level and quality of the surroundings of neighbourhoods labelled as problematic;
3 the city's housing policy must pay special attention to the problem of social exclusion, when defining its objectives;
4 one of the most important measures to fight against social exclusion must be against unemployment, especially to improve labour market qualifications and improve the employment rate of the long-term unemployed;
5 to encourage the realisation and continuation of neighbourhood projects and ensure the participation of the departments of the city administration;
6 preparation of an immigrants' integration programme;
7 improve training, employment possibilities and normalisation of mentally disabled people and those suffering from severe social exclusion;
8 improve the local child welfare and youth and family counselling, as well as share it between the local administration, NGOs, voluntary organisations and the police;
9 setting up of the *Year of Partnership* in the city administration in 1999;
10 promote the implementation of the latest information technologies in the prevention of social exclusion.

Part of the Strategy is the introduction of the principle of positive discrimination, which means that the most underprivileged areas will get extra resources for specific public services. Introduction of this principle is a break with the Finnish tradition that every citizen is entitled to the same treatment by the government. Based on eight indicators (unemployment, income, education level, single-parent families, etc.) districts are ranked according to their welfare level. The ones in the tail of the ranking (below a minimum level set) receive extra attention.

The Year of Partnership project (point 9 of the list of objectives of the Strategy) was the main subject to analyse in this case study. This project and its most important actors will be introduced in the following two sections.

The Year of Partnership

On 1999 the Year of Partnership was established as a part of the Strategy against Social Exclusion and Segregation (Final Report, Partnership Working Group, 2000). The programme has two levels:

* to stimulate cooperation of the city departments with each other and with external actors;
* the financing of small projects, which contribute to relieve social-exclusion problems.

The Year of Partnership was intended to be a new way of treating social problems in the city. It meant joining the forces of several actors in society to reach a common goal. The main practical objective during the Year of Partnership was to make the city's offices and departments ready to create and participate in partnerships. Three categories of actors, the public sector, private sector and the 'third sector' participated in the Year of Partnership. Some of the projects selected for the Year of Partnership existed already and have been taken as examples of cooperation between different actors in the fight against social exclusion. The project was settled by the city government and offered to the other actors (such as the private sector, neighbourhood or district associations, parishes, and NGOs).

About 250,000 of the 1999 budget appropriations of the city government were designated to the prevention of social exclusion and the setting-up of partnership projects. The idea was to stimulate citizen participation and community development as a bottom-up contribution to prevent social problems on the neighbourhood level. In fact every person or group could submit a project proposal. The projects were submitted by heterogeneous groups of people, from private persons, communities and enterprises. The degree of experience and cooperation with the municipality was also very different from one project to another. Four broad criteria were used to select the projects eligible for (financial) support. These criteria were based on the objectives of the Strategy:

1 prevention of social exclusion;
2 the implementation of a partnership;
3 the degree of innovation;
4 the degree of realism of the project.

Special attention was given to projects from areas labelled as problematic. A total of 161 projects were submitted, together applying for an amount of about 2 million. Among the 161 applications, 54 projects were selected, 43 of them were subsidised with this source and 11 from other sources within the city. A consequence of the approach chosen was that more than 100 projects had to be rejected. Given the fact that the submitted proposals did not differ very much in quality, this led to rather negative reactions from people involved in projects that were refused.

In the final report of the Partnership Working Group several examples of the projects undertaken under the Year of Partnership can be found. The projects could be divided into four main groups:

* Those that create models for sharing the responsibility for bringing up the youth of a district. For instance, in the Ruoholahti a group of parents arranged a local forum for young people. In the Käpylä project afternoon care for the children was organised.
* Projects led by residents to increase civic participation at the district level.
* Activities among district associations and parishes. For instance, the league of Helsinki district associations has stimulated the interest of residents in their own district and has constructed a data network on a district basis. This facilitates the access to information about one's own district and creates a sense of participation.
* Good practices: training days on partnership and prevention of social exclusion for headmasters in the city's Education Department; morning and afternoon pursuits for school children and District Forums to discuss themes on the district level.

Actors Involved in the Strategy

In this section the role of some of the relevant actors participating in the Strategy is described. In Figure 7.1, the organisational structure of the city of Helsinki is showed. There are four deputy mayors with specific responsibilities for urban policy fields and the respective urban organisations. The Deputy Mayor for Cultural and Personnel Affairs is responsible for, amongst others, the Training and Development Centre, Helsinki Urban Facts and the Education Department. The Training and Development Centre coordinated the Year of Partnership project and managed the decision process with respect to the subsidising of local projects. Helsinki Urban Facts provides statistical and strategic information on socioeconomic developments in the Helsinki region.

It has produced strategic reports on the need for a more comprehensive social-policy in the Helsinki region. The Urban Facts Department appears to be of high strategic value in the policy development process. Policy measures are often based on evidence provided by the excellent urban information system. In many cases sets of indicators and their maximum or minimum values are set and agreed by the council. When the facts show that in certain districts problems go beyond threshold values, this will be a sign for policy attention and/or measures.

The Education Department The Education Department supports participation and equality in the education system, and includes the prevention of discrimination in its main vision. In this sense, much attention is given to special education at secondary level also. Special education refers to children with educational deficiencies, handicaps and behavioural problems. These kinds of problem are often considered a consequence of increasing social exclusion. About 4 per cent of the students are in special education units. To avoid discrimination against these students, the Education Department tries to integrate them into mainstream schools. This implies in practice that more financial means have to be allocated to these schools. Special education is also oriented to reduce the number of dropouts. There are seven geographic areas in Helsinki where the special education is done inside normal schools.

The attention to immigrants also plays an important role in the department's vision. There is intensive instruction in Finnish, as well as additional comprehensive school classes for immigrants according to specific needs. There is also Finnish language instruction for adult immigrants. The Education Department ensures that all immigrants have the right to study their own language. To this end, education is now available in 39 languages.

The Education Department (in cooperation with the Social Services Department, third sector organisations and parishes) takes care of the morning and afternoon activities for children, so the schools also have an important role in social care before or after school hours. Another important point in the prevention of social exclusion is the already-mentioned principle of 'positive discrimination', aiming at dedicating extra resources to problematic areas. The application of this principle is accepted by most school directors, but some schools near to each other (but located in the 'right' or 'wrong' district) are not very happy about the different standards of treatment.

Social Services Department Before the economic recession of 1990s the Social Services Department had already started to collaborate with employment

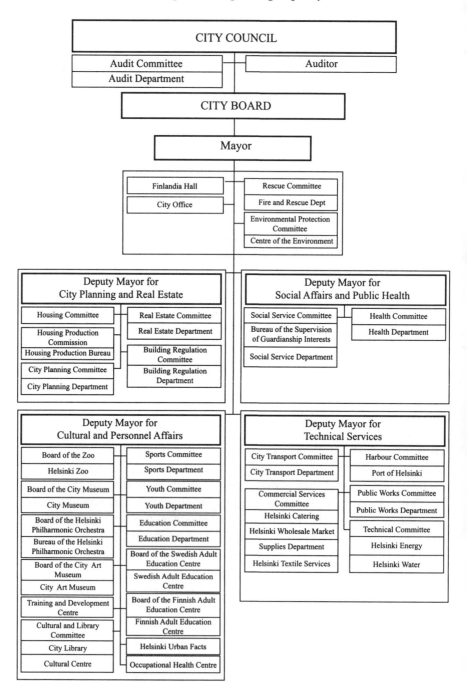

Figure 7.1   The organisational structure of the City of Helsinki

agencies to get young homeless people back to work. In that period employment was high in the city. This is considered the start of the strategy to prevent social exclusion. Before the recession there were only small points of exclusion (such as children in social care and alcoholism). The Social Services Department and the Urban Facts Department had by then already elaborated a set of indicators to define a deprived area, so they could better allocate resources to prevent social problems. However, at that time there was insufficient political support to the idea of area-based allocation of resources. During the recession years the social services in Helsinki were cut back. That meant that social problem groups who used to be protected by the department now had to deal with their problems themselves. Policy development and implementation of the Social Services Department in the framework of the strategy are described in section 7.5.

The Lutheran church In Finland the Lutheran church plays a big role in the life of the citizens as the formally established church ('state church'). About 70 per cent of the population of Helsinki are members of the church (compared to 85 per cent in the whole country), which is financed by a 1 per cent surtax on the income tax of the members, collected by the official tax office. In this situation the Lutheran church is considered almost as a public actor. In Helsinki there are 30 parishes spread all over the city. These parishes are autonomous in deciding the type of services and work they offer to their community. When the municipality started the project they invited the church to participate in the elaboration of the programme. The municipality also contacted the church when the Year of Partnership started. Cooperation between the municipality and the church already existed, but the programme helped to make this cooperation clearer. The application of the principle of 'positive discrimination', implying that parishes in problematic areas get more resources than the rest of the parishes, is still not really accepted. However, discussion on this issue is continuing.

7.5 Two Examples of Local Projects within the Year of Partnership Project

Local Partnership in Maunula – Helsinki

Maunula is a neighbourhood of Helsinki with about 10,000 inhabitants. It was created in the 1940s and grew quickly in the 1960s. In the following decades it was provided with services such as shops, hospital, church, etc. About 60 per cent of the housing in the area is social housing, a high rate for Finnish standards. Those houses are small or medium sized, with few lifts and most of them are for rent. Due to the characteristics of the apartments, many elderly people and single parents, as well as unemployed people and those with drug addictions, and so on, comprise the social structure of the area.

In 1964 some inhabitants began meeting in the Maunula Club and later, in 1978, an inhabitants' association was established. From its origins it has been a very active association and nowadays counts on the collaboration of professionals and a social worker. The inhabitants' association succeeded for instance in bringing back some shops and banking services. They also created a Local Forum, where all inhabitants can discuss issues about the neighbourhood. They meet six times a year and also organise two seminars. The concentration of 'problem' people in their neighbourhood – the result of priority allocation of dwellings to these households – is considered a serious matter by the association. Their main objective is to improve (balance) the social structure. They also complain that the area is weak in commercial services as a consequence of the social problems.

In 1999 the inhabitants association submitted a cooperation project with the municipality in the framework of the Year of Partnership. Their application was selected and they received a subsidy to rent a space in the neighbourhood as a meeting place. The so-called 'Maunula-Mini Partnership' started a project for the unemployed of the area, the 'Local Training Project'. Its aim is to provide people with skills to help them to find a job. This project is intended to help about 20 participants from the area. They received an amount of 64,000 Fin Marks (11,000) from the municipality (they asked for 74,000). The inhabitants have received the project well and local businesses also participate. For the next three years the project will receive money from the European Social Fund.

The association is critical about the role of the municipality because they only support financially, and do not listen (sufficiently) to the demands of inhabitants. The inhabitants claim that they informed municipal representatives about the increasing problems, but action was only taken when the statistics showed the true situation. The association thinks that a way to revitalise the area is to construct new, bigger apartments that will attract families. They also propose the demolition of an old low-quality shopping centre (which is now a centre for drugs traffic) and the building of new houses and a new shopping area instead. According to the association, the Real Estate Department (owner of the land) does not have an adequate vision for this development.

This Department again rented the land to the shops for exploitation reasons; thus the suboptimum situation remains.

According to the Maunula partnership, social workers are not used to cooperating with the inhabitants. In addition, they deal with problems from a divisional point of view. There is one social worker who actively participates with the Maunula Club. The Year of Partnership helped many of these workers to realise that it is possible to collaborate with residents, and this was clear both through the Forum and through the 'Local Training Project'.

Horisontti – the Jobseekers Association

The Horisontti (Horizon) project is situated in Malminkartano, a neighbourhood in northern Helsinki. This project started as the initiative of a woman who lost her job during the crisis of the early 1990s. Due to the increase of social problems (especially unemployment), the local population realised that the social services could not cope with them. Therefore, a small unemployment association began. The idea was to develop a kind of 'unofficial employment agency' where working skills could be developed. It was a very locally and practically oriented initiative that received some financial help from the city through the 'Healthy Cities' project. In the course of time 'new' problems like the integration of foreigners presented themselves and attracted the attention of the Horisontti group. A few years ago a vacant commercial building was acquired where the rapidly expanding activities could be located. They wanted the municipality to buy it for them, but up to the time of writing, all that is on offer is a subsidy to pay the annual rent. Because no long-term agreement about this subsidy exists, the leaders of the centre feel the future is rather insecure.

At the moment, the Horisontti group organises many social activities that go far beyond the original objective of seeking jobs for unemployed people. The objectives now involve the stimulation of the local economy (by offering room for some start-up companies), the improvement of its inhabitants' capabilities (language lessons for foreign people, computer lessons, etc.) and acting as a social care and activity centre for the neighbourhood. It has grown into an important neighbourhood community centre, also providing a wide range of activities for children and young people. Figure 7.2 shows the activities of the Horisonti group.

The Horisontti Association participated in the Year of Partnership in 1999. It received €170,000 from the budget to develop several small projects for immigrants, long-term unemployed, youth in danger of social exclusion and

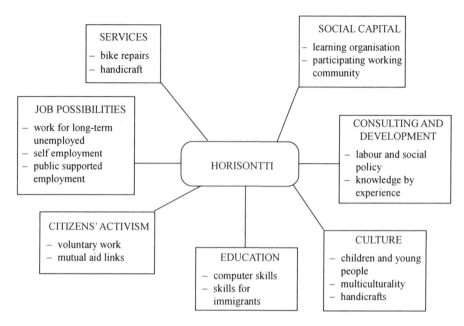

Figure 7.2   Activities of the Horisontti group in Helsinki

Source: Interviews, Helsinki.

mentally disabled people. One of the positive effects of the Year of Partnership was that the relationships with the mental hospital and the Employment Office improved. They consider the project as a good opportunity for forging better contacts with the municipality. It is now felt by the organisers that, in the interests of the centre, more energy should be put into the evaluation of results to convince the municipality of the value of the work. They feel that they do very valuable work that often complements the work of the municipal social workers. The municipality, however, does not give a clear role to the centre, which results in some dissatisfaction especially while the future remains uncertain.

Although question marks can be placed on the professionalism and the continuity (dependent on some key persons) concerns, the inhabitants feel that they can easily access the centre (no bureaucracy) and this gives the centre exactly the charm that makes it so popular among residents of the neighbourhood.

7.6 Analysis of the Organising Capacity

Vision

In a welfare state like Finland the socio-political culture can traditionally be characterised as a striving for equality in society. In Helsinki, where unemployment used to be a rather unfamiliar phenomenon and where the share of immigrants is still low, problems of social exclusion and spatial segregation are new phenomena. In this case study we deal with the set up of an approach to prevent the kind of concentration and accumulation of social problems that have become more or less common in many cities in western Europe. This situation implies that a well-articulated vision on the problem does not yet exist, nor are these 'new' problems embedded in a coherent urban strategy on what to achieve, and how to achieve it. Only within some city departments (for instance, Social Services and Education) are there ideas on how the strategy has to be carried out to fulfil certain goals. There seems to be, however, no agreement on these 'subvisions', or there is insufficient mutual communication on this. Some explanations for the lack of an adequate vision on a 'citywide' level are lack of experience with these new social problems (there is not much know-how available yet), that part of the social problems have become less pressing (the economy is doing very well again and the unemployment rate has been decreasing for some years), and that not much political priority seems to be given to the strategy (if the limited allocation of funds and the temporary character of the strategy are taken into account).

Start of policy development Ten years ago the municipality was not as independent as today. The main decisions were taken at state level. Also, with respect to social policies, the city mainly executed state directives. It thus hardly developed an independent tailor-made social policy. But by the process of decentralisation, municipalities have acquired the responsibility of defining their own problems and to find their own solutions. The city has started to develop policies which better fit the needs of the population. But the initiation of such policies has proved to be no easy task. There is a lack of knowledge about the specific approaches needed to fight problems in an efficient and effective way. Few lessons can be drawn from earlier experiences in this field in Helsinki. There is thus an urgent need for the evaluation of programmes and projects which are carried out in this field and to learn from the experiences of cities coping with similar or worse problems.

Vicious circle of socially excluded people Socially excluded people often face a complexity of problems, which cumulate over time. Such complexities of problems need a coherent approach. It makes no sense to fight only the symptoms of a much larger problem. A social exclusion process can start with the loss of a job after which other problems evolve such as a divorce, addiction to alcohol and drugs, criminality, deterioration of houses and districts, and closing of shops in urban areas. Simply trying to set up programmes to fight a part of this chain of problems, such as projects against drug abuse, does not solve the problems of social exclusion and segregation. One of the first lessons drawn from earlier experiences is that the approach adopted in Helsinki has been too divisional. The ideas of the strategy prove that there is a growing awareness of the limitations of such a traditional approach in the social policy field and a growing awareness of the need for a more comprehensive one. Still there appear to be tensions between the divisional and the area-based approach. Most departments still operate in a divisional way. A more coherent area-based approach seems to demand organisational changes and changes in attitude.

Strategic Networks Cooperation between the Actors Involved

Cooperation between municipal departments The Year of Partnership was also meant to stimulate cooperation between urban actors involved in policies preventing social exclusion. There was awareness that, especially between the different departments of the local government itself, there was too little cooperation to realise a comprehensive approach. During the Year of Partnership there were however no really clear incentives and sanctions to achieve better cooperation. Some improvements have been achieved, but in general municipal departments keep working quite independently and are not inclined towards partnerships. The project did not change this situation noticeably.

An important example could be found in the existing cooperation between the business sector and the education system. It contributed to make Helsinki a centre of education and research. There is however a widespread conviction that there is insufficient cooperation of this kind between the urban departments involved in social policies. At execution level the actors involved (sometimes) cooperate; this is however often not the case at the management level.

Only those departments that are traditionally 'socially oriented' (like education, youth, social services) did collaborate. Other departments such as real estate and housing were not so involved in the project. A possible explanation for their lower commitment to participating in social policies is that their primary tasks are different; they are 'technical' and directed at raising income from exploitation rather than participation in social policies. Such fundamental differences are difficult to overcome. They demand a change in attitude, maybe stimulated by specific financial incentives and/or sanctions, or by societal and political pressure, for instance if social problems are becoming a major threat to society.

Some discussion partners claim that the Real Estate Department did not cooperate sufficiently to achieve the aims of the strategy against social exclusion and segregation. In Figure 7.2 of the Final Report from the Partnership Working Group, however, it seems that it was especially the Real Estate Department that took most of the measures to ward off social exclusion and segregation:

- a third of new council flats have been reserved for existing city tenants who want to move to a new council flat;
- tenant criteria of council flats have been unified with other municipalities of the Helsinki Metropolitan Area;
- in certain areas labelled as problematic applicants with a job have been accepted faster if this has been likely to have a favourable effect on the area's population structure;
- the production of owner-occupied housing has been stimulated in areas labelled as problematic.

Despite the fact that the Real Estate Department has changed its housing policy, some still perceive it as insufficient to really contribute to the aims of the strategy.

Leadership

No clear statements can be made about who has the formal or informal power in the strategy. A possible explanation for this might be the lack of clear concrete goals in the programme. This lack of goals confirms the impression that there was no clear vision on how to tackle this complicated problem. Without a vision on how to prevent social exclusion, it is also difficult to see how different projects can complement each other. When actors involved do not understand the dynamics of the process and if no clear objectives have been formulated, the need for strong leadership to overcome these shortcomings increases. But under these uncertain conditions (insufficient ideas concerning which actors in which policy fields have to cooperate, and thus no clear ideas on who has to lead what) assuming leadership can be a tricky undertaking. Leadership has not been assumed by a specific department or private party.

Leadership has to start with adequate knowledge of and a well-elaborated vision and strategy on the problem field. When there are specific goals, and knowledge on desirable cooperation between actors involved, formal and informal leadership in the field will be (almost automatically) developed.

There will be a good leadership only if there is belief in improving the situation. Then there will be the setting up of projects that really matter. And if there are clear targets, the project can be monitored and evaluated to see whether adequate measures are taken. The impression is that Helsinki still has to start such a process.

On the level of the Year of Partnership project, the leadership role seems to have been filled according to the expectations, but the scope of the project was rather limited and especially oriented to tap private initiative. Leadership in the individual projects submitted within the context of the Year of Partnership is a kind of natural leadership, usually assumed by private persons who sacrifice time and capabilities to start and maintain local initiatives. However these initiatives are rather vulnerable and person-related. If natural leaders resign and some kind of formalisation does not take place, projects run the risk of failure.

Communication and Support

Communication No large campaign on the strategy was started. The fear was that too much would be expected from the programme and this would put pressure on the civil servants involved.

Because the resources were limited there was not a lot of diffusion of the Year of the Partnership programme. Only a small number of cooperation programmes could be financed; there was even the fear that too many actors would apply(!). During one month there were advertisements in a newspaper to announce the available funds. There were however more applications than expected. In November 1999 two seminars were organised to give the projects exposure. Attendance was high from the third sector but this was not properly communicated in the mass media.

There was hardly any communication regarding the results of the programme. A main reason for this was probably the lack of evaluation information. Only a list of subsidised projects could be given, but little could be said on the impact of these projects on the seriousness of the social exclusion problems. As a pilot project it could have been of interest as a learning process for the municipality.

Political and societal support There was a lot of political support for the strategy at the start. The mayor, the chair of the City Board, the Green Party and the Swedish Party were the main supporters. They all have different political colours, but all felt that something had to be done after the recession. If the budget allocated to the programme is taken into account, one could doubt the real value of the political support; politicians could, of course, not really impress with the programme because only minor changes could be expected. The lack of *ex-post* information gives the impression that the politicians involved did not give much priority to the strategy. If they had been sincerely interested, they would have allocated dedicated means for evaluation to assess the achievements of the policy and to build up knowledge for future policy development.

The intention of the strategy was to avoid some areas in Helsinki becoming 'deprived' with concentration of social problems, and to establish acceptable living conditions for all neighbourhoods. However, it is said that politicians tend to avoid negative qualifications of social problems and do not want to label some areas as problematic. This can be seen as positive, because it prevents stigmatisation of those neighbourhoods, but on the other hand it makes it more difficult to justify extra resources for them.

Finnish society strives for a high level of equality between people. This is worked out in practice by setting welfare norms (expressed by a set of indicators) that any person should be able to meet. Consequences of this are that acceptance of positive discrimination (to give more financial means to lagging districts) is difficult and that acceptance of maps indicating problem areas is also difficult. Only in education is positive discrimination now being applied. Schools in problem areas receive more funds to support the extra efforts they have to make to fight specific problems. These schools have started to carry out additional social tasks such as care for children after school hours. The Lutheran church also faces lack of support for the introduction of the positive discrimination principle in some parishes.

Policy Development and Implementation

As stated, the strategy did not include clear goals. The formulated 'objectives and measures' were quite soft, and more like policy starting points. This made it impossible on the one hand to develop a coherent policy and to evaluate the achievements on the other. Furthermore, there was only a relatively small budget available to support projects for the strategy. There was €1.7 million available of which less than one-quarter was set aside for the private project proposals. Compared to the total annual budget of the Social Services Department (€250 million) the budget made available was less than 1 per cent of the annual budget.

It has to be realised that the strategy was meant as an answer to the situation of recession. The idea of giving money to develop small projects (through the Year of Partnership project) is considered as good one, because it allows the development of new ideas. However, it is said that it is also necessary to 'formalise' the bottom-up approach and to give the projects a more concrete framework of reference. The bottom-up approach was insufficiently complemented by a top-down strategy.

Implementation: need for some kind of formalisation   During the Year of Partnership all kind of projects could be proposed in order to get financial support from the local government. Many of the accepted projects were already in existence, but they got an extra impetus during that year. For some of the projects the continuation seems insecure, because their financing for the coming period is not guaranteed. Some of the rejected project submitters were rather bitter. This certainly did not stimulate their motivation.

The tenth point of the strategy was to use the new technologies in the prevention of social exclusion, giving to unemployed and unqualified people the possibility to learn them. But no specific work was done in the programme because all city departments already undertook some activities related to information technology.

The programme has been considered as a positive step in the fight against social exclusion. However, many actors stated that it was not sufficient, for it does not help to solve the problems in a more structural way. The projects are too limited in their scope and there is a serious risk that the initiated activities will not last, for instance if leaders resign. Some kind of formalisation seems necessary.

Housing policy   One of the most important points of the strategy was the housing policy. The municipality realised that people with social problems (such as unemployment, and drugs abuse) usually occupy social housing. This means that areas with more social housing also become the areas with the highest concentration of social problems. To avoid this, some social housing has been given to less deprived people, to create a more mixed social structure. However, there are no concrete results of this policy. Another goal related to housing was to involve the other municipalities in the Helsinki region in a common housing policy. However this had no support from the other municipalities themselves. Thus a common regional approach of the housing policy could not been achieved.

Effectiveness/Outcome

No clear statements can be made about whether there has been an increase or decrease of social exclusion phenomena as a consequence of the strategy. Due to economic progress the unemployment rate has decreased, but there is still quite a substantial group of people who are to a certain extent excluded from 'normal life'.

'Let all the blossoms blossom' and wait if there is some result, seemed to be the device of the strategy to prevent social exclusion and segregation. Many small initiatives in the social field were supported. The expectation was that at least some of them would generate positive results. However, due to the lack of evaluation this can not be demonstrated. This means that few lessons can be drawn from the initiatives taken. Although the projects may have generated positive effects on social exclusion phenomena, the lack of evaluation unavoidably decreases their value.

Information needed To develop an adequate social policy, the city also needs to have good information on new social problems. The city possesses an excellent statistical information system, but statistics sometimes do not tell everything regarding social problems and how these problems are perceived in society. Besides, statistics can be slow to indicate which problems are arising and where. Thus part of the information needed has to be gathered in another way. An adequate way to achieve this seems to be to listen to people living in the districts themselves, workers in the field (social workers) and the parishes. They often are the first to notice the seriousness of social exclusion phenomena. A more systematic approach of gathering such bottom-up information should be recommended. Perhaps the presence of a kind of neighbourhood service centre might be helpful. They are closer to the citizens, their daily problems and perhaps to their solutions. Currently the distance between the citizen and the municipality seems to be quite substantial.

7.7 Conclusions

Social policy development in Helsinki still in its infancy Social exclusion and segregation are considered a serious threat to Helsinki but the concentration and cumulation of typical big city problems are still limited compared to many European cities. Helsinki faces social problems mainly as a result of the economic depression in the early 1990s. The unemployment figure is decreasing but still relatively high, despite the recent favourable economic development in the Helsinki region. In the 'lifecycle' of social policies Helsinki can be classified as a city in transition from a development stage to a stage of institutionalisation. In the development stage social policy is usually started via special needs of people with social problems, but there is hardly any coherence between projects. In Helsinki the approach is to stimulate cooperation between sectors and partners, to bring the need to combat social problems to the minds of the municipal departments and to support small-scale mostly neighbourhood based bottom-up initiatives by private actors and/or the third sector. 'Let all the blossoms blossom' and wait to see if there is some result seemed to be a device of the Strategy to Prevent Social Exclusion and Segregation.

In the strategy's project Year of Partnership many small initiatives were taken and supported in the social field. The expectation was that at least some of them would generate positive results. At this stage there is hardly any top-down approach. However, there is a growing consciousness of the need for a more comprehensive approach to fight the growing problems in a more effective and efficient way. There is felt the need for cooperation of public and private actors with respect to social policies.

The variety of local initiatives as a product of the strategy need some institutionalisation, not by killing valuable private initiative, but by searching for a balance between top-down strategies and bottom-up initiatives. This balance should be supported by an adequate overall framework, better cooperation and tuning among the parties involved, better coherence between the projects and more sustainability in the social policy. In most of these elements Helsinki still has a way to go. In this final section we will briefly mention some of our conclusions.

Summary of the elements of organising capacity There does not yet exist a well-elaborated vision on how to approach Helsinki's 'new' social problems, nor are the social problems embedded in a strategy for the region or the city. With respect to leadership no clear statements can be made about who has the formal and informal power in the strategy (and some of its elements). A possible explanation for this is lack of clear goals in the programme. This confirms the impression that there is no clear vision on how to tackle this complicated problem. Without a vision on how to prevent social exclusion, it is also difficult to see how different projects will complement each other. When actors involved do not understand the dynamics of the process and if no clear objectives have been formulated, assuming leadership is a tricky undertaking. Our impression is that the strategy lacked strong leadership.

The Year of Partnership was especially meant to stimulate cooperation between urban actors involved in policies preventing social exclusion. There was awareness that, especially within the municipal organisation itself, there was too little cooperation to realise a comprehensive approach. However the Year of Partnership programme did not offer important incentives or sanctions to achieve more cooperation. Rather, it aimed at a change in mind by taking the social component also into account. Some improvements have been achieved, but in general municipal departments took the message to improve cooperation for granted and continued working quite independently.

The sectorial approach within the city administration is considered a main bottleneck for effective and efficient policy. Socially excluded people usually have an accumulation of problems, which demand a comprehensive approach. Cooperation between the 'social' municipal departments and the more technical ones remains weak. To improve the effectiveness of social policies more cooperation between all relevant departments (physical, economic and social) is necessary. The setting-up of programmes that stimulate this cooperation (by directives or specific incentives) is recommended. These programmes should, of course, have to fit into a comprehensive strategy that should offer guidance for actions.

The communication of the programme was limited. Explicit reasons not to start a large campaign were the fear of raising expectations and too much pressure on civil servants involved, which sounds realistic given the limited funding and scope of the programme. There was hardly any communication regarding the results of the programme. A main reason for this was probably the lack of evaluation information. The impact of the projects has not been evaluated.

If the budget allocated to the programme is taken into account (less than 1 per cent of the annual budget of the Social Services Department) one would doubt the degree of political support. Politicians were very positive when the programme was launched, but given the limited scope and funding politicians could not really score with the programme because only minor changes could be expected.

There is also some doubt with respect to societal support. This has to do with the introduction of the principle of 'positive discrimination' in the Finnish society, where equal treatment is considered a sacrosanct principle. The idea that positive discrimination will help to achieve a more desirable distribution of well-being (by fighting the most severe problems of social exclusion and segregation) is accepted in the Education and Social Services Departments, but it does not seem to be an issue at the entire municipal level. Support among citizens seems not to be very high in a society that has traditionally been oriented to provide the same level of services for everyone. Now that the idea of fighting social problems by positive discrimination is accepted by some actors as indispensable, it will be worthwhile to evaluate its impact. When its effects are found to be positive, it might be expected that other actors too will employ the idea of positive discrimination.

No clear statements can be made whether there is an increase or a decrease of social exclusion phenomena as a consequence of the strategy. As a consequence of the objectives set, measurable results of the strategy cannot be given. These objectives were predominantly in the abstract, without aiming at concrete results.

The idea of tapping into private initiative (by stimulating project proposals) has been rather successful, as some examples of local initiatives clearly show. These projects, however, are rather vulnerable as regard their continuation. A kind of formalisation is required to aim at more sustainable effects.

Final remarks Finnish municipalities possess a high degree of autonomy and have to raise their own income. This stimulates competition (for well-to-do residents and business investments) and hampers cooperation on the metropolitan level. Forced by international competition, better cooperation within the metropolitan area should become an important policy issue for the future.

The impression is that social actions have to wait for the facts (statistics) to show that somewhere in the city something is coming below the indicator values agreed upon. This could lead to a delay in policy development and implementation. A kind of social service office at neighbourhood level could be of help to trace social problems earlier and to develop more effective solutions.

Notes

1   This section is mainly based on van den Berg et al., 1999.
2   In this chapter we will sometimes refer to it as the strategy.

Chapter 8

A District Service Centre in Northeast Utrecht

8.1 Introduction

To comply with the growing demand for housing and business accommodation, considerable investments have been made in and around Utrecht. On the west side of the city a completely new district is evolving, called *Leidsche Rijn*, with 30,000 dwellings, 700,000 m² of office accommodation and 780 hectares of land for other activities. For its growing population, the expanding city needs to increase its central provisions. At the time of writing, there are plans, for instance, to redevelop the area around the central station, increasing the capacity and raising the quality of the environment. However, these plans have met with considerable resistance from the local population, so much so that a political protest party called *Leefbaar Utrecht* (Liveable Utrecht) won many votes on that score, enough to gain admission to the public administration. In the hope of lessening the resistance to changes in the city, policy is now trying to involve the population more and earlier than before in the decision-making. In particular, to shorten the distance between the local government and the actors active in neighbourhood development, experiments are being made with pilot District Service Centres, where citizens are welcome with a variety of questions and problems. One such pilot centre has been established in community centre '*De Leeuw*' (The Lion) in the district Northeast Utrecht. That experimental service centre is the object of the present case study. The data of the metropolitan profile of Utrecht are summarised in Table 8.1.

8.2 Socioeconomic Profile of the Utrecht Region[1]

The Utrecht Region

The city of Utrecht has 234,000 inhabitants and is the fourth city of the Netherlands, after Amsterdam, Rotterdam and The Hague. The Utrecht region has approximately 548,000 residents. The population reached a peak at the

Table 8.1   Data of metropolitan profile of Utrecht

Characteristic	Utrecht
Population of the city (1996)	234,000
Population of the urban region (1996)	548,000
Growth of the urban population (city, %, 1980–96)	+1.0
Share of the population of foreign extraction (city, %, 1999)	30
Proportion of population of working age in employment (city, %, 2000)	67
Unemployment rates (city, %, 1997)	7.0
Proportion of employment in industry (city, %, 1998)	9.5
Proportion of employment in services (city, %, 1998)	85.8
Number of administrative tiers (including state and boroughs)	3
Borough Boards	No

Sources: van den Berg, Braun and van der Meer, 1998, p. 257; Centraal Bureau voor de Statistiek, http://statline.cbs.nl/statweb/index.stm; Gemeente Utrecht; www.utrecht.nl/cijfersinter/.

end of the 1960s, when Utrecht housed about 280,000 citizens. After that, it fell to some 230,000 by the end of the 1980s, and has since been once more on the wax. The large-scale residential project *Leidsche Rijn* is expected to raise Utrecht's population again to about 280,000 inhabitants by 2010. Thirty per cent of the residents are of foreign extraction. The largest ethnic groups are the Moroccans (nearly 8.7 per cent of the total population), the Turks (4.7 per cent), and the Surinam group (2.8 per cent). As in the other major cities, the number of residents of foreign descent is increasing. In 1999, twice as many foreigners settled in the city than left it (2,500 against 1,300); moreover, natural growth is higher among the non-indigenous than among the indigenous Dutch nationals.

The housing stock in Utrecht consists of 101,000 dwellings, of which 39 per cent are owner-occupied, 16 per cent private tenement houses, and 55 per cent corporation tenement housing. Some two-fifths of the dwellings are one-family houses; the remainder are apartment buildings.

In parallel with the development of the *Leidsche Rijn* expansion scheme, the area of the municipality of Utrecht has been enlarged with the territory of the municipality of Vleuten-de Meern, also located to the west of Utrecht. Such new urban settlements reflect the national spatial policy. This so-called VINEX policy sets out to create new large residential areas on the outskirts of existing cities. To accommodate *Leidsche Rijn*, the highway A2, which now cuts through the area, will in part be shifted and another part laid underground, with new urban functions to be developed on top.

Utrecht occupies a central position within the Netherlands, at relatively short distances from the economic centres of Amsterdam, Schiphol and Rotterdam. The city is eminently accessible, lying at the junction of main traffic axes that connect Amsterdam and Rotterdam/The Hague with the east and south of the Netherlands and with Belgium and Germany. Utrecht Central Station is the busiest railway junction of the Netherlands. Utrecht is also on the borderline between the highly urbanised metropolitan west and the middle and eastern parts, which are full of natural beauty spots. Utrecht and its surroundings are therefore very attractive as living and work locations. The appeal of the city is enhanced by the historical centre with its picturesque canals and narrow shopping streets, a favourite shopping and entertainment area. The multitude of students from the State University (22,000 students), the Utrecht *'Hogeschool'* (University of Professional Education, 25,000 students), and the Utrecht School of Arts (3,000) add flavour to Utrecht's inner city.

Economically, Utrecht has fared well in recent years. Because of its central situation, the easy access, the pleasant surroundings, the convivial historical inner city and the absence of polluting industries have made this provincial capital an attractive location for all manner of service activities. The northern part of the Dutch Randstad (the Haarlem-Schiphol-Amsterdam-Utrecht ring) in particular shows a healthy economic growth, concentrated around Schiphol and in the Amsterdam and Utrecht regions. Utrecht is very much the place for meetings, as is evident from the success of the Royal Dutch *Jaarbeurs* (trade fair and exhibition centre), one of the greatest in Europe. Besides, Utrecht holds some strong trump cards in the business services, the ICT sector and the biomedical and biotechnical clusters ('life sciences'). In employment growth, Utrecht ranks second after Amsterdam. In the creation of office space, too, Utrecht scores high: third after (again) the capital Amsterdam and the government seat The Hague. In comparison to the other three major Dutch cities, Utrecht houses but few branches of international companies: Utrecht is first and foremost a national centre. The composition of the employment in Utrecht is represented in Table 8.2.

The Staatsliedenbuurt in the District of Northeast Utrecht

The *Staatsliedenbuurt (Statesmen's Neighbourhood)* is one of the weaker neighbourhoods within the district of Northeast Utrecht, which itself counts among the stronger districts of the city. Northeast Utrecht is favourably situated,

Table 8.2   Composition of employment in Utrecht

Sector	Absolute	Percentage
Agriculture, fishery	298	0.2
Industry, public utilities	11,307	6.4
Construction	5,517	3.1
(Retail) trade, hotels, catering	30,426	17.1
Transport, communication	17,889	10.1
Financial/business services	47,889	27.0
Public/nonprofit services	56,266	31.7
Remaining	8,101	4.6
Total employment	177,616	100.2

Source: Gemeente Utrecht, http//www.utrecht.nl/cijfersinter/.

not far from the central station and on the attractive east side of Utrecht. The average income and the proportion of house owners are relatively high in this district, which counts 34,000 residents, among whom 7,000 (21 per cent) of non-Dutch descent, and relatively many senior citizens. It is a post-war district where many renovation projects are in progress. The expectation is that the upgrading will attract the higher income groups and that a portion of the lower income groups will move to such underprivileged regions as Overvecht and Kanaleneiland.

Two smallish areas within the *Staatsliedenbuurt* are underprivileged in comparison with the rest of the district, namely, the environments of the District Service Centre *De Leeuw* and the *Stieltjesstraat*. Most problems in the *Staatsliedenbuurt* spring from the composition of the population (high proportion of non-indigenous residents), the comparatively high unemployment rate, the incidence of (petty) crime (often associated with drug abuse) and the emergence of black schools. There is no question, however, of these problems extending into other parts of the district. Any subsidies are allocated on the district level, which means that on the basis of average indicators (number of residents, educational level, age structure, generation of start capital) the district receives relatively little money to take the social problems in hand. Moreover, unlike North Utrecht, *Overvecht* and *Kanaleneiland*, Northeast Utrecht does not benefit from the Major Cities Policy.

The *Staatsliedenbuurt* is undergoing a drastic physical restructuring. Many houses are unattractive, are being demolished, and their residents allotted other dwellings by the municipality or the housing corporations. However, there will not be enough new social tenement houses to replace all those demolished. Instead, some owner-occupier houses will be erected for the sake of a differentiated housing supply. It means that not all displaced tenants will be able to come back to their own neighbourhood. Those who fail to find a new apartment and cannot afford an owner-occupier house, will have to move to other neighbourhoods.

8.3 District Service Centres

The Involved City

Unlike Rotterdam and Amsterdam, the municipality of Utrecht has no borough structure, being considered too small for that. The city is divided into nine districts, in which district committees have been created that are comparable to the borough councils of the two largest cities of the Netherlands. All nine districts have a district office, where a limited number of municipal tasks are carried out. The district offices constitute a municipal service which the local administration hopes will bring it closer to the citizens. The municipal departments all have a representative at the office, and local residents are welcome with their questions. However, for a passport or to apply for a social allowance they still need to go to a central location in the city.

The municipality of Utrecht is trying to improve the service to its citizens, and understands that the supply of physical and virtual municipal services should match the demand better than it does at present. In the programme '*Utrecht in Uitvoering 2001–2006*' ('Utrecht under Construction, 2001–2006') the Board has expressed that intention under the title '*De Betrokken Stad*' ('The Involved City'). The title stands for a programme of measures and activities intended to strengthen the relation of residents, entrepreneurs and social organisations with the city and its administration. The programme builds on to what has already been achieved in Utrecht by district-oriented action and citizens' participation. The concept developed to that end rests on three cornerstones: better orientation to customers, a more comprehensive approach to several problems, and closing the gap between government and citizen.

One of the 17 points of the 'Involved City' programme is to establish District Service Centres. A District Service Centre is a place which offers both municipal and private assistance as well as digital services. The idea is to create 'desks' where the local residents are welcome with a range of questions about housing, working and living in the district. The District Service Centres are supposed to fulfil a high-grade intermediary function. Matters that bother the local residents can be reported there immediately, and if necessary channelled through to other bodies. The municipality also wants to enlist the centres in its efforts to increase citizen participation in all manner of municipal activities. Again in the framework of the 'Involved City' programme and together with external partners, the municipality wants to invest more than before in the provision of digital information. Indeed, e-government may open new opportunities for services to be delivered directly to the citizen.

Local politicians could not reach an agreement on the practical application of the district service centre concept, and therefore chose to begin by starting up some pilots. District Service Centre *De Leeuw* was one such, and a second service centre was opened in the *Kanaleneiland* (Southwest Utrecht) at the end of December 2000. Unlike *De Leeuw*, that latter centre is combined with a municipal district office. A third pilot is being created in *Vleuten-de Meern*, recently added to the municipality of Utrecht. That centre is slightly different in nature and reach. At the time of the municipal redivision an agreement was reached that the level of services in the previously autonomous *Vleuten-de Meern* was to remain the same as before. The centre will be a kind of subsidiary city hall, where people can be married and have their passports renewed.

The Development of the District Service Centre in the Staatsliedenbuurt

The planning for the revitalisation of the *Staatsliedenbuurt* focused at first on physical aspects. Much attention was given to the physical restructuring, the demolition of unattractive houses and the building of a new differentiated supply of owner-occupier and tenancy dwellings. Little was done or thought about social aspects, and too little attention given to the perception and wishes of the residents and the stimulation of social networks. However, experiences with earlier city-renewal projects and other undertakings have shown that the reinforcement of social structures is often a necessary condition for the long-term improvement of a city district. In that vein, a broader, comprehensive vision was drawn up later, in which the social infrastructure ranks more prominently. It was indeed the consolidation of an idea that had already been nurtured by some actors, to create a so-called 'broad district centre' with a wide variety of social-cultural activities.

The District Service Centre *De Leeuw*, opened on 31 August 2000, comprises among other things an infant playroom, a club for teenagers, an activity room for senior citizens, exhibition halls, and a meeting room. The intention was alongside such regular functions of a community centre, to accommodate, if possible at the same location, representatives of various public agencies, such as the municipality and the police, concerned with district affairs. In that way local citizens would have one easily accessible address to pose questions and lodge complaints. When such a concentration at one address proved difficult to accomplish, the compromise opted for was a desk, which would take questions from local citizens destined for the official bodies. The bodies to be thus represented should obviously be chosen in conformity with the wishes and needs of local citizens. A comprehensive, demand-oriented approach was the aim to strive for.

The idea of a broad community centre-cum-district service centre (a community centre plus) had been first conceived in the neighbourhood itself. At a later stage, when it appeared to match ideas playing around in municipal minds, the concept was included as a pilot in the municipal programme 'The Involved City'. *De Leeuw* distinguishes itself from the other two pilots by the participation of non-municipal actors. The District Service Point has evolved into a joint desk of five agencies: welfare work (UNO), the municipality (the District Office), the housing corporation (Mitros), the police, and the residents' committee (see Figure 8.1). The project is controlled by a steering committee on which all partners have seats. The daily management is in the hands of UNO. Because the service centre is a pilot in the municipality's political programme 'The Involved City' and on that basis draws additional funding, the management is answerable to the municipality.

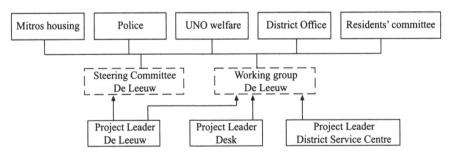

Figure 8.1   Project organisation of District Service Centre *De Leeuw* in Utrecht

Financing of the district centre   In the course of time the costs of the project have mounted from €0.5 to 1.8 million. Several money flows could be combined on behalf of the service centre: €0.4 million have come from welfare money and €1.3 million from city-renewal funds. The rising costs are due in part to technical questions. For instance, the foundation of the building required additional research. The tight demand on the property and building markets has also boosted the costs. The OGU (the municipal real estate department) administers the real estate of all public organisations in Utrecht and charges market-geared tariffs, no matter what functions are performed, as required by the OGU council. There is no municipal strategy to take not only the commercial but also the social relevancy of certain areas or buildings into account, thus permitting price differentiation. The UNO (Utrecht Noord-Oost) is now the main tenant of the building and pays the rent, which has risen with the building costs, to the OGU.

Actors involved in the District Service Centre

Welfare organisation UNO UNO (*Utrecht Noord-Oost*), the main tenant of the building, is a welfare organisation that is not only engaged in social-cultural work, but also offers many other services, such as a day nursery for children, playgrounds, youth provisions, services for senior citizens, general social work, community and club centres. Since 1994, such welfare activities have no longer been a municipal but a district concern. The UNO (annual turnover €5.5 million) is 50 per cent financed by the municipality with the remainder from the revenues of commercial day nurseries (some €3 million). The municipal Department for Social Development (DMO), responsible for welfare, social affairs, sports and education, is a major principal and sponsor of UNO.

District Office The municipal District Office is established at a separate location. The district offices, described in the previous section, have a district manager representing the municipal Department of District Administration and City Renewal of Utrecht. Citizens tend to look upon the office as not easily accessible. That is one reason why District Service Centre *De Leeuw* has chosen to operate as front office to the *Noord-Oost* district office rather than to combine the two agencies. Moreover, the Office serves a larger area than the Service Centre, namely the entire northeast district. Another reason is that the municipality does not think the time ripe for a fully-fledged neighbourhood-oriented organisation. In time, integration of the district offices with the District Service Centres is not excluded, however.

The police The police were great supporters of a District Service Centre right from the first planning. That can be explained from their immediate involvement with local living problems; very often the police are the first to be confronted with crime and alcohol- or drug-related problems. Besides, the police are lacking the human and financial resources to act adequately on their own. Moreover, they admit that the relatively great psychological distance between themselves and the local population may hold citizens back from taking their questions and problems to the police station. Participation in the District Service Centre is indeed a lot cheaper than setting up an additional police station.

Housing corporation Mitros Mitros developed early in 2000 as a merger of three housing corporations, and counts Utrecht and Nieuwegein to its jurisdiction. Most of the 124 dwellings to be demolished in the *Staatsliedenbuurt* belong to the Mitros housing stock. A prominent task of the District Service Centre is to accompany the physical renovation process. The expectation was that the relatively large-scale demolition and new building activities would provoke a lot of questions from residents, since these activities may well cause nuisance and unease among residents for quite some time. Emotions may run high, for the demolition of their houses and sometimes the forced removal from their own neighbourhood is seen as a devastating experience to the residents. The District Service Centre can give them information about how the demolition and renovation are going to proceed. People may address themselves either to the desk of the Service Centre, or to the Mitros neighbourhood manager, who holds a daily office hour there.

Access to the service centre for concrete complaints and well-defined questions is believed to be easy, because citizens can express these when they come to the community centre for other functions. Because Mitros considers respect for the tenants' privacy of the essence, the information systems of the District Service Centre and Mitros are not coupled, so that the District Service Centre desk worker has no insight into possible rent arrears problems. To Mitros, one advantage of the service centre is the easy coordination with representatives of other partners.

Remarkably enough, the housing corporation Amnes is not represented in the service centre. This organisation owns a substantial number of tenement houses (social housing) in the *Staatsliedenbuurt*. The desk worker of the service centre can do no more than refer clients to Amnes. The body that registers housing candidates in the whole of Utrecht and offers them accommodation, called *Woonservice*, is not a participant in the service centre either. It is seen as a potential partner for the future, possibly on an ad hoc basis, if, for instance, relatively many houses were to be demolished and many people needed new housing.

8.4   Analysis of the Organising Capacity

Vision

On the municipal (and the regional) level, there is no long-term vision of the desirable urban development. The Board's programme ('Utrecht under Construction, 2001–2006') is the context supporting the present administrative coalition. Furthermore, to be eligible for the funds set aside for the national Major Cities Policy, Utrecht has drawn up a 'Municipal Development Plan', which covers the period from 2000 to 2005. The ambition of that plan is to preserve Utrecht as 'a major city of human dimensions', with controlled sustainable growth as a priority. The greatest challenges confronting Utrecht in the coming years are the development of the entirely new district of *Leidsche Rijn*, considered the motor of a host of innovations (in the new and the old city alike), and the restructuring of the station area by the public-private Utrecht City Project. Both projects fit neatly into the national policy, which is to consolidate municipal competitive positions by encouraging the construction of large-scale residential areas and massive multifunctional projects. There is, however, no well-defined overall vision for the separate municipal departments to hold on to, or to fall back on for their decision-making. For that to happen, one discussion partner believes that a cultural turnabout is required on all levels, from aldermen and heads of departments down to the civil servants charged with implementation, a shift in thinking from subsidy-following to proactive, from supply- to demand-oriented, from divisional to comprehensive. A change of attitude is needed to operate in a really customer-oriented and comprehensive way. The municipal account managers in the districts can do much to match supply and demand. They can help to counter compartmentalisation by adopting a comprehensive approach and pointing out to the municipal departments how they can improve their services.

Shift to client orientation The District Service Centre can be perceived as the outcome of a shift in Utrecht thinking towards client orientation. A process of *rapprochement* between actors engaged in local problems has been in progress for some time. The District Service Centres pilot is the provisional acme of that vision. If it is successful, then perhaps every district of Utrecht will set up such a Centre, where relevant actors can work together to solve local problems and where citizens can seek the assistance they need.

That the District Service Centre has become reality is due not solely to a well-defined strategy; there have been some helpful coincidences, which resulted in synergy between the decisions and the vision evolved. For one thing, the timing was good: money and a location were available. The concept for the District Service Centre developed from inside the district. A limited number of those immediately involved conceived and elaborated the idea, with the client's point of view as first priority. An inventory was made of residents' needs and wishes, and partners were sought who were engaged in district services and might help to meet those needs. Only then was attention given to the possible organisation, with what provisions and in what buildings it would be located. The trajectory chosen combined architectural (spatial) and organisational aspects; a suitable location had to be found and developed and an adequate organisation created. A primary principle was that the contents were to be directive: to meet the needs of future users so that the local quality of living would be raised.

Strategic Networks: Cooperation between the Actors Involved

Positive cooperation of partners The service centre is at the receiving end of a variety of questions from residents. The workgroup will discuss the matters put before them and draw up a joint strategy. The parties work together because they have certain objectives in common and realise that they cannot solve the problems on their own. The experiences with the Centre so far suggest a reasonable cooperation between the actors involved, thanks among other factors to the investments made in the preliminary trajectory. At brainstorming sessions organised by UNO, the missions of the partners were compared. Means were invested in contents and support, so that later obstacles (mostly of a financial nature) were easier to overcome. The cooperation has increased gradually. Most resistance came from the municipality, which indeed, as holder of a near-monopoly in district policy, had most to lose. The municipal departments were loath to give up some of their identity and be forced into a more cooperative attitude and a more effective and efficient way of working. Slowly the municipal agents began to understand the usefulness and advisability of cooperation. After all, seeing the cooperation between the housing corporation and the police, the departments would not want to miss the boat. Indeed by now, the municipality seems to have become one of the most enthusiastic partners.

Compartmentalisation: a municipal organisation is counterproductive The adjustment between the municipal district office and the District Service Centre could be better. Indeed, the adjustment of the front and back offices is felt to be the weakest link in the project. There are a lot of questions which the District Service Centre cannot answer itself, but has to refer to the proper agencies, that is, to the municipal back offices. If the latter are unable to treat satisfactorily the matters referred to them by the front office, then the complaining citizens readily blame the District Service Centre. Obstacles are the many partitions erected among the municipal departments. The compartmentalisation of the municipal organisation may be counterproductive to the dispatch of residents' complaints. Department officials do not always feel inclined to solve problems put before them, or may show themselves unwilling to cooperate to that end with other departments.

Sometimes the District Service Centre is regarded by municipal departments as an unwanted supervisory organ, in particular when complaints about their own action reach them through the Service Centre. In the past, individual citizens used to have much trouble getting their complaints and questions through to the departments, and even more getting them answered and solved. Things are a bit different when a complaint is made not by an individual citizen but by a quasi-public, well-informed body like the District Service Centre. The Centre is supposed to give satisfaction to the complainant, and will therefore in turn expect a decisive and effective attitude from the municipal departments. Such expectation may come up against a lack of understanding or a shortage of staff on the part of the municipal department. There may ensue a sort of competition between the Centre and the Departments about who may intervene in what policy area. If the Departments remain doubtful of the desirability of a District Service Centre, a demand-oriented approach might well be a long way off.

Another problem for the District Service Centre may be the combined channelling of money flows. Subsidies are given by several organisations, who tend to put constraints on joint channelling to certain projects. Political responsibilities may play a role in that context. The constraints limit the decisiveness of the Centre. Demand-oriented action implies a certain flexibility in allotting the financial means. If the spending of budgets is fixed beforehand, any response to change or unexpected questions is impossible. In that case, there is no way to match the supply of services to the demand.

Difficulties in financing the accommodation for the District Service Centre At the time efforts were made to acquire accommodation for the District Service Centre *De Leeuw*, the relationship between the two municipal departments DMO (social services) and OGU (real estate) was troublesome. Almost all real estate in the Utrecht municipality is administered by the OGU, whose mission is to draw as much profit as possible from the property by acting in conformity with the market, regardless of the kind of real estate. Private tenants and agencies with a social mission in the community have to pay market prices. No thought seems to have been given to a system of cross-subsidising among functions. But the market forces cannot really work freely, since once a building has been acquired for a certain function, the OGU has a virtual monopoly and can set its tariffs to its own discretion. DMO is fully dependent on OGU, without recourse to another supplier for a competitive offer.

The attitude of OGU has given rise to conflicts with DMO, which saw itself confronted with costs for the realisation of the Service Centre far above the original estimates. The final outcome is a higher-than-expected annual rent, which means a higher burden on the welfare budget. If the budget remains the same, other welfare provisions must suffer. UNO, as the main tenant of the building, thus finds itself forced to operate in conformity with the market and increasing its charge to clients for what it has to offer. The question then arises whether the underprivileged, the prime target groups, can still be reached, as they are likely to be unable to pay for welfare services.

Leadership: Inside Initiators of the Process

The plans for the District Service Centre were initiated by a small team from the *Staatsliedenbuurt*. The district manager, the director of the UNO and an external adviser developed the concept of a broad district centre and set in motion the process to accomplish it. There were incidental stimulating factors (availability of the building and resources), but there were also powerful stalling influences. Notably in the municipal organisation, considerable resistance to the realisation of the provision had to be overcome. The serious financial drawbacks during the process were another obstacle (in the event, the costs proved three times as high as expected). The perseverance of a small number of project pullers finally crowned the efforts with success. From the discussions, leadership appears to have been the crucial carrying factor. The existing organisational structures constituted a high barrier, but the initiators, keeping their clear vision in mind and basing their objectives on that vision, have doggedly persevered against the establishment to achieve what they wanted.

Support for the District Service Centre

The idea to participate in a District Service Centre was initially received with mixed feelings by the housing corporation Mitros. As far as the object to improve the service to the clients, Mitros was in favour, but it rejected at first a possible association with the municipality. Mitros values its independent role and sets great store by its own identity. Moreover, the corporation does not have too high an opinion of the services rendered by the municipal departments, and shies away from a full association with them towards its clients. In that connection Mitros voiced its preference for the title *Neighbourhood* rather than *District* Service Centre, the latter term giving rise to confusion with the municipal district offices. However, the municipality insisted on the title District Service Centre.

Strangely enough, the District Service Centres come under the portfolio of the alderman for Financial Affairs. He soon showed himself a supporter of the project, as it was aimed at a raised level of services. The alderman for Social Affairs also gave his support, insisting however on the name 'District Service Centre' rather than the originally proposed 'Neighbourhood Service Centre', to safeguard its eligibility as a pilot project. The fact is that the municipal policy is oriented to districts rather than neighbourhoods. Moreover, the creation of neighbourhood centres next to municipal and district provisions would be hard to get accepted politically.

Communication

According to one discussion partner, communication is on the whole not the municipality's strongest point, neither among the individual departments nor with the outside world. The rapid rise of a protest party may have something to do with that. The opening of the District Service Centre did indeed get due attention within the district. By free local papers, mailings from the partners and the opening celebration as such, residents were kept informed. The idea is that the residents have easy access to the service centre through the combination with other provisions in the community centre. To make the District Service Centre and its activities better known, its communication should be further developed, but this will be delayed until the back and front offices are better linked, among other things by harmonised automation systems. For a proper response to complaints and suggestions as well as adequate feedback and evaluation, much investment in automation is needed.

The advantage of the District Service Centre is that it offers one desk for questions and problems about housing, working and living in the district. The disadvantage is that the partners are apt to be identified with one another, which is not always what they want. Perhaps some people shun the centre 'because it is where the local policeman is', or perhaps the housing corporation would rather not be identified with the municipal organisation. That makes high demands on communication. Each participating organisation needs to make its essential autonomy quite clear. The service centre should in fact be advertised as a '*social shopping centre*'.

There is a danger that some people will consider the service centre as 'just one more link' in the bureaucratic chain. Naturally, that would be undesirable. The basic idea is that the citizen will have better and prompter services at his disposal. To that end it is vital that the centre is managed by the 'independent' UNO and that the desk workers are highly qualified to answer any questions properly or refer them adequately to the right organisations. Of course, that boosts the costs: highly qualified desk workers imply high staff costs. However, the quality of the associates of the service centre is considered crucial. The employment of good staff shows that the partners want to respond seriously to the questions of residents, and gives the residents a reason to be proud of their centre.

High demands are made not only on the quality of the associates but also on the architecture and interior appointment of the building, in contrast, for instance, to the rather dilapidated municipal district centre. No concessions have been made as far as the construction and design are concerned. Even a 'social' building can look attractive. Those concerned believe that the outer appearance contributes to the objectives of the project and as such is an element of communication.

Policy Development and Implementation

For a long time, the social sector has been mostly supply-oriented. In the last decade it has more and more shifted to demand-orientation: more attention is now given to existing needs and the question whether there is really a demand for the social products which have – until now – been offered. Demand-oriented operation requires a new way of working, directed to participation and involvement. To that end, the social sector cooperates closely with residents' associations and develops networks to get to know people and their needs. That requires a well-qualified staff of people who do not just sit back until someone comes along with a question. The new approach is manifest everywhere in the Netherlands, but especially in the major cities where the problems are most serious. It inspires a continuous development of products. The supply of the social sector has thus changed tremendously in comparison with 10 years ago. At that time, the products offered were geared to target groups, while currently the groups have a flexible choice from a more general service offer.

However, certain target groups are hard to reach and difficult to involve in the district concerns. Participation forums often miss their goal; they draw too few residents and certain groups are not represented at all. As a remedy, specific gatherings are planned, such as lessons for children and thematic evenings for senior citizens, in the hopes of getting an insight into the needs of local residents. To adjust the supply to the demand seems particularly important in contacts with citizens of foreign extraction, who often turn out to have other needs than the indigenous citizens. A case in point was a project to activate Turkish and Moroccan women in the district. The target groups consisted of nearly 140 Moroccan and over 100 Turkish women. They showed themselves positive about integration by intensive contacts among themselves and with other local residents, but were averse to taking a job like many indigenous Dutch women. They did not want to go out to work: they much preferred to remain housewives.

To bring together actors who can help raise the quality of the local housing and living environment is the primary objective of the District Service Centre. While it is true that its reach is shorter than that of the district office, their existence and functioning side by side still causes amazement. To combine them for better service would have been more logical. Another question that suggests itself is whether more functions could be added. Health and care are two aspects that come to mind. At the time of creation a consultation centre had indeed been suggested, but was rejected as not fitting the policy. Other possibilities are home care and the Area Health Authority. A library is not (yet) provided either, but a digital service for on-line searching and reservation is being considered.

Evaluation and Monitoring

The District Service Centre pilots carried on in Utrecht are all monitored, and from the observations conclusions will be drawn regarding the creation of regular district centres. A helpful tool is the software program *Regipro*, which registers the activities of the desk workers. Much attention will be given to the relation between *front and back offices*. The District Service Centre *De Leeuw* has been in function too short a time for a well-founded judgement of the output, but it is only fair to say that to have brought some social services together at one location is already an organisational success. Some conclusions can at any rate be drawn.

- Whereas formerly residents had to take their complaints and their ideas about their quality of living to the rather forbidding district office, now they can express them to the desk at the District Service Centre where most of them are already calling in for one of the other functions located there. Strikingly, the district office has also recorded more reactions; evidently, the easy access to the service centre makes people more inclined to open their minds. The challenge for the district office now is to satisfy their clients by efficient and effective response.

- For better and accurate answers to questions, the relation between front office and back office should be improved. Many people expect their problems to be instantly remedied, but in many cases the solution cannot be that prompt. A serious handicap for the functioning of the centre is that the back offices of various organisations, such as the police and Mitros, fail to give feedback on what has been done with the problem, so that the front office cannot inform the clients properly and definitively.

- No concrete targets (for instance as to the number of visitors) have been laid down. The incoming questions are registered by the two desk workers. In the first three months, some 200 questions were posed about the quality of the living environment (waste matter in the streets, for instance) and certain provisions in the neighbourhood (where to find a playgroup, a toy library, etc.).

- Most problems put before the desk at the District Service Centre have to do with the client's rented apartment or housing in general. The question is whether people come to *De Leeuw* because it is conveniently to hand, or because they know they could have gone directly to the housing corporation's office. The next question would be whether it makes sense to keep the service centre going when four-fifths of the questions are really destined for the housing corporation.

- To communicate clearly to the residents that the service centre is open for matters other than housing, a survey has been drawn up of the services on offer, and how they can be rendered: instantly, indirectly, by the provision of information, or by referral. From this list, the number of immediately available services appears to be limited. A difficulty often encountered is that organisations want to keep their decision competency in their own hands. Back offices do not want their tasks to be taken over and they claim to be the ones with the necessary professional knowledge. Even for the supply of concrete services, problems of competency seem to arise.

No zero or result measuring The impression is that the municipality of Utrecht does not sufficiently analyse the (desired) return on subsidies. Because the municipal organisation is so compartmentalised, departments may be inclined to optimise their own profitability without looking at the total service package. Notably with common projects the targets are often not set beforehand, or the concrete actions towards their accomplishment defined, or when and how to perform interim and end evaluations. Such a situation is hardly suitable to encourage organisations to work efficiently and effectively.

With respect to the District Service Centre, the announced zero measurement of the perceived service rendering in the *Staatsliedenbuurt* has not been performed. The reason given is that this measurement was too abstract and the comparison between 'before' and 'after' too artificial, indeed a comparison between apples and oranges. No concrete targets had been set in advance by which to judge the result. A judgement will be made on the basis of some objectives, which had indeed been formulated for the process. So the output, not the outcome, will be evaluated. Actually, even if the pilot were a failure, the building will be maintained. In that case the desk will disappear and the other functions kept up. Perhaps the district office and the district service point will then after all be combined in one new building.

8.5   Conclusions

Changing Role of the Government

The realisation of the District Service Centre reflects the changing role of the government. One of our discussion partners described the change as follows: first the government played the role of a strict father, then that of a caring mother, and is now that of a facilitating and cooperative big brother (not the one that is watching you!). No longer does the government dictate the enhancement of a living environment in the conviction that it knows what is good for its citizens. There is no longer a need for citizens to be pampered with supply-oriented services. Nowadays, efforts to raise the quality of living imply the cooperation of the government, NGOs, business companies and residents. The government has a valuable facilitating role and with experiments like the District Service Centre seems to be taking a significant step forward. Whether the Utrecht approach will prove to be the right form cannot yet be verified. The answer to that question will have to wait until the teething problems (such as the too strong dependency on the cooperation of back offices) have been solved and adequate and valid evaluations have been performed.

Comprehensive demand-oriented thinking has been professed for years, but in practice seems to be a difficult proposition. Pilot projects like *De Leeuw* can help to develop the relevant knowledge and understanding. To that end, a drastically new way of thinking among municipal departments is indispensable. The expertise they undoubtedly possess should be put to the benefit of society, that means, adjusted with great care to the real needs of society.

One of the most important challenges for the future will be to substantiate the demand-oriented supply of products. Next to a cultural revolution, great organisational changes are called for, for one thing a new and different way of financing the services. At present, additional flows of money are used to initiate pilot projects, but the final aim should be to bend the regular financial processes in such a way as to enable all actors involved to work in a client-oriented fashion.

Demand-oriented and Comprehensive Working at the District Service Centre

Although admittedly its final realisation was helped along by favourable coincidences (availability of an appropriate location and means, and the simultaneous development of a municipal programme to stimulate District Service Centres), still the initiation and development of the District Service Centre was based on a vision. Its prime object was and is to unite all actors concerned with the quality of life in the district in a joint effort to meet the needs of the residents. No longer should each agency offer products without heeding the others and without verifying whether or not there was a demand for those products. In that light, the community centre cum District Service Centre may indeed count as a considerable step towards demand-oriented and comprehensive cooperation of all stakeholders in the welfare of the district. Easy access and convenience are the prominent concerns.

Canvassing for Like-minded Supporters

The *De Leeuw* project is considered a success for the sole reason that it is the embodiment of the original idea. From the beginning the project has been conducted with content in mind. The neighbourhood centre was the creation of demand-oriented reasoning. Once the authorities had discovered exactly what the demand was they went ahead to find the necessary suppliers.

A provision like the District Service Centre cannot be created without the support of actors with a stake in the local quality of living. Sometimes it is necessary to proceed ruthlessly without heeding any established structures and cultures. That implies, however, the earliest possible enlisting of all relevant actors. Adequate communication, calling upon all actors to think and decide along with the initiators, may reduce or overcome any resistance to structural innovation. The required commitment will grow and the whole plans will not be looked at as 'somebody else's business'. On the whole, a more constructive attitude will ensue.

Relationship between Front and Back Offices

The troublesome relationship between front and back offices is one of the main obstacles to the exploitation of the Service Centre. The success of the front office depends very much on the capacity and organising power of the back offices. The back office's failure to answer a question or solve a problem received through the intermediary of the front office, has to be explained by the latter to the client. Especially when the feedback fails or is delayed, the residents will be inclined to blame, and lose trust in, the District Service Centre in its capacity of front office.

Conflicts of competency between front and back offices can also obstruct the healthy functioning of the District Service Centre. For good results, all actors must have trust in the others to perform their respective tasks properly, and all must understand why those tasks have to be divided among them. The mutual trust would certainly be disturbed if the thought were allowed to take root that back and front offices were checking up on each other. Failure of the back offices to deal satisfactorily with any questions and problems referred to them by the front office might well entail a negative evaluation of the whole concept of District Service Centres.

Final Remarks

That citizens in the present situation have two addresses at which to pose their questions and lodge complaints directed to the municipality – the District Service Centre and the District Office – must be confusing to the citizens and does not make for a friendly relationship. Perhaps in the end they should be joined, despite the risk of too strong a 'municipal' signature.

One final remark we want to make in this case is concerned with the evaluation of the project in hand. No endeavour seems to have been made to set concrete targets in advance, nor has the promised zero measurement been performed. The records seem to show a disproportionate amount of questions asked at the service desk which should by rights have been addressed to the housing corporation that owns most of the tenement apartments. Perhaps the local residents' greatest concern will turn out to be their own dwellings and the direct living environment. Such an outcome would put the usefulness of the chosen approach in question, and should be seriously taken into account.

Note

1   Part of the text of this section has been borrowed from van den Berg and Pol, 1999.

Chapter 9

A Chain Approach to Addicts in Eindhoven[1]

9.1 Introduction

In social policies, drug addicts can be counted among the most complex target groups. Firstly, their comprehensive personal problems in the sphere of unemployment, finance, homelessness and health (including mental illness) are responsible to a considerable extent for general problems (that affect others) such as crime and a bad perception of safety in the city. Secondly, the target group is hard to reach. On the one hand, many addicts do not have a fixed address and on the other, those who have a home (and a job) are very good at hiding their problems. Therefore, an effective drug policy demands the cooperation of all organisations that deal with the target group, including the police, health care, psychiatry and the judiciary. In this chapter we analyse an innovative project set up in the City of Eindhoven, called 'Handles for Recovery' (*'Handvatten voor Herstel'*), that aims to respond to this need for organising capacity.

The remainder of this chapter is structured as follows. Section 9.2 presents an introduction to the Eindhoven region, including some general information on demography, the regional economy and the city vision. Section 9.3 describes the Handles for Recovery project. What are the social problems related to drug use and how does the city of Eindhoven try to solve them? In Section 9.4 we will analyse the project on the basis of our model of organising capacity with regard to social policies. The final section concludes. The data of the metropolitan profile of Eindhoven are summarised in Table 9.1.

9.2 Social-economic Profile of the Eindhoven Region[2]

The foundation of Philips in 1891 marked the beginning of the transformation of Eindhoven from a small town with about 5,000 inhabitants into the fifth city of the Netherlands, with more than 200,000 citizens (Adang and Van Oorschot, 1996). Today, the city covers an area of five villages that have

Table 9.1   Data of metropolitan profile of Eindhoven

Characteristic	Eindhoven
Population of the city (2000)	202,000
Population of the urban region (2000)	700,000
Growth of the urban population (city, %, 1980–96)	+1.0
Share of the population of foreign extraction (city, %, 2000)	20
Proportion of population of working age in employment (city, %)	Data not available
Unemployment rates (city, %, 1999)	4.4
Proportion of employment in industry (city, %, 1999)	40
Proportion of employment in services (city, %, 1999)	60
Number of administrative tiers (including state and boroughs)	3
Borough Boards	No

Sources: van den Berg, Braun and van der Meer, 1998, p. 257; Gemeente Eindhoven, 2000, p. 37, internet: www.eindhoven.nl/.

grown together. The genesis of Eindhoven might be an explanation for the village mentality that can still be observed in various districts. A typical characteristic of Eindhoven is the presence of social networks on a small scale, often a continuation of old districts or parishes (Stadsvisie, City of Eindhoven, 2000). Eindhoven is the centre of the southeast Brabant region, which is often referred to as the Greater Eindhoven Area or 'the Eindhoven region'. This region comprises 22 municipalities. Like the city of Eindhoven, the population of this region has grown rapidly in the last century. Today, it counts some 700,000 inhabitants. Apart from Eindhoven, the most important centre in the region is Helmond, with 80,000 inhabitants.

The appearance of the city of Eindhoven is determined by urban design of the twentieth century. In the city centre, buildings and housing estates offer a cross-section of twentieth century (housing) architecture. The city's rapid growth and Eindhoven's preoccupation with technology have also left their mark on the city's appearance. Although Eindhoven is the fifth city of the Netherlands, up to the 1980s the urban environment did not live up to that status. The town centre was considered unattractive, and apart from the Evoluon there were no special attractions vital to boost the image. Since the 1980s, Eindhoven has put much effort in city renewal. A high quality shopping centre (*Heuvelgalerie*) and a concert hall (*Muziekcentrum Frits Philips*) have been opened, as well as a multifunctional building (the *Witte Dame*, a restructured large Philips building). Eindhoven is trying hard to bring its urban environment in line with its economic, social and cultural position.

Geographically, the region of Eindhoven is situated some 100 km east of the Randstad, the cultural and economic 'centre of gravity' of the Netherlands. Nevertheless, its location is by no means peripheral, in particular in a European perspective. The region is situated within the rectangle formed by the Randstad, central Germany, the Ruhr Area and the Belgian cities of Brussels and Antwerp.

Economic Development and Structure

The Eindhoven region ranks among the more prosperous in the Netherlands. Incomes per capita are well above the Dutch average. The region of Eindhoven is an important centre of employment. It has some 320,000 jobs in a population of 700,000.

During the last 15 years, the economic fortunes of the regions have changed several times. Up to the mid-1980s, the region did relatively well, with growth rates higher than the national average. From then on, however, regional employment growth has lagged behind national averages. Between 1986 and 1991, the yearly employment growth rates dropped from 5.3 to 0.9 per cent. From 1991 onwards, things got worse. On balance, the region started to lose jobs. Up to 1994 the regional employment figures continued to drop. The main factors behind the economic problems of the region were the severe difficulties of the two leading industrial firms in the region: Philips (electronics) and DAF (lorry construction). In the early 1980s, Philips employed 35,000 people in the region. This figure had dropped to 21,000 by 1993. In 1993, the DAF company collapsed, meaning the loss of another 2,500 jobs. Additionally, the large network of external suppliers in the region that worked for DAF was also severely hit. After the few difficult years, the region had strongly recovered by the mid-1990s. Along with a general recovery of the Netherlands economy in the second half of the 1990s, the severe restructuring of Philips and DAF in the beginning of the 1990s has generated a positive spin-off in the form of newly started businesses and the outsourcing of activities.

The Eindhoven region is the most industrialised region of the Netherlands (Stadsvisie, City of Eindhoven, 2000), and the leading area in technology and research and development activities. Industry produces 46 per cent of the regional turnover, against 32 per cent on the national level, and employs more than 21 per cent of the regional labour force. The employment structure of the Eindhoven region is depicted in Table 9.2.

Table 9.2   Employment structure, Eindhoven region, 1999 (%)

Sector	Eindhoven region	The Netherlands
Agriculture	4.3	5.3
Industry	21.4	15.2
Construction	7.0	6.6
Trade and repair	18.1	18.1
Hotel and catering industry	4.3	4.0
Transport, storage and communication	4.3	6.2
Financial services	3.3	3.7
Business services	15.5	12.4
Public administration and government	3.0	6.0
Education	5.3	6.0
Health and welfare services	9.9	12.5
Other services	3.0	4.0

Source: 'Werkgelegenheid in Noord-Brabantse gemeenten' ('Employment in North-Brabant Municipalities'), ETIN, 1999.

City Vision

The national government and major Dutch cities have agreed that cities need to present a long-term vision and a development programme, if they want to claim money from the national Major Cities Policy budget. The City of Eindhoven has formulated a vision in *Stadsvisie 2010* (City Vision 2010), in which four objectives are emphasised. Eindhoven wants to be(come):

* an innovative knowledge centre focusing on technology;
* a city with an attractive centre;
* a city where people feel at home, as individuals and in their social environment;
* an effective administrative centre.

Social policies are mainly related to the third objective. In the vision, the city expresses its strategic choice for an approach that stimulates socially weak people – youngsters, the homeless, drug addicts, old people and the long-term unemployed – to be self-supporting. These target groups of social policy are concentrated in the city centre and a number of weak neighbourhoods. In Eindhoven, the weak parts of the city have been labelled restructuring neighbourhoods, in accordance with the district approach of the national Major

Cities Policy. The city wants to find solutions that meet the demands of the target groups. According to the vision, the municipality is challenged to mobilise its organising capacity to create strategic alliances with social partners that are able to respond to changing demands and developments in the external environment, which demands an outcome-based and cross-sector approach. One of the instruments to reach the fourth objective is the creation of strategic alliances and co-productions with social partners in the city (citizens, companies and institutions). Another administrative challenge refers to the decompartmentalisation of the municipal policies and the reinforcement of coherence between policies. The well-supported city vision that links various policy objectives has laid the foundation for such a development. Investment and project proposals are judged by five criteria that are related to the vision as described above. One of these criteria touches upon seven keys to success: safety, sustainability, interculturalisation and integration, accessibility, social return, cooperation and co-production, and innovation.

The vision has been translated into an urban development programme for a four-year period (1999–2003), which consists of four pillars: an economic, a spatial, a social and an administrative pillar (more or less related to the four objectives). The urban development programme is closely related to the Objective 2 programme that has been formulated. Eindhoven is one of the nine Dutch cities that receive money from the European Commission to fight urban decline.

9.3   'Handles for Recovery'

The drug policy of Eindhoven cannot be analysed without knowledge of the Dutch drug policy. The main aim of the national drugs policy is to minimise, if not prevent, harm to users, the people around them and the public in general.[3] Soft drugs and hard drugs are dealt with in different ways, because the health risks associated with their use differ.[4] The possession of soft drugs for personal use (up to 30 grammes) is a summary, nonindictable offence. Coffee shops can sell soft drugs without being prosecuted, providing they observe strict rules. The aim of this policy is to prevent users of soft drugs from becoming marginalised and from being exposed to more harmful drugs. It is illegal to sell, produce, possess, import and export either hard or soft drugs. The demand for drugs and the harm they cause to users and the people around them are kept to a minimum by professional care and preventive strategies. Addicts are encouraged to give up drugs and can seek help in doing so. The ultimate aim is to help them recover their physical and mental health, and function better in society. The fact that they will not be prosecuted or stigmatised makes it easier to seek help. Addicts who commit indictable offences may be eligible for a special scheme which allows them to get treatment instead of serving their sentence. In such cases the courts may suspend or waive their sentence. Those who opt for treatment have to obey certain rules; one is that they have to stop using drugs and take tests to prove they have done so. In the case of failure they will be required to serve the original sentence. Schools conduct campaigns to deter youngsters from using drugs by informing them about the danger of all addictive substances, including nicotine and alcohol. Drug supplies are reduced by tackling organised crime.

Policy is also aimed at maintaining public order and preventing drug-related nuisance. To reduce the nuisance homeless addicts cause in the streets some cities have opened special centres, with care workers in attendance, where addicts can use the drugs they need. Local residents are amenable to the scheme and take part in consultations on running the centres. No drugs may be sold or supplied. One of the instruments to reach addicts is the methadone programme. This synthetic opiate (a substance containing opium) enables addicts to function more effectively and helps to reduce drug-related crime. It is prescribed only in serious cases, either as a part of a detoxification programme or as a form of treatment to stabilise addiction.[5] An interesting development is the 'socialisation' of social services, including the care of drug addicts, implying that services increasingly are delivered outside the institutes, which calls for good cooperation between the various suppliers of services. One of the problems is that not all neighbourhoods are equipped with these services and that the city attracts many customers from out of town (Stadsvisie, City of Eindhoven, 1999).

The Target Group

Drug addicts and homeless people are counted among the vulnerable groups in the city vision. Care of the homeless in Eindhoven is confronted with an ageing target group. Most customers are male. More than 70 of the about 290 registered chronic addicts (1997 statistics) do not have a fixed address. That group is exhibits a range of problems (debts, bad health, problems with their families) and is responsible for a considerable part of local nuisance and crime. The number of registered addicts is relatively low compared to other cities in the Netherlands. The addicts are concentrated in a limited number of neighbourhoods: the city centre and two other neighbourhoods: Woensel-West and De Bennekel (see Figure 9.1). Their ages are between 15 and 53, with 35 as average. Men are in the majority (230) and about one fifth of the women are registered as heroin prostitutes.

Many people associate drug addicts with crime. In practice, however, the number of troublemakers is relatively low. About 60 clients are known by the police as such and among them are 30 so-called systematic perpetrators (people who commit crime on a regular basis). More than 70 clients do not have a fixed place of residence; among them are 30 real tramps. Approximately 60 clients are entitled to an allowance. Some remarkable differences between the concentration areas can be observed. Clients who are registered in the city centre are mainly troublemakers without a fixed place of residence. Those registered in Tongelre cause inconvenience, but they do have a place of residence. All heroin prostitutes – without a place of residence – operate in Woensel-West. A considerable share of the other registered clients in this neighbourhood are troublemakers and/or lack a place of residence.

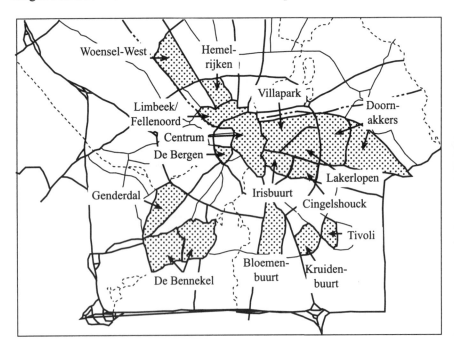

Figure 9.1   Restructuring neighbourhoods in Eindhoven and other areas that suffer from drug-related nuisance

Source: 'Onderzoek Handvatten voor Herstel' ('Research Handles for Recovery'), City of Eindhoven, 2000.

Eindhoven's Drugs Policy

The drugs policy of the city of Eindhoven consists of action programmes on several levels (van Gerwen, 2000):

- pre-active (prevention and proactive policing);
- active (care and aid);
- post-active (aftercare);
- judicial addict care (criminal reception of addicts and the systematic perpetrator procedure).

One of the main elements of this policy is Handles for Recovery, a project that was launched in 1995. Its main objectives are a decrease in the inconvenience caused by drug and alcohol addicts, and care for, and social integration of the target group: chronic addicts who are not (yet) able to or do not want to solve their problems. The project mainly focuses on troublemakers, systematic perpetrators, people without a fixed place of residence and heroin prostitutes. Handles for Recovery includes a chain of services, delivered by several actors, to reach those objectives. Such an integral approach is needed because addiction problems are related to numerous other social problems (housing, crime, safety, education, homelessness, psychological and psychosomatic problems, etc.). Moreover, many 'customers' are getting more and more difficult to treat as they increasingly use both alcohol and drugs or several types of drugs. An increasing number of clients can be characterised by a double diagnosis – the combination of drug addiction and mental disorders – resulting in very complex and unpredictable behaviour. The chain approach demands a close cooperation between the various actors, including the police, the judiciary, municipal services, business companies and neighbourhood organisations.

Initially, the chain was composed of five elements: night care, day care, process supervision, day structuring and social reintegration, and supervised living. Before the start of Handles for Recovery, night and day care were absent. Drug addicts could make an appointment with one of the ambulant consultation desks for alcohol and drugs. Furthermore, addict clinics were available. During the programme three other elements have been added: the multifunction unit for clinical and ambulant addict care, the criminal care of addicts, and 'meddle care'. Table 9.3 contains some additional information on these elements.

Table 9.3   The elements of Handles for Recovery in Eindhoven

Night care	A place where a limited number of clients (20) can stay the night and get a meal (bed, bath and breakfast).
Day care	A well-equipped facility where clients can stay from 9 a.m. to 7 p.m., take a shower, get a meal and their methadone, and attend (entertainment) programmes.
Process supervision	Coaching by a permanent social worker who writes a personal plan to guide the client through the various stages of the process.
Day structuring and social reintegration	Programme that aims to get clients accustomed to work, to help them to find a job, to educate them, to teach them social skills and stimulate them to practise a sport.
Supervised living	Teaching addicts how to live on their own and how to spend the day in a useful manner (including personal care and budgeting), under supervision of a social worker.
Multifunction unit for clinical and ambulant addict care	Facility that takes care of the so-called double-diagnosis patients, who have to deal with addiction and mental disorders at the same time.
Criminal care of addicts	Compulsory treatment of chronic addicts who are constantly involved in criminal acts.
Meddle care	A team that literally meddles with the target group by direct contact (ringing their doorbell).

Actors Involved

Several actors are involved in this project. The main contractor of Handles for Recovery – the spider in the web – is Novadic. Novadic is a network for addict care in the Eindhoven region (Oost-Brabant). The organisation offers a range of services from the treatment of addicts living at home (ambulant services) or in a clinic, to preventive action and criminal care. Novadic stresses the need for an integral approach and hence, cooperation with doctors, mental care, the police, judiciary and various other institutes (Novadic, 1999).

The night care facility has been set up in cooperation with the *Nieuwe Eindhovense Opvang Stichting* (the New Eindhoven Social Care Assocation), which is financed by the municipality. The multifunctional unit for clinical and ambulant addict care has been set up in cooperation with the Dutch ministry of health, health services, client organisations, psychiatric institutes and the municipality. The element 'day structuring and social reintegration' is a joint venture of Novadic, the job centre and the municipal department for social affairs and employment. The meddle care team consists of representatives from the police, Novadic, (mental) health services (GGD and GGZE), and social care. The partners of meddle care have also signed a protocol to fight nuisance in residential areas, neighbourhoods just outside the city centre. Citizens will report nuisance to the police (for instance by calling a special 24-hour emergency number), who then communicate these reports to the relevant organisations. The participating actors try to observe early signals and to react to nuisance in an adequate way. The leading role differs among individual cases. Together, partners attempt to find an appropriate solution in terms of care and psychiatry. In general, the lead is taken by the organisation with which the client already has a confidential relation. Behind the scenes they work together with the municipal health authority (GGD), the municipal department of social affairs and employment, and several other social services.

The municipal department of social affairs and employment welcomes approximately 70 customers who receive a weekly tramp benefit (about €90). Many clients use that allowance to buy drugs or alcohol.

Day and Night Care

Since February 2000, the night care has been located underneath a parking garage. It offers space for 20 persons. This bed, bath and breakfast facility is only accessible with a 'sleep card'. The use of drugs or alcohol is not allowed. Professional guards and supervisors are present. The night care can be characterised as sound, proper, sober and hygienic, showing respect for the customer. The overnight stay costs €3.40 and is deducted from the allowance.

The new permanent day care is situated at *De Kade*, a business park. This new facility will replace the current day care at the Tongelresestraat which is located right in the middle of a residential area, causing a lot of nuisance to the residents. Moreover, the current facility is too small to function as day care seven days a week, the living room is unsuitable as accommodation for the target group and there is no private outdoor space.

The night care facility is one of the places where addicts get their daily allocation of methadone; most addicts are obliged to consume their methadone in front of the distributor, in order to avoid trade. They get their allocation twice a day, from Monday until Friday. On Friday, they also receive their allocation for the weekend; trade is then impossible to avoid. Some addicts who are trusted not to deal in drugs (most of them have a job and/or a family) are allowed to take away their methadone for the whole week.

In general, drug and alcohol addicts (and tramps in particular) feel attracted to the city centre with its warm places (for instance shopping malls). Obviously their appearance does not contribute to the status and image of the (inner) city, and in that respect frustrates the city-marketing activities of the municipality. Nevertheless, the City of Eindhoven has decided to keep the day and night care facilities in the (periphery of the) inner city, taking the addicts' radius of action into account.

9.4   Analysis of the Organising Capacity

Vision

The Handles for Recovery strategy is based on the assumption that only a chain approach can effectively and efficiently reduce the nuisance caused by addicts and reintegrate them into society. A non-coherent approach can lead to compartmentalised treatment of the addicts, among other things, and to miscommunication between the actors involved. The objectives of the programme are clear and supported by all actors involved. Moreover, most people agree that a cooperative approach (like that of Handles of Recovery) is needed to tackle the complex drug-related problems. The project objectives fit well in the national and local policy visions. The national drug policy aims to minimise harm to the users and the general public. In 1995, a steering committee of the government pleaded a decrease of inconvenience caused by addicts and improved support for the integration of addicts in society. Money would be made available through the national Major Cities Policy programme, which stimulates the various actors in the region to cooperate in a network organisation. In several other Dutch cities, similar chain-like projects have been launched, such as *De Oversteek* (The Crossing) in Tilburg and Escape in Den Bosch. In its city vision, Eindhoven expresses its wish to stimulate socially weak people to become independent, and stresses the need for organising capacity and a demand-driven, outcome-based and cross-sector approach.

One very important element of the programme vision is its focus on the customer, the target group. Novadic constantly monitors the match between the supply of services and the demand from (potential) clients, which may result in changes in the supply (new or improved services). People who are in contact with the customer monitor the trends in the demand, so that the model (the supply) can be adapted to reality. Developments in the world of addicts and tramps are monitored in order to meet their demands. Social projects are never complete (unlike physical projects), which calls for process management and continuous product development, especially since the lifespan of social products is becoming narrower. For instance, it appeared that – in general – drug and alcohol addicts could not get along with each other. Therefore, the new day care facility will have several rooms to separate them. From the experiences of Eindhoven we can learn that a concept or vision should not be treated as a blueprint. It is a matter of learning by doing.

Strategic Networks

The chain approach demands close cooperation between the various actors, including the police, the judiciary, municipal services, business companies and neighbourhood organisations. Novadic has the clients and expertise to help them, while other organisations have their own specific expertise in the fields of housing, care, psychiatry, homelessness, etc.

The characteristics of the target group are continuously changing, making constant monitoring necessary. Therefore, Novadic provides the partners in the chain with up-to-date information. Informal contacts between actors have turned out to be important for formal cooperation. The participating actors have been stimulated by the project to change their internal focus for an external one and to understand their own problems as well as the problems of others. The chain approach of Handles for Recovery has changed the attitudes of participating actors. Because institutions have extended their borders, they have become more willing to participate in other projects as well. The creation of various networks with the same organisations makes the participating actors less inclined to shift their responsibilities to others, since they increasingly need one another. If you refuse to take responsibilities in network A, your partner in network B could refuse to participate as well. An interesting finding is that the activities of Novadic go across several municipal departments and initiatives. Several times civil servants have appeared unaware of initiatives taken by other departments. Such lack of openness complicates the realisation of the project. Handles for Recovery can be regarded as an incentive for participating actors to change their internal organisations. The relevant organisations have been invited and challenged to present visions that cross their borders. Discussions about competence have been avoided as much as possible.

Actors that operate on another scale than the city level turn out to complicate the chain approach. The Prosecution Counsel (*Openbaar Ministerie*), police and the aftercare and resettlement organisation work on different levels. The cooperation between those actors is clearly a weak link of the chain. Recently, the Prosecution Counsel opened a front office to allow faster actions towards the target groups (including addicts). In 1999, this had already resulted in a higher inflow of clients who are obliged to follow process guidance. Another problem relates to the internal organisation of the participating actors. Complicating factors in the process of cooperation are bureaucracy, compartmentalisation and internal problems such as a lack of manpower. One of the partners that deal with capacity problems is the police. For the year 2000, the police had agreed with the other partners to put a number of policemen at the project's disposal, but serious incidents (such as murder cases) have claimed more capacity than could have been foreseen. Apparently, these problems are caused not only by the situation on the labour market, but also by the fact that the workload (of the police, but also of other actors) is determined by external factors. In some cases, the exchange of information between partners is weak, because the priorities of most participating organisations are mainly determined externally (outside the chain, in their regular tasks) and not internally (within the chain).

Leadership

Although the Municipal Department of Social Development (DMO) directs the programme, there is not just one leader in the chain of Handles for Recovery. It is a network in which chain managers, network managers and case managers interact. None of them has the power to really navigate the whole process. However, the behaviour of partners can be influenced by certain interventions, provided that clear objectives have been formulated and accepted by all. In general, the chain approach calls for a manager who thinks in terms of networks and has good communication skills.

Figure 9.2 illustrates the complexity of leadership in social policies. Several interrelated problem areas can be distinguished, such as drug addiction, the integration of minorities (foreigners) and the observance of compulsory education. The network manager – the municipality and the municipal Department of Social Development in particular – takes care of the entire network, being responsible for the development of an integral vision on social policies. The chain managers look after the coordination of the elements of one chain. Obviously, the chain manager of the problem area 'drug addiction' is Novadic, the so-called 'spider in the web'. They coordinate the activities of other actors and stimulate them to participate. Case managers are in charge of one specific element of the chain. For instance, the police force is one of the three leading actors in 'meddle care', together with Novadic, the mental health services (GGZE) and the municipal health authority (GGD). However, the police are also involved in several other chains, as illustrated by the vertical lines in the figure.

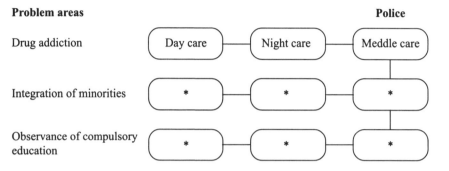

Figure 9.2 Chain managers, network managers and case managers

Political and Societal Support

Addict-care services can be counted among the facilities that most people admit are important, but few people like to have in their backyard. Not surprisingly, the realisation of day and night care facilities in Eindhoven turned out to be very difficult, causing a lot of discussion among politicians and citizens. The current location policy is a combination of concentration and deconcentration: services are concentrated in two facilities (day care and night care), which have been located relatively remote from each other, because addicts need 'break-out moments'.

In the case of the night-care service, Novadic, the police and a number of municipal departments deliberated about the location, and agreed on a place that was suitable for a temporary facility (*'t Eindje*) and a location for a definite one (underneath a parking garage). The municipal council came to a temporary decision and started to communicate with the people involved; first with small groups, later with the entire neighbourhood (*Limbeek*). The municipality wanted to show the residents that they really could influence the decision process. The citizens submitted about 90 written objections, which were all discussed and answered. After several participation sessions the council made its final decision. In the period until the opening, the inhabitants were involved in the process all the time to keep their commitment. At the day of the opening, a covenant – signed by all actors involved – was presented. This covenant embraces all improvements (on surveillance and safety) the city of Eindhoven will realise in the neighbourhood. A covenant with regard to the permanent night care is considered unnecessary.

For the temporary and permanent day care facility, a soundboard group has been called into being resulting in the 'Covenant Day Care' signed by Novadic, the municipality, the police and several neighbourhood and business associations. The covenant embraces agreements on the ways to deal with drug- and alcohol-related nuisance in the neighbourhoods concerned. The covenant specifies opening times of the day care facility, police supervision, permanent supervision by Novadic at the day care facility, the registration and handling of complaints (the installation of a 24-hour telephone number), evaluations and physical improvements of the neighbourhood, such as the maintenance of playgrounds and the installation of lighting and alcohol-prohibition signs.

Strikingly, most business companies support the construction of the new facility, with the exception of one of the immediate neighbours, a clothing manufacturer. Together, Novadic and the business association try to create a win-win situation by minimising the negative effects, for instance by not fitting the opening times of the day care facility to the visiting times of regular customers of the companies. The companies involved are cooperative because it is in their own interest to minimise the nuisance caused by addicts. In this case, the companies had also suffered from the location at the *Tongelresestraat*. They showed understanding for the municipality's decision to move the day care facility from a residential to a nonresidential area, especially since the business park is located in the centre of the city (within the radius of action of the target group), which is quite unique in the Netherlands. Furthermore, the business association attaches much importance to a good relation with the local government, in view of their power in the field of spatial planning. *De Kade* even took the initiative to start an employment project for addicts, together with Novadic (part of day structuring and social integration). The association of entrepreneurs has forced the municipality to include two user rooms (places where addicts can use drugs or alcohol) in the new facility, in order to get more grip on the addicts and to diminish the inconvenience caused by them.

Output and Outcome

Before the project started, evaluation indicators had been defined for each element (day care, night care, etc.) of the chain. The indicators relate to the number of customers (the total reach of services and the average day occupation), reduction of the number of complaints with regard to nuisance caused by addicts, reduction of crime, the outflow of clients and the use of drugs (see Table 9.4).

To what extent have these targets been accomplished so far? The results of the campaign to reintegrate drug addicts cannot be measured unambiguously. A positive sign is the decrease of the number of drug addicts from 290 to 250, but that success should be ascribed mainly to the prevention policies (at schools for instance) and the economic growth of the last few years, resulting in a lower inflow of new addicts. The outflow of addicts did not increase which can be explained for one thing by the rising complexity of the target group (for instance double-diagnosis patients). As a consequence the clients are ageing.

From the 1999 statistics it can be concluded that 105 clients (different persons) visited the night care facility one or more times (above target), with an average of 10.5 a night (below target). Since the opening of the permanent night care facility in 2000 (with a capacity of 20 instead of 16), the occupation rate increased considerably. The average number of addicts that use the day care facility has increased from 15 (1997) to 37 (1999). This number is below target but will undoubtedly rise above target after the opening of the permanent day care facility. In 1999, the inflow of clients into process supervision was higher than intended (90), but the number of clients who were obliged to participate was below target (21). However, the 'obliged inflow' has increased since the Prosecution Council opened its front office in Eindhoven (see *Strategic Networks*). The client base of day structuring reduced from 42 (1997) to 26 (1999), which is below target. Novadic attributes these results to the rising complexity of the drug-related problems and the increasing number of potential clients who avoid any form of care. So-called 'care avoiders' are now to be reached by the meddle team. In 1999, social integration programmes were attended by 34 clients (most of them also participating in day-structuring programmes). Finally, the client base of 'supervised living' consisted of 20 persons, right on target.

By means of surveys, the city of Eindhoven has measured the changes in the (experienced) nuisance caused by addicts (the other objective). The degree of nuisance has been measured in two ways (City of Eindhoven, 1999):

• By a question in the survey Quality of Life and Safety which is conducted in Eindhoven every two years within the framework of the Major Cities Policy: 'Do you think there is drug-related nuisance in your neighbourhood?'. An evaluation of Handles for Recovery can be made by comparing the results of three surveys (spring 1996, autumn 1997 and autumn 1999).

Table 9.4   Evaluation indicators and targets in Eindhoven (1995)

Element	Clients a year	Complaints	Crime	Outflow	Drugs use
Night care	50 (12 a night)	-30 %			
Day care	200 (45 a day)	-20 %	-5%/-10%*	40 (to day structuring)	
Process supervision	60 (30 obliged and 30 voluntary)				
Day structuring and social reintegration	50		80% of the clients commit no offences	30% to education, 60% to work	90% no illegal drug use, 70% no methadone use
Supervised living	20			60% to independent living	

*   5 per cent reductions in housebreaking, bicycle theft, and car theft and a 10 per cent decrease in shoplifting.

Source: Original project description (City of Eindhoven, 1995).

- By more specific questions in some neighbourhoods where drug-related nuisance can be observed. Among these are all eight restructuring neighbourhoods as well as some neighbourhoods near the day care facility (Villapark, Irisbuurt, Lakerlopen). This survey has been conducted twice (autumn 1997 and autumn 1999).

It appears that on the city level the experienced drug-related nuisance increased from 14.3 per cent (1996) to 17.9 per cent (1999). The statistics show that the increase of that percentage slowed down after 1997, when the project started (see Table 9.5). In the restructuring neighbourhoods and the areas around the day care facility the drug-related nuisance is higher than on the city level, and most districts experienced increased inconvenience.

Table 9.5 **Experienced drug-related nuisance on the City of Eindhoven and neighbourhood levels** (in % of the number of inhabitants)

	City	Restructuring neighbourhoods*	Woensel-West
Spring 1996	14.3	33.9	55.8
Autumn 1997	17.0	35.8	51.3
Autumn 1999	17.9	38.0	74.8

* Non-weighted average of the neighbourhood-level percentages.

Sources: 'Onderzoek Handvatten voor Herstel' ('Research Handles for Recovery'), City of Eindhoven, 2000/'Enquete Leefbaarheid en Veiligheid' ('Survey Quality of Life and Safety'), adjusted by the authors.

The experienced inconvenience is significantly higher than average near the temporary day care facility (*Tongelresestraat*) with percentages of 64.5, 51.2 and 67.3 in *Lakerlopen, Irisbuurt* and *Villapark*. Another neighbourhood that suffers a lot of nuisance caused by addicts is *Woensel West*. Table 9.6 presents statistics related to some more specific questions. The percentages are non-weighted averages of neighbourhood-level percentages. Regrettably, *Irisbuurt* and *Villapark* (and *Lakerlopen*) could not be included, as these districts did not participate in the 1997 survey.

As well as by surveys, the results can also be analysed by looking at actual crime rates. First, we can analyse offences that are indirectly related to drug use such as theft from cars, housebreaking, bike theft and shoplifting.

Table 9.6   Specific questions on drug-related nuisance in Eindhoven

	1997	1999
Do you think drug-related nuisance increased over the last months?	12.5	11.6
Did drug-related nuisance decrease your perception of safety in your district?	14.3	16.3
Are facilities for drug users a nuisance to you?	5.5	7.0

Source: 'Onderzoek Handvatten voor Herstel' ('Research Handles for Recovery') (City of Eindhoven, 2000)/Drugsmodule, adjusted by the authors.

From research (Bieleman and others, 1995), at least half of all recorded offences in some major Dutch cities appear to have been committed by drug addicts. Second, the number of offences that are directly related to drug use can be analysed. In general, we can conclude that neighbourhoods where people complained of drug-related nuisance (as resulted from the surveys), have to deal with more crime and rising crime rates than other neighbourhoods. The number of reports on drugs-related nuisance tripled in the 1996–99 period. Most reports were made by inhabitants of *Lakerlopen* (where the day care facility is located), *Doornakkers*, *Hemelrijken* and *Woensel-West*.

The statistics presented above could be explained as a failure of Handles for Recovery as far as the objective of reducing nuisance is concerned. However, we have to keep in mind that two important elements of the chain – permanent day and night care – were not yet realised in 1999. Furthermore, external factors make it hard to compare surveys conducted at two or three different points in time. For instance, the rising number of reports on nuisance can be explained by an increase of problems, but also by the fact that more people mention the same problems.

Within the framework of the Major Cities Policy, the department for research and statistics also gives an account of the quality of life in the neighbourhoods involved (so-called quality of life monitors). Those reports are more comprehensive than the Handles for Recovery reports; they also deal with infrastructure and economy. The exact effects of the project are not quantifiable owing to causality issues. Changing context factors complicate the comparison of two measurements at different points in time. The fact that the participating actors use their own registration methods makes effect measurement more difficult too. For instance, police statistics cannot be linked to individuals. Strict privacy laws limit the possibilities to link databases together.

At the moment, the chain is not yet complete, which leads to the loss of control of some addicts. Some elements still have to be developed. In general, the chain functions very well with regard to social integration, but not optimally with regard to the reduction of nuisance. An interesting question in the case of Eindhoven is whether the high service level attracts drug addicts from other cities in the Netherlands. However, such a tendency has not yet been observed.

9.5   Conclusions

As a concept, the programme 'Handles for Recovery' comes up to the requirements of organising capacity. The vision and objectives are clear, and largely correspond to national and local policies. Coordination and achieving mutual contact between actors (leadership) are tasks of the local government and Novadic. The latter organisation is acquainted with the expertise of other actors. The concept attaches much importance to the exchange of information and knowledge through formal and informal networks. Furthermore, changes in the context and the demand of the customers lead to changes in the concept. The municipality and the other actors involved are very much aware of the need to obtain social support, notably by reaching the objective of nuisance reduction.

In practice, however, the programme is not yet functioning in an optimum way. From the results (outcome) can be concluded that both objectives – to reduce nuisance and to reintegrate addicts – have not yet been reached. The low performance on nuisance reduction in particular is a critical factor, because social and political support are closely related to it. The actors involved give a range of reasons for the poor results.

- Some criticise the national drugs policy. They ask themselves if the government should let people walk around and treat them as customers (and spend many euros on them), while they cause so many problems in the sphere of crime, insecurity and an unattractive townscape. This complaint can clearly not be treated on the local level, but should certainly be considered in the assessment of the concept.
- Some put the lack of success in perspective by pointing at external circumstances or the temporary character of problems. For instance, they claim that the chain is not complete as long as the permanent day care facility has not been realised, that there is no rise of nuisance, but an increase of complaints, or that patients (addicts) are getting more difficult to treat.

- Some criticise the participating actors. They accuse actors of not keeping their promises (notably the police of not delivering the arranged number of policemen, which can be explained by structural and occasional capacity problems) or a surfeit of red tape in the internal organisation (for instance the organisation of the municipality). Some mention the fact that the actors involved operate on different spatial levels. We claim that the quality of the people and their willingness to cooperate are critical factors of failure and success. Since people are confronted with an increasing number of very different tasks, they should be appointed with an eye to their competences, instead of their tasks and functions. There are various theories on how to organise a network, but in practice it matters that people get along. A comprehensive approach to social problems demands a flexible network, in which actors participate in various chains to avoid compartmentalisation of social policies.

- Some criticise the concept itself. Handles for Recovery is clearly a concept that needs to be adapted to reality over and over again. On the other hand, one could argue that – unlike physical concepts – social plans cannot be designed fully beforehand. In view of the lack of knowledge on the chain approach at the time and the dynamism of the environment in question, the trial-and-error method seems useful to develop social concepts such as Handles for Recovery. In the evaluation reports, the disappointing results are attributed to the external factors mentioned above. However, the success of the trial-and-error method is in part based on the willingness of participating actors to admit poor performance: people can learn from (admitted) mistakes.

- What counts most is for the people involved to be determined with respect to the aims to be achieved. Most of them are convinced of the necessity of tackling the social problems related to drug addiction, and do try to develop those policy measures that seem best to reach the stated goals. For them it is important to continue, notwithstanding changing circumstances, the activities that are desired under the chain approach.

The poor performance on nuisance reduction makes it more difficult to obtain social support, as illustrated by the problems with respect to the location of a new day care facility. The questionable decision of the local government to locate the temporary day care facility in the middle of a neighbourhood could well explain the lack of confidence towards the municipality among citizens and their organisations, although the municipality does its best to reduce nuisance as much as possible. An interesting finding is that business companies (united in business association *De Kade*) can function as a link between citizens and local government. These companies acknowledge their self-interest in contributing to solutions for social problems and making their business location more attractive.

Notes

1   Co-author: drs. A.H.J. Otgaar
2   Borrowed in part from 'Growth Clusters in European Metropolitan Cities' (van den Berg, Braun and van Winden, 1999).
3   See 'A Guide to Drugs Policy' (The Netherlands Ministry of Foreign Affairs, 2000).
4   Hard drugs are very harmful to health. Examples are heroin, cocaine and ecstasy. Soft drugs such as marijuana and hashish are less harmful.
5   In 1998, a programme was launched (with pilots in Amsterdam and Rotterdam) to study the effects of treating chronic heroin addicts with a combination of medically prescribed heroin and methadone. It targets people who have failed to respond to other forms of treatment, whose physical and mental condition is poor and who are unable to function properly in society. The aim is to see whether treating them with a combination of heroin and methadone achieves better results than methadone alone.

Chapter 10

Summary and Conclusions

10.1 Introduction

This final chapter recapitulates the principal findings of the case studies. The structure is as follows. In the first section the reason for this study, the problem statement, the objectives and the theoretical framework for organising capacity will be recapitulated briefly. Section 10.2 summarises the facts of the case studies, namely the urban context, the social problems of the city in question, the programme or project submitted for the analysis, and the results of this programme or project up to now. Section 10.3 presents a comparative study of the case study analyses, confronting the theory with the facts. What can be learned from the experiences in the eight cities involved? Each element of the theoretical framework will be briefly introduced, before the main findings are presented. Section 10.4 will be devoted to what can be indicated as one of the outcomes of the study, the idea of an evolution of social policies in urban areas. This evolution is based on differences in the approach to social policies (top-down versus bottom-up approach) and the dominance of the actors involved (private and public actors and the third sector). The synthesis will be concluded in Section 10.5.

Why this Study?

Fundamental changes in the economy, technology, demography and social preferences are reshaping the environment of cities in Europe. This environment has become increasingly competitive and complex. One of the threats to a balanced urban development is the accumulation of social problems. This is not only unacceptable from a societal point of view, it may also hamper the cities in their functioning as engines of the economy. In these circumstances cities need to anticipate and respond to opportunities and threats that influence their position structurally.

Increased social polarisation seems to be connected with the restructuring of the welfare state, a consequence of the emerging information society and increasing competition. Social problems, such as unemployment, lack of education, poverty, crime, youth delinquency, drugs or alcohol abuse, homelessness and other social deprivation, accumulate in parts of cities. In many of the larger European cities a polarisation is defining itself, between the dynamic well-educated segment of the population and another segment that is falling into economic and social exclusion. Such a concentration of distressed groups is especially manifest in cities that have been hit by industrial decline, but also occurs in cities that have managed to reverse a downward economic trend as well as in cities that have been prosperous for a longer time.

To combat social polarisation seems to be the most important, but at the same time the most difficult challenge. The conviction is gaining ground that only a comprehensive approach will lead to long-term solutions. A change from problem-led to opportunity-led policies can also be observed, with opportunities for the economy being grasped.

To enhance the effectiveness of social policy is, in that context, considered a spearhead for many cities. In practice, social policy does not always seem to be carried out effectively. To create organising capacity seems to have become a *conditio sine qua non* for a coherent comprehensive approach to urban social problems. Organising capacity can be defined as the ability of those responsible to solve a problem to convene all partners (public and private, internal and external) concerned and jointly generate new ideas and develop and implement a policy that responds to fundamental developments and creates conditions for sustainable economic growth.

Problem Statement

What social strategies do urban actors develop in response to social problems and how are they implemented to contribute in an effective and efficient way to an economic and social revitalisation?

Main Objectives

1   To deepen the theoretical knowledge of 'organising capacity' in cities confronting social challenges.
2   To generate practical knowledge and tools by which cities can strengthen their 'organising capacity' on behalf of social revitalisation.

Methodology

The method used is that of an international comparison of experiences with strategies (programmes, projects) in the social sphere. For the analysis a theoretical framework has been drawn up, based on international literature and the results of previous empirical research. This framework has been elaborated and agreed upon by experts in the field of social policy and by representatives of the cities involved. The eight cities involved submitted a local programme or project for the analysis. The analysis of the cases is based on written documentation and on interviews with more than 90 key persons involved in social policy in the eight participating cities. Table 10.1 presents some demographic data of the cities involved in this study.

Limitation

Programmes and projects in the sphere of social policy should offer solutions for (multiple or cumulated) complex social problems in cities. Of necessity, the present investigation does not cover total social policy in the eight cities. A major part of the social problems (and the policy addressing them) has to be left out of consideration. Nevertheless an attempt has been made, with the help of well-chosen examples, to find an answer to the problem as stated and attain the objectives. The limitation of the relatively small number of cases should be considered while interpreting the results of the study.

Introduction of Theoretical Framework

Figure 10.1 represents the theoretical framework of the investigation. The elements have been grouped into three categories: context, tools, and policy process. The context constitutes the specific spatial-economic, administrative and sociocultural circumstances in urban regions, which might possibly explain discrepancies among cities. The tools are the elements of organising capacity, which together, interactively, determine its strength. The policy process is the chain of policy elements that have to be passed through for implementation. As the figure shows, the elements of the three categories are mutually influential. In each case study the three categories have been considered to permit a comparison of the social strategies presented by the cities. The different elements will be explained below and will be dealt with in detail and illustrated by examples from the cases in section 10.3.

Tools for Organising Capacity

Vision Vision can be regarded as a comprehensive view of the future prospects of a city. How can the strengths and opportunities of a city or region be

Table 10.1 Demographic data of cities involved in this study

City	Population of the city	Share foreign extraction (%)	Population of the urban region	Year	Growth city population (%)	Year
Rotterdam	593,000	44	1,080,000	1996	+2.9	1981–96
Strasbourg	264,000	14	451,000	1999	+6.5	1990–99
Antwerp	456,000	14	1,161,000	1995	−2.5	1991–96
Malmö	247,000	11	618,000	1996	+1.1	1991–2001
Stockholm	762,000	10	1,762,000	1996	+11.0	1981–96
Helsinki	539,000	5	1,155,000	1998	+10.2	1980–96
Utrecht	234,000	29	548,000	1996	+1.0	1980–96
Eindhoven	202,000	20	700,000	2000	+1.0	1980–96

Sources: see tables within the case studies.

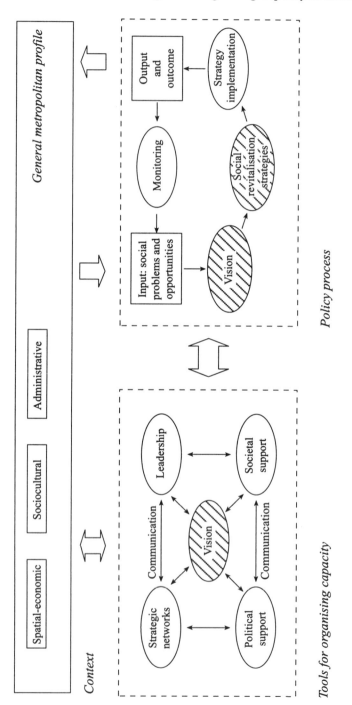

Figure 10.1 Theoretical framework of social organising capacity

adequately responded to, and weaknesses and threats be taken into account as well? In the present research, an opportunity-oriented approach is central. In this approach, vision is defined as an idea developed by an actor or group of actors as to the way sustainable solutions can be achieved by responding to certain chances and use them to take certain urgent problems in hand. An adequate vision should be ambitious but realistic, visionary and comprehensive, and widely subscribed to. Such a vision gives direction to strategies and policy, and to that end should have a broad support among all actors involved. Without an adequate vision, social projects can become unguided missiles. Once sufficient support has been won, the vision will have to be translated into a strategic plan pointing the way for the development of the various policy fields.

Strategic networks In view of the complexity of the present society and the disappointing results of social policy in the past, governance in the form of one-way traffic between public and private sectors is no longer acceptable. Strategic networks can be conceived of as patterns of interaction between mutually dependent actors, evolving around policy problems and/or policy programmes. Activities related to 'governing efforts' are by definition interactive between public actors and involved (public or private) target groups or individuals. Social problems are the result of various interacting factors and cannot be attributed to a single one, and possible solutions are spread across many (public, semipublic and private) actors. And thus the cooperation and tuning of municipal actors and partnerships with other parties involved have become crucial pillars of organising capacity.

Leadership Leadership is necessary to utilise the potential of networks and to give direction to the efforts of parties involved. Every organisation, programme or project needs a leading actor to initiate, manage and complete the activities required. Presumably, leadership substantially contributes to the design, development and implementation of programmes and projects. It is an indispensable element of organising capacity, whether relying on specific competencies or on the charisma and spirit of private individuals. Leadership is required on all levels, not only on the project level itself, but also on the municipal level (political leadership) and on the level of the target group or neighbourhood.

Support and communication Social policy frequently depends on the political will to tackle social problems. Politicians are often key actors when it comes to introducing new social programmes. Programmes drawn up on the higher government levels can serve as catalysts for the development of social programmes on the local level. No matter how valuable a project might be for sustainable metropolitan development, lack of support from those directly involved, notably the population, may curtail the chances of successful implementation. To obtain political and societal support, the local government and other relevant actors will have to work out a communication strategy to explain to the population at large the importance of social problems and of the policy to be conducted to solve them.

Policy Process

Strategy implementation and output The implementation of policy consists in the acquisition of means, the allotting of partial tasks, and the execution of the strategy. What interests us in particular is the output: how adequately has the strategy been implemented? Were there sufficient financial and human resources available for the effective execution of the measures as proposed in the strategy? The quality criteria have not been thoroughly treated in this investigation, for cities have already gained much experience on that score and we did not want the research to lose itself in a surfeit of details. However, on the strength of the knowledge gained from the cases, some comments can be given.

Monitoring and outcome The orientation of social policy is observed to shift from input to result. The implication is that more attention should be given to evaluation and monitoring. That is useful to gain insight into the degree to which the formulated objectives of social strategies have been attained. The outcomes of monitoring enable those in charge to decide whether the strategy should be cancelled, adjusted or continued. Without periodic monitoring there is not much that can usefully be said about the success of a social strategy. The outcomes of monitoring permit comparison of the actual results with those envisaged or with the benchmarks formulated in the strategy.

10.2 Cities, Programmes and Projects

For each of the participating cities this section briefly describes the programme and/or project submitted as an example of an opportunity-oriented, innovative approach that deals with social problems, and the results of this programme or project, if already available. The descriptions start with some characteristics of the city and its social problems. Table 10.2 presents the social programmes submitted by the participating cities, including the main sponsors and the aimed functions of the programmes. At the end of section 10.2 a summary will be given in three tables of the administrative and economic (Table 10.3) and the employment (Table 10.4) characteristics of the cities involved. Moreover, Table 10.5 presents characteristics and finances of the submitted strategies.

Integrated Area Approach in Rotterdam-Hoogvliet

Rotterdam is the second city of the Netherlands. The city has 593,000 inhabitants, of whom 28 per cent belong to ethnic minorities (people from Surinam, Turkey, Morocco, the Antilles and Cape Verde); a total of 44 per cent is of foreign descent. Since the late 1970s Rotterdam has, through the decline of several port-related basic industries, suffered from a high rate of unemployment. Thanks to energetic opportunity-oriented strategies and a more favourable economic tide Rotterdam's economic position, physical appearance and quality-of-life reputation have changed for the better. Because port and transport are no longer major job creators, the Rotterdam authorities try to support the diversification of the economy. Employment (especially in business services) has grown substantially, but Rotterdam still lags behind other Dutch cities and the national average.

The social dichotomy is still very much in evidence. In many respects (income, educational level, unemployment, crime, etc.) the city belongs to the most disadvantaged of the country. Although Dutch municipalities are financially strongly dependent on state payments, they are fairly free to formulate their own policies and spend their own budget. The national Major City Policy (initiated in 1994) contains a clustering and coordination of city-oriented payments and policies from nine ministries. The 25 cities involved in the programme have to draw up an integrated strategy that needs approval by the state.

Rotterdam has combined this national policy with some existing divisional policies and the European Urban programme into the Integrated Area Approach (IAA). The IAA, a local political spearhead, has heralded a new phase of urban and social renewal. Whereas the 'old' urban renewal (during the 1970s and 1980s) was predominantly physical and strictly oriented to social housing, the new approach aims at the integrated economic, physical and social revitalisation of backward boroughs, among them the borough of Hoogvliet. Hoogvliet is a post-war 'satellite', built close to the port area (spatially detached from the rest of the city), with 45,000 inhabitants, most of them living in unattractive apartment buildings. Some years ago Hoogvliet's socioeconomic

Table 10.2 Strategies submitted by the cities

City	Programme name	Sponsors	Functions
Rotterdam	Integrated Area Approach	National government City	Physical renewal, social investment, employment
Strasbourg	Masterplan for Social Intervention	City National government Département	Reorganisation, physical renewal, employment
Antwerp	Social Impulse Fund	Region City	Reorganisation, integration, employment, physical renewal
Malmö	Metropolitan Initiative	National government City	Employment, integration, education
Stockholm	Territorial Employment Pact	European Union City	Employment
Helsinki	Strategy against Social Exclusion and Segregation	City	Employment, stimulating partnerships
Utrecht	District Service Centre	City	Reduction of distance between city-citizen
Eindhoven	Chain Approach to Addicts	National government City	Reintegration, reduction nuisance

situation was considered tragic in several respects. For the 2000–2010 period, €90 million has been allocated to Hoogvliet for the more than 60 projects within the framework of the IAA. Next to the social pillar (among other things reinforcement of social cohesion and educational levels, fight against youth crime, help to young Antillean single mothers) and the economic pillar (revitalisation of the borough centre and business locations, enhancing the image) the Hoogvliet IAA concentrates on a drastic physical restructuring of the housing stock; one quarter of the low-quality apartments will be demolished and replaced with more attractive and varied housing. The vision is that to be able to stop the downward spiral, first the quality of life has to be improved. Much attention is paid to the social aspects of the demolition and rebuilding process, aspects that have been neglected in the past. Intense communication is considered of the utmost importance and the Hoogvliet citizens are intimately involved in the process. The message is: demolition offers you a golden opportunity! The IAA demands strong cooperation between actors on the municipal as well as the borough level. Most directly involved are the borough board (among other things responsible for welfare policy and project management), the privatised housing corporations (providers of social housing), the municipal departments (to implement projects) and the local businesses and residents' associations. At the time of writing, because the programme is only halfway through, final results are not yet available. Although the programme is comprehensive, there is no integrated evaluation; each actor involved calls for its own evaluation, given specific responsibilities.

Preliminary results in the fields of economic structure, safety, quality of life and citizen involvement/appreciation look promising. The favourable economic tide has certainly helped to reduce the number of unemployed, but weak points and threats, especially in the field of education, still abound.

Restructuring Social Policies in Strasbourg

In general terms Strasbourg – with 264,000 inhabitants the seventh city of France – is a comparatively prosperous city. The service sector is dominant in the city's economy, for one thing because of the presence of European and some international institutions. Thanks to foreign investments, the industrial sector has remained quite important for the regional economy. From 1945 onward, the French state took care of the development of social policy. However, in the 1980s a process of decentralisation started and lower levels of government have been given more responsibilities in social policies. The *Département* has fairly many responsibilities in the social field. According to the French law, the municipalities do not. They are not obliged to provide services, but they can if they want to, which is a matter of political choice. Strasbourg, for one, has traditionally played a fairly strong role in the delivery of social services.

Strasbourg is confronted by some severe social problems, such as comparatively many long-term unemployed people, and deteriorated neighbourhoods. Neuhof, in which a *Grand Projet de Villes* (GPV) is being carried out, is one neighbourhood seriously beset with social problems. The GPV aims to stimulate cultural and social inclusion, improve living conditions and accomplish urban and economic transformation. Much attention is given to the physical restructuring of the urban area.

By its approach to social policies Strasbourg seems to be ahead of other French cities. This approach changed drastically after the development and implementation of the 'Masterplan for Social Intervention'. In Strasbourg several institutions provided social services, a situation which sometimes led to fragmented social help. Historically, all kinds of NGOs have intervened in social policies. Since the 1980s, the *Département* has had relatively many responsibilities, such as mother and child care, health and funding care centres for the handicapped and the elderly. Influenced by its German periods, the city government of Strasbourg has traditionally taken care of social services, which is an exception in France. The Masterplan aims to reorganise the existing structures to achieve a more comprehensive approach to social policies in which the client has a central position. It aims to restructure the social policy field according to:

- a territorial dimension: by introducing a district approach, social services should be set up in the direct vicinity of the clients, and differentiated according to the specific needs of individual districts;
- a thematic dimension: intervention according to themes related to the competencies attributed or delegated to the urban Department for Social Action;
- a logistic dimension: comprising activities that complement those of the former two dimensions.

The fact has been stressed that the new approach requires a change of attitude of the actors involved more than a change of laws or regulations. In particular the way social workers operate in the field, their attitude, their ideas about how best to help the clients, needed change if the envisaged goals were to be achieved. These thoughts developed in particular after two important French laws were passed in 1998, one concerning the mimimum social allowance (RMI) and one concerning the fight against social exclusion. One consequence of this law was the drive to make clients more independent and self-sufficient. Much attention has been given to the creation of an adequate monitoring system. A number of associative and governmental actors cooperate in a so-called 'social observatory'. The idea is that anybody can provide information to this system and use its results. The observatory can help to identify social problems at an early stage and to give more coherent help to customers. It also serve as a powerful tool to evaluate the results of the new approach to social policy.

It is too early to judge the results of the Masterplan. At the time of our analysis, the last stage of implementing the Masterplan had just started. In this stage the first evaluations of the new approach are to be made. We could conclude that the first changes required in the framework of the Masterplan have indeed been carried through.

Organisational Reforms in Antwerp

The city of Antwerp has 456,000 inhabitants, and its administrative region houses nearly one million. The port of Antwerp is still the motor of the economy but no longer the eminent generator of jobs. Antwerp has accomplished the switch to a modern service economy, but is still behind its direct surroundings. Starting in the early 1970s, Belgium went through a process of federalisation, which was completed in 1995 by the first elections for the three regional parliaments. For many purposes, the Flemish government then became the prominent centre of address for the Antwerp administration.

Social problems in Antwerp are most painfully evident in the high and persistent unemployment rate, the unequal spread of prosperity and the poor quality of housing. The accumulation and culmination in some underprivileged neighbourhoods of such urban problems is considered societally unacceptable and a threat to the future (economic) attractiveness of the city.

In Antwerp a new approach to social policy has been stimulated by the Flemish Social Impulse Fund programme (SIF). It helps cities to carry out a policy intended to restore the living and environmental quality of backward neighbourhoods to raise prosperity and fight deprivation. On the basis of a contract concluded between the Flemish government and some Flemish cities, financial support is given for that purpose. In the city of Antwerp, the first part of the strategy concerns organisational changes. Currently social programmes and projects are developed by special organisations that have been set up jointly by the municipality and NGOs to combat social exclusion and to stimulate social revitalisation in backward districts. The prospect is to integrate these organisations into the city administration. The vision behind this strategy is that the current social organisational structures have not been able to adapt to changing societal circumstances. Changes are indispensable to enable action in an opportunity-oriented way.

An important actor in the social field is the public body OCMW, that has responsibilities in the area of welfare and health care. The OCMW is accountable to the city council, but functions in full independence. In the framework of SIF some of its tasks are allotted to RISO, a NGO for Community Development. SOMA, another NGO, coordinates and orchestrates the spending of external funds, in particular those made available for the SIF scheme. Furthermore, the NGO CISO accommodates public organisations that cannot find a place within the regular bureaucracy, but nevertheless need to be close to it. Examples are units for housing and neighbourhood development. These satellite structures are considered necessary for a successful social policy. Admittedly, it is a second-best solution. Ideally, their tasks are carried out within the existing bureaucratic structure.

As the SIF scheme was implemented, social policy evolved from an inward to an outward orientation; instead of just trying to alleviate the pain of deprivation, explicit endeavours are now being made to attack social problems in a structural way, for instance by relating to the economic prospects of city neighbourhoods. The idea of the SIF programme is to focus on a limited number of districts with a concentration of problems. An example is the NOA business centre for new entrepreneurs, which opened in 1995. Its location in a deprived neighbourhood was considered highly innovative. The economic effects were supposed to benefit the immediate neighbourhood. Starting entrepreneurs are offered accommodation and administrative support at relatively low prices. Meanwhile, a great variety of companies have settled here.

So far, the SIF-programme cannot yet boast great tangible achievements. It has been appraised primarily on the programme level. Such evaluations were very broad and in the eyes of some people lacked significance, since certain successes on the implementation level remained obscure. Evaluation of the operational objectives and actions is still in progress.

Integration and Employment Programme in Malmö-Hyllie

Malmö, Sweden's third city, has around 247,000 inhabitants, of which 28 per cent have foreign roots. The Malmö-Lund region has 618,000 inhabitants and the permanent Öresund link has created a polycentric conurbation with around 2.4 million inhabitants. Located in Scania, the southwestern part of Sweden, Malmö serves as a gateway to the EU. Malmö used to be Sweden's leading industrial city, but around 1960 industry started to slow down and in the early 1990s the economic recession brought heavy job losses. The poor economic performance of the city has reduced Malmö to one of the least wealthy cities in Sweden. In recent years a more positive trend has appeared. Malmö expects that the Öresund link will create new opportunities for economic growth. In this region especially the knowledge cluster, with four universities (Copenhagen, Roskilde, Lund and Malmö), is considered a valuable catalyst for further growth. Local autonomy is the cornerstone of the Swedish system. Municipalities have taxation authority and operate more or less independently. In 1996 Malmö was divided into 10 city districts, each with an appointed District Council in charge of some municipal, mainly social services.

Compared to the other Swedish cities, Malmö suffers from high unemployment rates, low education levels, and a high concentration of immigrants (mostly refugees from Afghanistan, Iraq and former Yugoslavia). People with low incomes and poor education also live in the areas which comprise massive, rather dull apartment housing. Together these problems threaten the social structure in Malmö.

The municipality has recognised this and in recent years much attention has been given to possibilities how to overcome this problematic situation. The interest has extended to the national government, which for the first time has launched an urban programme, the Metropolitan Initiative (MI) oriented to helping the seven most disadvantaged cities, including Malmö. The idea of the programme is for residents, NGOs, municipalities, regions and county councils and the state to join forces to create growth in vulnerable areas and to integrate foreigners in the Swedish society. For Malmö the crucial need is for methods to stimulate the integration of the foreign inhabitants. Hyllie (population 30,000) is one of the four districts that participate in the MI programme. Although the quality of the apartments is good, the surroundings lack identity, attractiveness and facilities. Within Hyllie the Holma neighbourhood displays the worst concentration of problems. The greatest obstacle to integration and employment is lack of Swedish language skills. Through the MI, Hyllie is receiving €5.1 million for a period of three years to be spent on various projects concerned with employability, education, integration, culture, public health, local development initiatives and crime prevention. For the Holma Employment and Education Programme a Local Job and Development Centre was created in 2000. The innovative approach adopted is to emphasise customer-oriented attention to clients, for instance by 'rebuilding' the participant's motivation into his/her capacity to work. Courses have been set up to teach illiterates first to read and write in their own language before starting on Swedish. Non-Swedish nationals have been able to help their compatriots with lessons in their own language. Another programme undertaken is to stimulate integration in society. 'Integration secretaries' have been selected from among the four largest ethnic groups. They get in touch directly with 'their' people, stimulate the creation of networks and associations of people with the same ethnic background, and invite them to present their own ideas on how to improve their situation to the centre and local politicians. Four times a year bottom-up ideas for new projects can be submitted. The MI is a public programme. Only actors from the public sector have been involved in the definition of the goals and the implementation of projects. The housing company MKB is an important partner as manager of the housing stock and provider of premises at no cost as meeting places. The programme specifies detailed objectives.

It is too early to say anything about the outcome. Lund University is involved in the evaluation; university associates measure the performance by interviewing 'customers' every six months. It is expected to take several years for the real effects to become known.

New Ways to Employment in Stockholm-Norrmalm

Stockholm is the largest city of Sweden, with 762,000 inhabitants in the city and 1.6 million in the Metropolitan Area. Approximately one tenth are foreigners, most of them from Finland (25 per cent), although recently other groups have also become significant (among others, Turks, Poles, Somalis). From 1998 the Stockholm economy has been growing, after an economic recession in the early 1990s. The development of the knowledge-intensive business sector has been the main engine of the recovery. Nowadays, unemployment in the Stockholm region is quite modest, 3.6 per cent in 2000, substantially below the national average of 6.8 per cent. In Norrmalm, the Stockholm district analysed, only 2.5 per cent of the population is unemployed. This small percentage is considered to contain the persistently long-term unemployed, threatened by social exclusion. The sound economic circumstances are considered a good opportunity to set up programmes aiming in principle for a job for every citizen.

The European Territorial Employment Pact (TEP) is a response to long-term unemployment. It aims to set up innovative approaches to that problem.

The underlying philosophy was the awareness that unemployment is a major threat to the cohesion ideal of the European Union. Welfare differences within regions had become more severe than those between regions, and the most appropriate way to deal with them was to try and reduce (long-term) unemployment. That awareness led to the formulation of the four EU goals of the TEPs: to improve employability, to develop entrepreneurship, to encourage adaptability, and to create equal opportunities. Stockholm translated these four goals into the vision explicitly laid down in the 1998–99 City Action Plan: all people should have the possibility of supporting themselves by gainful employment. As in the other 88 European Pacts, the concept of the Stockholm TEP is to mobilise all the players in the city's districts to combat unemployment, as well as to strengthen the employment effects resulting from European Structural Fund contributions. In the Stockholm TEP projects both public actors (such as the city of Stockholm, the County Council, and the Public Social Insurance Office) and private ones (like the Swedish Association of Enterprises, and Sweden 2000) participated. In Stockholm, development grants were received from EU Objective 3 and Objective 4 Structural Funds to develop the TEP. Almost one half of the technical assistance for the Pact has been financed by the European Commission and the national government. The remainder comes from the City of Stockholm's Labour Market and Education Committee. The total costs of the TEP programme in Stockholm were €5.3 million, of which €2.1 million was financed by the EU Structural Funds and €3.1 million by national and local budgets. For the implementation of the TEP programme four districts were chosen in which 21 projects could be carried out. In the projects, participants were involved in daily activities aimed at creating routines and group dynamics that should result in a feeling of power, energy and self-esteem and an identity other than that of 'jobless social benefit recipient'. During the project, the participants were given opportunities for personal development through guidance, project work, vocational orientation for contacts on the labour market, as well as help to gain practical experience.

The project allowed participants successively to develop their competence on the basis of individual action plans. Four-fifths of the former long-term unemployed participants found work while the projects were in progress. However, the projects analysed were relatively small; the first project had 20 participants, the second only 10.

Preventing Social Exclusion and Segregation in Helsinki

With 552,000 inhabitants, Helsinki is by far the largest city in Finland. The Helsinki region (with a population of 1.2 million) is still growing considerably. During the last decade, the economic development of the Helsinki region has been characterised by considerable dynamics. Up to the late 1980s, income levels were rising and the unemployment was very low (3 per cent). In the early 1990s, the situation changed dramatically mainly because of the collapse of the Soviet Union, at that time an important trading partner. Finland's GDP dropped by 10 per cent and unemployment (especially in cities) rose to 18 per cent. From 1994 onwards, the economic situation has improved considerably. The Helsinki economy is based on knowledge intensity: research and development are considered the key to economic success. Internationally the Helsinki region ranks high for its economic performance. There has been a boom of IT enterprises in the Helsinki region.

However, given the heavy international competition, Helsinki's position seems vulnerable. Finnish society is well known for its emphasis on equal welfare distribution. Until the early 1990s Helsinki was a socially balanced city. However, the recession brought the city massive unemployment and other previously unexperienced social problems, related to education, age, gender, and housing. In the last few years the acute problems that hit the city seem on the way to being solved. Unemployment decreased to 10 per cent, but from the statistics, long-term unemployment persists and differences in income are widening. Moreover, immigration has increased to 5 per cent of the population, which is still low compared to many other European cities.

The idea is that the prevention (rather than combating) of social exclusion should become a policy objective for the Helsinki government. The Strategy against Social Exclusion and Segregation is a first response to the situation. This strategy is based on recommendations made by a special committee in 1998. These recommendations are, among other things: to alleviate unemployment (by improving labour market qualifications as a basic tool against social exclusion); to bring the prevention of social exclusion into the activities of all municipal departments; to encourage internal and external partnerships and citizens' initiatives to fight social problems especially in (potentially) weak neighbourhoods. One project of the strategy, the Year of Partnership, was intended to stimulate cooperation among city departments and external parties and to finance small-scale projects submitted by citizens. About €250,000 (of a total budget for the strategy of €1.7 million) was made available for such small initiatives. One hundred and sixty-one projects (together applying for €2 million) were submitted, of which 54 were financed. The projects were aimed among other things aiming at influencing youth behaviour, increasing civic participation and enhancing interest in the living environment. Actors involved were municipal departments, citizens' associations and the Lutheran church (the state church). Two examples of neighbourhood projects (which were already in progress) are a neighbourhood association trying to improve the quality of life in their living area, and a privately set-up job-seekers initiative (during the recession period), which evolved into a fully-fledged neighbourhood community centre with a wide variety of cultural, social, recreational and educational activities.

For lack of evaluation, no statements can be made as to whether the strategy has helped to decrease or prevent social exclusion. Local income differences have continued to widen, while unemployment has decreased. Partnerships between 'soft' and 'hard' city departments appear to remain difficult and neighbourhood projects seem too small and vulnerable in their continuation to achieve much against social exclusion.

A District Service Centre in Northeast Utrecht

Utrecht, the fourth city of the Netherlands, has 234,000 inhabitants of which 31 per cent are of foreign extraction. The Utrecht region has some 548,000 residents. A large-scale housing project (*Leidsche Rijn*) is expected to raise Utrecht's population to about 280,000 inhabitants by 2010. Economically, Utrecht has fared very well of late. By its central situation, easy access at the junction of some main road and rail lines, the pleasant surroundings, the convivial historical inner city, the active student community and the absence of polluting industries have made this provincial capital an attractive location for all manner of (nationally oriented) service activities. Utrecht holds some strong trump cards in the business meeting function (trade fair), the ICT sector and the biomedical and biotechnical clusters. In growth of employment and office space Utrecht ranks second and third, respectively, in the Netherlands.

Although Utrecht can be considered a rather affluent city, to some extent it suffers from the same social problems as other major cities. They are concentrated in some neighbourhoods, for instance in two smallish areas within the relatively prosperous northeast district. Problems here spring from the high proportion of foreign residents, the high unemployment rate, the incidence of (petty) crime (often associated with drug abuse) and the emergence of black schools. The Staatsliedenbuurt, a small neighbourhood, is undergoing a drastic physical restructuring. Many houses considered unattractive are being demolished, and their residents are being allocated other dwellings by the municipality or the housing corporations. Unlike Rotterdam and Amsterdam, Utrecht has no borough structure, but there are district committees and district offices where a limited number of municipal services are carried out.

The strategy in Utrecht is to bring the city closer to its citizens. The municipal board has initiated a special programme ('Involved City') intended to strengthen the relation of residents, entrepreneurs and social organisations with the city administration. One of the 17 points of the 'Involved City' programme is to establish District Service Centres (DSC). A DSC is a low-threshold 'desk', run by a welfare NGO, and supposed to fulfil a high-grade intermediary function. Matters that bother residents can be reported there and, if no immediate answer is possible, channelled through to the public and private organisations involved in the DSC. No longer does the government dictate the enhancement of a living environment in the conviction that it knows what is good for its citizens. Efforts to raise the quality of living now imply the cooperation of public and private actors. The government has a facilitating role with experiments like the District Service Centre. The DSC, established in neighbourhood community centre *De Leeuw* (a reconstructed former school, opened in August 2000), serves as a pilot project. Within *De Leeuw* are found an infant playroom, a teenagers' club, a room for senior citizens' activities, exhibition halls, Internet facilities, meeting places and the DSC, which is a joint desk of five agencies: a welfare NGO, the municipality (branch of the district office, located at some distance), a housing corporation, the police and the residents' association. Other functions (for instance health care and the second housing corporation) were not added because at the time of the creation they were rejected as not fitting the policy. The daily management rests with the NGO. The costs of the project have mounted from €0.5 to €1.8 million. The rising costs are due in part to technical construction questions and to the high-quality design, corresponding to the adopted vision on how to treat the 'customers'. The NGO is the main tenant of the building and pays the rent (which has risen considerably along with the building costs) to the municipal real-estate department.

The DSC has been in operation too short a time for a judgement of the output; however, the very feat of bringing several partners together under one roof is as such considered a success. The weak point is the feedback by the back offices to the front office. Because objectives and evaluation procedures are not properly defined it seems difficult to learn a lot from this pilot project.

Eindhoven: a Chain Approach to Addicts

The foundation of Philips in 1891 marked the beginning of the transformation of Eindhoven from a small city with about 5,000 inhabitants into the fifth city of the Netherlands, with more than 200,000 citizens. The Eindhoven region ranks among the more prosperous in the Netherlands. Incomes per capita are well above the Dutch average. The region of Eindhoven is an important centre of employment with 320,000 jobs in a population of 700,000. It is the most industrialised region of the Netherlands. Industry produces 46 per cent of the regional turnover, against 32 per cent on the national level, and employs more than 21 per cent of the regional labour force.

In the city's vision, the 290 registered chronic drug addicts (a relatively low number compared to some other cities in the Netherlands) are judged to be among the most vulnerable groups in society. That group suffers from a range of problems (debts, health, living, relations) and is responsible for considerable nuisance and crime. They are concentrated in the city centre and two other neighbourhoods: Woensel-West and De Bennekel. An increasing number of clients can be characterised by a double diagnosis – the combination of drug addiction and mental disorders – resulting in very complex and unpredictable behaviour.

In 1995, Eindhoven launched the strategy Handles for Recovery, a chain of services delivered by several actors. Its main objectives are the decrease of inconvenience caused by drug and alcohol addicts and social integration of the target group. The underlying vision is that a chain approach is the only effective and efficient way to achieve the reduction of the nuisance caused by addicts and their reintegration in society. Indeed, one disadvantage of an approach lacking coherence is that it can lead to compartmentalised treatment of the addicts and miscommunication among the actors involved. The project focuses on troublemakers, systematic perpetrators, people without a fixed abode, and heroin-addicted prostitutes. The chain approach demands close cooperation of the various actors, including the police, the judiciary, municipal services, business companies and neighbourhood organisations. The core actor is Novadic, a network for addict care in the Eindhoven region. The organisation offers a range of services from the treatment of addicts living at home (ambulant services) or in a clinic to preventive actions and criminal care. Novadic stresses the need for a comprehensive approach and hence cooperation with doctors, mental care, the police, judiciary and various other institutes. Initially, the chain was composed of five elements: night care, day care, process supervision, day structuring, and social reintegration and supervised living. As the project

Table 10.3 Administrative and economic characteristics of the cities involved

City	Employment in industry (city, %)	Employment in services (city, %)	Year	Number of administrative tiers (incl. state and boroughs)	Borough Boards
Rotterdam	18.2	81.7	1997	3	Yes
Strasbourg	23.3	76.6	1990	4	No
Antwerp	24.9	71.1	1997	5	No
Malmö	21.0	76.0	1999	3	Yes
Stockholm	14.6	85.2	1996	3	Yes
Helsinki	14.4	83.8	1995	4	No
Utrecht	9.5	85.8	1998	3	No
Eindhoven	40.0	60.0	1999	3	No

Sources: see tables within the case-studies.

Table 10.4 Employment characteristics of the cities involved

City	Proportion of population of working age in employment (city, %)	Year	Unemployment rates (city, %)	Year
Rotterdam	53	1996	7.2	1996
Strasbourg	45	1999	6.1	1999
Antwerp	61	1991	8.3	1991
Malmö	61	1997	11.0	1997
Stockholm	76	1996	6.5	1997
Helsinki	55	1996	10.5	1997
Utrecht	67	2000	7.0	1997
Eindhoven	58	1996	4.4	1999

Sources: see tables within the case-studies.

Table 10.5   Characteristics and finances of the submitted strategies

City	Object	Duration	Allocated funds (in €million)	Period	Scale
Rotterdam	District	Temporary	90	2000–10	District
Strasbourg	District, Individual	Permanent	0.9	6 years	District
Antwerp	District	Temporary	136	1996–99	City
Malmö	District, Individual	Temporary	5.1	3 years	District
Stockholm	District, Individual	Temporary	5.3	3 years	City
Helsinki	District	Temporary	1.7	1999	City
Utrecht	District	Pilot	1.8	–	District
Eindhoven	Target group	Permanent	2.1	1995–2004	City

Sources: see tables within the case-studies.

advanced, three other elements were added: a multifunctional unit for clinical and ambulant addict care, criminal care of addicts, and 'meddle care'. One very important aspect of the strategy is its focus on the customer. Because the composition of the target group and its needs change, the programmes set up to treat the addicts need to be adapted regularly. Novadic therefore constantly monitors the match between the supply of services and the demand from (potential) clients, and changes the supply as found necessary (new or improved services).

The concept is not yet functioning in an optimum way. Neither of the objectives – to reduce nuisance and to reintegrate addicts – has been reached. It appears that on the city level, drug-related nuisance has increased from 14.3 (1996) to 17.9 (1999) per cent. The outflow of addicts has not increased which can be partly explained by the rising complexity of the target group. A positive sign is the decrease in the number of registered drug addicts from 290 to 250, but that success should be mainly ascribed to the prevention policies (at schools for instance) and the economic growth of the last years, resulting in a lower inflow of new addicts.

10.3   Assessment of the Theoretical Framework of Social Organising Capacity

In this section the elements of the theoretical framework of social organising capacity will be confronted with the facts from the case studies. Successively, the elements of the left-hand part (tools) and the right-hand part (process) of Figure 10.1 will be treated. The upper part, the context, has been concisely described in the section preceding this part, which recapitulates the cities and their programmes and projects. Our first subject will be vision, as the central element of the theoretical framework of social organising capacity. Figure 10.1 represents vision as a tool as well as part of the policy process.

Tools for Organising Capacity: Vision

Introduction Besides the vision on the urban or regional level, the framework of this study distinguishes two other levels, namely, that of the social policy field and that of a concrete programme or project. The levels are hierarchical: the visions on the higher level determine the orientation on the lower ones. A vision of social policy should ideally be evolved on the basis of the overall vision of the urban region. Failing that, a vision will have to be developed just for the social policy field as such, without being imbedded in a wider perspective. Characteristics of an adequate vision on the level of social policy are multidisciplinarity and surpassing of the narrow policy field. Social policy is traditionally oriented to the solution of social problems. An opportunity-oriented approach responds to chances. However, chances are often found in other fields, for instance that of the economy, spatial development, or quality of life.

Once a vision on the entire field of social policy has been formulated, ideas can be developed from it for concrete programmes or projects. Without a comprehensive vision of social policy, separately evolved programmes or projects may suffer from a lack of insight into possible chances and strengths in other parts of the urban region or in other sectors. Comprehension and transgression of close policy limits may then be out of reach. The chance of inconsistent policy thus increases and synergy will be hard to accomplish.

Practices on the level of the functional urban region In not all the cities analysed did we find an explicitly formulated general vision on the urban level elaborated into a strategic plan. The exceptions were Eindhoven, Rotterdam and Strasbourg. The city of Eindhoven has developed a long-term vision of the city in the framework of the national Major Cities Policy. Rotterdam has laid down its ambitions in 'Vision 2010'; the main themes of the current council programme follow that lead: a strong city, valuable neighbourhoods, concerned citizens, and enterprising government. The other cities have no explicit vision and/or strategic plans, although they do boast overall policy programmes, usually formulated by the current municipal board and approved by the city council. The development of social projects in Strasbourg were based on an urban vision on sustainable development giving attention to amongst others social cohesion.

Practices on the level of social policy field: national policies point the way to change Social policy practice seems to be based primarily on social values and standards agreed upon on the national level. There is not so much a vision as a set of politically agreed social rights, such as the right to education, accommodation, health, care, benefit, safety, etc. National social policy has tended to be divisional, without spatial dimension, and decisive for the lower authorities, which mostly had only limited opportunities to give it substance. Local social policy was mostly confined to the implementation of national policy by public actors or by NGOs financed by the national government. In the last decade, however, a remarkable shift has been perceivable. Increasingly, social policy in the major cities (especially the problems of social segregation) has become a national policy concern. While formerly social differences among regions were dominant, nowadays social discrepancies are most poignant in cities. That is one reason for the switch from a purely divisional, spatially dimensionless approach to one that is directed explicitly to social problem concentrations. That switch is accompanied by others: from a problem-oriented to an opportunity-oriented and from a fragmented to a comprehensive policy. Those switches seem to be related to the trend of policy decentralisation manifest in many countries. The awareness is growing that the nearer one comes to the problems, the more effectively a policy can be evolved. With the exception of Finland, the same trend can be observed in all the countries of our study. In France, cities have since the late 1980s gained more independence regarding social policy, which now should be made comprehensive and opportunity-oriented as well. In the Netherlands (Major City Policy) the shift occurred in the mid-1990s, to be followed by Flanders (Social Impulse Fund), and very recently by Sweden (Metropolitan Initiative). Especially in Sweden, where regional policy had always been dominant, the introduction of this explicitly urban policy forms a clean break with the past. In all four countries budgets of various policy fields are combined, and the cities are expected, in partnership with other actors (mostly NGOs), to develop comprehensive policy strategies. Characteristically, the national government and the municipalities present themselves as contract partners. The state undertakes the orchestration and fixes the preconditions, while the cities formulate social strategies and are financed on the basis of an implementation commitment. In Finland, a first step in that direction was taken in 1998, but the Finnish state has not yet offered an incentive for (or imposed the 'duty' of) a cooperative approach, so that initiatives have to come primarily from the cities themselves. The new trend to address the problems from closer by, in a neighbourhood- or customer-oriented approach, is remarkable. We shall now look more closely into the second switch.

Practices on the level of social policy: the central aim of social programmes is to make target groups self-supporting The visions formulated for social programmes in the various cities all seem aimed at one objective, namely to make the target group self-supporting (or emancipated). That objective seems the recurrent theme in the investigation. Stockholm formulates it as follows: *all people should have the possibility of supporting themselves through gainful employment.* However, the opportunities seized in the individual cities (whether or not incorporated in their vision) differ. In Rotterdam and in Strasbourg, measures to raise the quality of life are seen as an opportunity to make the population more self-supporting. The measures are often concerned with physical restructuring. Utrecht wants to supply citizens with made-to-measure social services in the neighbourhood itself, responding better to demand and persuading suppliers to join their forces. In Antwerp, the economic revival of the Central Station area is seen as an opportunity that can benefit a wider part of the city and with which employment for the long-term unemployed in depressed neighbourhoods can be created. To accomplish that, Antwerp adopted the 'partial vision' that reorganisation of the civil service is a necessary condition for social revitalisation.

The central vision of the chain approach to drug addiction in Eindhoven can be split into several levels of ambition. Preferably, those addicted should be encouraged to build up a 'normal existence' including a job. The highest level of ambition, in other words, is to make the target group self-supporting. A somewhat lower tier of ambition is to reduce the nuisance caused by the addicts. However, the city strongly depends on the national drugs-policy. Moreover, the city government of Eindhoven is aware that addiction can never be banned entirely. Attempts are therefore made to keep the phenomenon in control. If the addicts are given facilities, such as a day shelter and a night shelter of their own, they need no longer be a nuisance to themselves and to the city since they would no longer be busy all day long with (in criminal ways) scraping together what they need for their next fix.

In Malmö and Stockholm, innovative programmes are run to try and prepare the long-term unemployed for a return to the labour market. Like Rotterdam, Strasbourg sees good chances in the physical restructuring of underprivileged neighbourhoods and in focusing on the individual. The same as in Antwerp, a reorganisation of the bureaucracy is carried through as a necessary condition to reach that objective. In Helsinki, the vision development on the emerging social exclusion problems is still in its infancy. A start was made on the basis of a 'partial vision' in the hope that it would be the base for a 'fully-fledged vision' (in fact, only two city departments came forward with ideas how to carry out the Helsinki strategy towards the aims).

Emerging hierarchy of visions Of the three levels of urban vision, the intermediate one, the link between the comprehensive urban or regional vision and the programme or project vision, was determined mainly by national governments (through social security laws, social allowances, Dutch drugs policy, etc.). This policy was essentially fragmented, spatially undimensional and oriented to solving problems but not to responding to chances. The resulting rupture of the 'vision hierarchy' may explain in part the fragmentation and compartmentalisation of social policy. That situation seems changing. Under the influence of a decentralising tendency, cities are more and more themselves filling in their social policy (and the vision of it). Thus, a logical succession of vision development can be achieved, with the lower-level visions hitching on to higher-level ones (see Figure 10.2). It means that the local visions (can) really connect to the concrete strengths and opportunities of a specific city, be developed in a comprehensive way and including a spatial dimension.

Tools for Organising Capacity: Strategic Networks

Existing administrative structures are inadequately equipped for a comprehensive approach In several cities, the administrative structure is so inert that the required comprehensive policy is all but impracticable. That is why Antwerp and Strasbourg want to reorganise their own administration before venturing to comprehensive strategies. In Antwerp, the social and care policy is in the hands of an independent public organisation, the OCMW, while within the city administration the Community Building Department

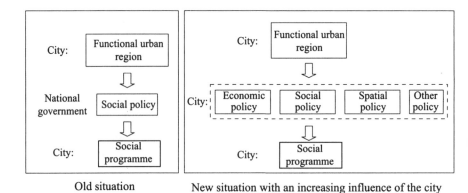

Old situation   New situation with an increasing influence of the city
                     and a more comprehensive approach

Figure 10.2 Hierarchy of visions and main actors behind these visions

gives shape to social policy. The situation sometimes gives rise to conflicts of competence between the city council and the administrators of the care sector. The OCMW believes that the municipality has wrongly assigned 'new' social tasks to NGOs. The innovative and flexible methods of these NGOs allow them to operate with an efficiency and effectiveness that are not (yet) feasible within the formal structures. The idea is in time to integrate such organisations (or at least their innovative manner of working) in the municipal apparatus. The reverse, innovation from the inside out, is considered a long and awkward road. The experience is that partnerships need time and opportunity to grow, in a growth process requiring much attention. In Strasbourg also organisational changes are considered necessary. Here, in spite of a particular history, like in other French regions, social policy was essentially carried out by the state and the *Département*. Since social problems call for comprehensive solutions, the city of Strasbourg claims a heavier role in social policy, with cooperation between social organisations as crucial factor. In Rotterdam, the comprehensive approach adopted (both functionally among sectors, and spatially between municipality and borough) has led to a complicated organisational structure, entailing long communication lines and a surfeit of consultation platforms. On the other hand, there is a sound cooperation on the level of the underprivileged neighbourhood. What with the seriousness of the problems and the jointly formulated vision and strategy, the local actors are cooperating in a sound way.

Cooperation of municipal departments is poorly developed Within the public organisations, networks of various sectors often appear to be poorly developed. The need for a comprehensive approach is understood (on paper), but its implementation is obstructed by rigid structures and traditional work cultures that are loath to work together. In the meantime, four of the five national governments of our study have stated that local social policy should be more result-oriented, mostly mentioning a partnership approach as a condition. Such an approach requires first and foremost better adjustment and cooperation among the parts (divisional and spatial) of the municipal apparatus itself. In Helsinki, the 'soft' departments (social services, education) cooperate better among themselves than with such 'hard' departments as that concerned with real-estate. In Utrecht there are complaints about the lack of cooperation of the real-estate department, which is reported to make no distinction between commercial projects and the exploitation of the social pilot, the District Service Centre. In Rotterdam, no fewer than eight departments work together within the Integrated Area Approach. Here, questions have been raised about the cooperation of the three 'soft' services (social, health and education departments) within the 'social platform'. In Malmö, an innovative, successful plan to involve ethnic teachers to teach Swedish to their illiterate compatriots is insufficiently supported by the education departments, which believe that the official, traditional approach (which has proved unsatisfactory in practice) has to be continued, merely because teachers have been appointed to that end. The education department keeps itself aloof, strictly adhering to the formal rules, and prefers not to be bothered with a possible role in social policy. In Strasbourg, social policies were spread among too many institutions that a drastic reform of the organisation structure was considered necessary. This reform intended to enforce coopation between relevant actors

Private parties hardly involved in social policy From the cases dealt with, the activities in the framework of social policy appear to be still largely reserved to public networks. The programmes are dominantly executed by (departments of) the local public sector. There are (secondary) parts for NGOs, housing corporations (as in Rotterdam, Utrecht and Malmö), residents' associations, local entrepreneurs and the churches (for example the Lutheran state church in Finland). Strikingly, private enterprise hardly figures at all among the actors. Despite the fact that opportunity-oriented policies such as the equipment of people for a position on the labour market (an explicit goal in Malmö and Stockholm), specifically aim to respond to economic opportunities, the participation of the private sector is below par. Local entrepreneurs are indeed involved, as in Rotterdam, but the influential Hoogvliet-neighbour Shell seems to take part largely to enhance its own image. Despite the intentions and trends towards social entrepreneurship, except for directly involved local entrepreneurs or companies, in not any of the projects is the (commercial) private sector a full partner – except for immediately involved local entrepreneurs or companies – neither in the formulation of vision and policy, nor in the implementation. Sometimes the need for more cooperation with private partners is expressed, but there seems to be no example of its practical accomplishment. Sometimes, competence problems are the handicap, as in Malmö, where contacts with the private sector (to match the schooling of unemployed people to the existing vacancies), are claimed by the traditional employment agency (which as a matter of fact is involved in the neighbourhood project).

Cooperation is achieved faster on the level of neighbourhoods: striking a balance between top-down and bottom-up strategy   The developments in Rotterdam-Hoogvliet have demonstrated that the closer to the problems, the easier to reach cooperation. On the other hand, however, it is also true that the closer one gets to the problems, the harder it is to keep sight of the whole and to give a problem its proper place in the urban or regional context. It is a matter of finding the optimum level of approach. The impression is that, when a customer-oriented or a neighbourhood-oriented approach is at stake (concerning youth crime, for instance), the municipal level is too far from the facts. With an approach on the level of boroughs (as in Rotterdam, Stockholm and Malmö) the communication lines are shorter and the actors concerned are more apt to understand the inevitability of cooperation to achieve efficiency and effectiveness. That depends, of course, on the size of the city. Rotterdam, Stockholm and Malmö have borough councils. In the city of Helsinki there is no level of administration below the municipality. In Antwerp, boroughs are in preparation. In Utrecht, the wish to bring the municipal government nearer to the citizen has been a political priority for some time. Through district offices, citizens are served in communal matters by a centre 'round the corner'. The latest form of service, the District Service Centre, adds a kind of 'social district shopping centre'.

Sectorial political responsibility is one cause of the lack of a comprehensive approach   One cause of the lack of cooperation within municipal organisations is the way in which the political administration is organised. Governors have to account for the policy fields in their portfolio. That gives the sectorial approach the ascendancy over the comprehensive approach. In Rotterdam, several aldermen have 'adopted' an underprivileged neighbourhood in addition to their normally allotted tasks. It does encourage comprehensive thinking, but even in their adopted neighbourhoods their competence remains confined to their 'own' political jurisdiction. In Utrecht, a special alderman for neighbourhood affairs has been appointed, which seems an interesting option.

Tools for Organising Capacity: Leadership

Leadership should be anchored on several levels; the required operational skills and the tactical and strategic insights vary among levels Leadership on the project level is focused on implementation; it should be operationally strong, and have a well developed relational component, because of the direct contact with the customers. A good project leader need not necessarily be a good strategist (or vice versa, although it is useful when both skills are present). On the level of policy formulation and (political) decision-making, strategic and tactical insights are expected. In Strasbourg the director of the social department (DAS) needed to convince the associates that a completely different way of working was necessary. In spite of initial resistance, sufficient credit to gain the involved parties' acceptance of the new approach way built up, which was indeed quite revolutionary by French standards. In Antwerp, on the level of programmes the search was predominantly for persons with leadership qualities. To that end the implementing organisations were placed outside the municipal structure, so that bureaucratic rules could be circumvented. That is evidence of tactical insight, even though politically the solution found does not seem optimum. In Utrecht, the District Service Centre is primarily the initiative of two persons (the leader of a welfare organisation and an external consultant). They acted at the right moment: a building and funds were available. Without that circumstance the chance of realisation would probably have been much smaller. They also managed to convince all parties involved and the competent alderman that participation would be to their own advantage. They overcame several formal barriers, despite some clashes of competence with traditional forces within the municipality. In Rotterdam, the leadership on the level of programmes calls primarily for intensive consultation, negotiating and adjustment to other programmes and with public and private parties involved, aspects inherent to the complex organisation structure needed to accomplish the functional and vertical integration (between municipality and borough) of the neighbourhood approach. For that reason, the 'implementing leadership' rests primarily with the project leaders.

How to fill in the part of the leader, and how effective his performance will be, are evidently dependent on personal qualities In Rotterdam, the inspiring leadership of the political leader of the Hoogvliet borough has strongly marked the joint undertaking of the large-scale local renovation process. This leader is regarded by many as the motor of the renovation. In Malmö, the foreign project leaders appear highly successful in their approach, thanks to their familiarity with the culture and language of their clients. The programme leader, being in the background, left room for the project leaders to make their own contribution. That stimulated the project leaders' to use their own initiative, which was greatly appreciated by them, as was the unconventional approach against the somewhat wary, traditionally thinking advisers and decision-makers at the level of the municipality or district. In the neighbourhood projects in Helsinki, leadership comes naturally because the work is done by volunteers, supported by social workers. In such circumstances, the leaders/initiators tends to show exceptional commitment. The vulnerable aspect of such very person-oriented voluntary projects is continuity, since successors tend to be less involved. Incentives to permanency (naturally under certain preconditions) seem required in Helsinki to find good successors – if and when needed – to continue this valuable voluntary work. Some measure of formalisation need not jeopardise the private initiative.

Without political backing or clear objectives there is a risk of diffuse leadership The lack of political leadership can impede the adequate execution of programmes. In Helsinki the formal and informal leadership had not clearly been defined as far as the Strategy against Social Exclusion and Segregation was concerned, which was due in part to the lack of well-defined objectives and of political interest once the programme had been put on the rails. The politicians kept aloof from the suggestion that there should be underprivileged neighbourhoods in Helsinki. That was one reason for the disappointing results of the strategy. In Strasbourg, the political support of the mayor and the alderman for social action was decisive for the purposeful way in which the Masterplan for Social Intervention was developed and implemented. Powerful political support was indispensable for the changes envisaged by this approach. It also meant essential support to those implementing the reconstruction of social policy in Strasbourg. The boroughs of Rotterdam may sometimes be heard to complain that 'the city' allows them little space to play around in and that they are too dependent on municipal departments for the execution of projects, although in actual fact municipal political leadership leaves the boroughs generous leeway to come up with their own ideas. Before the Flemish

SIF programme was set up, new social policy (such as neighbourhood and community development) in Antwerp was mostly initiated and carried out by NGOs. Because the 'traditional' social policy is entrusted for the most part to the OCMW, which operates outside the municipal bureaucracy, the latter displayed hardly any involvement with social policy. Since the SIF called for a comprehensive, outward-oriented policy, adequate propelling of all separate public and private actors was the first concern. The organisational and content-related changes that were needed for effective control could be put in motion mostly thanks to the leadership of an experienced and politically strong alderman. He promoted the founding of an ex-municipal organisation (SOMA) to coordinate the spending of external funds more adequately than existing public agencies could have done. The problem remains that the political leadership seems invested in one person, while other aldermen involved show less interest.

Tools for Organising Capacity: Support and Communication

Support by national governments has apparently been of great importance for the recent renewal of practical local social policy The main political support appears to come from national governments. Because on the national level the increasing social dichotomy has become a major political item almost everywhere, this support for a substantial change of policy in favour of a more effective and efficient approach on the local level is well accepted in most of the cities involved, as was already pointed out with respect to the development of a vision of social policy. In Belgium (Flanders), the Netherlands and Sweden, cities having serious social problems have been designated to receive extra funds on the basis of their self-evolved vision, as well as greater freedom to strengthen their own social policy. That has proved a strong incentive. Only in Helsinki is such an incentive sadly lacking, with the result that on the local level as well the political support remains on the meagre side.

Explicit support from responsible governors turns the signal to green: weak political support makes implementation a lot more troublesome Political support on the municipal level has already been touched upon under the heading of political leadership. An alderman's explicit and convincing attitude as puller of a programme or policy, simplifies the implementation, the more so if without such support that implementation cannot count on much applause. In Strasbourg and Antwerp, the purposeful intervention of governors appeared necessary to get some planned changes accepted by the implementing agents. In Utrecht as well, the support of the governor involved was necessary to get the signals turned to green. In Helsinki, the need to undertake something against the advancing social segregation was admittedly subscribed to by governors, but for the rest it was not really an urgent political item. That fact has obviously influenced the degree of implementation and also the fact that none of the parties assumed the leadership of the strategy against social exclusion.

Societal support is gained by explicitly involving the clients in the decision making: trust is of the essence The successful developments in Rotterdam-Hoogvliet are mainly due to the high degree of solidarity and involvement of the population. In spite of its serious social problems, this somewhat isolated city quarter still displays the feelings of togetherness and solidarity that characterise a village. Just as characteristic is the manner in which the (real) desires of the customers are listened to and taken into account. As a result, popular trust in the leaders and the plans is relatively large. In Malmö the social support among citizens of foreign extraction increased tremendously when their 'own' trusted people were enlisted to explain the (worthy) intentions of the Swedish approach.

The lack of societal support for 'positive discrimination' of backward regions or groups in society (such as foreigners or drug addicts) is sometimes an impediment to political support and thus hampers certain policy programmes Social policy is not always recognised by (parts of) the population as necessary or desirable. Notably in the Scandinavian cities the fact was emphasised that large portions of the population were not in favour of preferential treatment for certain neighbourhoods or groups in the community, for instance by granting them extra money for special education. That form of 'positive discrimination' seems to be hardly acceptable within the Scandinavian equality culture. Even the Lutheran church in Helsinki stated that opinions vary within its parishes concerning the unequal treatment of neighbourhoods or groups and the gravity of their social problems. Integration and equipment programmes are negatively affected by such attitudes. In Sweden, the city governments could give a good example by themselves employing foreign workers. The Swedish private sector does not seem to have progressed as far as that, and is still averse to employing foreigners. In Antwerp the rise of an extreme right-wing party (*Vlaams Blok*) has induced a tightening of social policy. The impression prevails that voters for this party are mostly citizens who want to signal their protest against the inadequate support from public agencies for improvement of their environment. In Utrecht, a political (local interest) party, which in essence wants to vent its disenchantment with the Utrecht local government, has gained many voters. To recover trust, the policy is to emphasise the rendering of direct services to the Utrecht citizens. The District Service Centre is an exponent of that policy. Societal support for measures to combat and solve the problems of drugs addiction, as in Eindhoven, is mostly poor. As soon as citizens or businesses have the slightest fear of bother, they set up powerful societal opposition.

Trust in policy flourishes when the results become visible: seeing is believing That thesis is defended notably in Antwerp. Only when the people observe improvements with their own eyes can trust in this approach grow. That is why such great store is set in Antwerp by physical improvements in under-privileged neighbourhoods, for instance around the Central Station, as a condition for gaining approval for the accompanying, less noticeable 'soft' social policy measures.

Once the private sector takes an active part, political support will increase In Stockholm, a greater input from the private sector in employment projects is considered a condition for more interest from politicians. On the other hand, the private sector will not take part unless it is explicitly involved in the making and implementation of policy measures. In Antwerp, a few providers of financial services have been found willing to invest in a local business centre, thanks to the business-oriented approach of this project on the basis of a business plan. The participating companies hope for a positive impact on their image and improved relations with the local authorities.

Communication is sadly underappreciated as a factor of social policy From the examples cited above, concerning the lack of societal or political support, the key factor has often been that the problems and the plans for solving them by programmes and projects were not or poorly communicated to those involved. The attention of policy designers and policy implementers tends to be focused on the product (programme or project); communication often comes at the bottom of the list. That is true not only of external communication but also internally, within the local government organisation or even within one and the same government department. Often those involved do not or not sufficiently know what the others are doing. Better information and communication are required to avoid working at cross-purposes. Most projects lack an adequate communication strategy, with a few positive exceptions. In

Rotterdam-Hoogvliet the intensive communication with those directly involved (through mailings, meetings, house-to-house newspapers) has provided a sound foundation for trust in the new-building propositions. In Malmö, the (labour-intensive) personal approach of the 'integrators' (by visits or personal notes) created trust among the target group. In Helsinki, the communication was consciously kept limited, for fear of raising expectations too high. Nevertheless there was an enormous response to projects submitted by the population. That only about one-third of all the suggestions could be realised somewhat depressed the societal support among those rejected. Notably the discrimination inherent in almost all measures that grant advantages to backward neighbourhoods or groups, calls for wise communication strategies. Actually, the matter seems first and foremost of national relevance. In the eight cases investigated, we have failed (perhaps with the exception of Malmö) to find any innovative local approach to such problems.

Policy Process: Strategy Implementation and Output

Comprehensive approach calls for much mutual communication The comprehensive implementation of social programmes calls for frequent communication among actors in different policy fields and on different policy levels. The danger then looms that communication gobbles up so much time that too little of it remains for other policy matters, such as contact with the clients. The impression is, for instance, that the actors of the Hoogvliet borough and the municipality of Rotterdam are disproportionally engaged in mutual adjustment and communication. What with the complexity of the integrated area approach and the rather diffuse distribution of tasks among the levels (municipality, borough) and parties (municipal departments), extensive communication is unavoidable. The relevant actors themselves indicated that other activities regularly were in danger of being crowded out. In Strasbourg the same difficulties were encountered as social policies were being implemented on the territorial level. The new approach was considered time-consuming because so much time was 'lost' in meetings to exchange ideas. However, one of the prominent ideas of the Masterplan is that the advantages of better mutual communication will outweigh the time spent on lengthy discussions.

Adjustment of the policy concept during the process Because relatively little is known as yet about a comprehensive, opportunity-oriented approach to social policy, and the problem fields are subject to much exogenous change, frequent adjustments are required during the implementation of a social strategy. Obviously, blueprints for new social concepts cannot be made in advance. During the process, learning effects as to the most advisable approach will occur, making certain changes in the implementation necessary. It is a matter of learning by doing, a trial-and-error process. In several cities that has become clear. In Eindhoven for instance, new chain elements have been added in the course of the process, and in Utrecht, the concept of the District Service Centre crystallised gradually over time. Through all adjustments of the social concept, it is imperative to hold on to a certain policy line that has gained consensus from a broadly supported underlying vision. Indeed, what is needed is a distinct overall concept to give direction to the policy implementation. Furthermore, a strong leadership is required to initiate the necessary changes. At the same time, a flexible attitude of those involved is desirable to learn from errors and to carry through adjustments. Earlier failures should indeed be admitted and recognised if the policy is to improve. Mutual trust of the actors involved seems an important precondition to that end.

New organisations and other skills demanded for an opportunity-oriented social policy Depending on the visions on social policies, new organisational structures might be requested. They can be structured according to a categorical, a functional or a territorial approach. With the exception of Eindhoven (categorical) and Helsinki (functional), all the cities investigated have chosen to submit a programme or project with an area-oriented approach. Strasbourg is actually carrying through a drastic reorganisation of the municipal social-policy service for that purpose. Antwerp is also carrying through organisational reforms to arrive at a more opportunity-oriented, comprehensive social policy. In the other cities there was no question of a reorganisation, although here too tensions between the organisational needs of the policy implementation required and the existing organisational structures were clearly visible. In many cities, the social policy still has a functional orientation, which may clash with an area-based approach. The fact is that an opportunity-oriented approach calls for a changed attitude of the employees involved. In all the cities, a stringent bureaucracy seems to be an obstacle to desirable reforms. Processes of social change are often slowed down by a conservative, non-innovative attitude among the civil servants. In Rotterdam-Hoogvliet the argument was that the new approach (the physical restructuring) called for innovation, creativeness, courage and deviation from standards. Therefore, the people employed in social policy should possess skills and a mentality that differed from those that had previously been the norm. That means generous investment in training and schooling for those people.

Policy Process: Monitoring and Outcome

Results of monitoring and evaluation are not always properly used The various programmes and projects offer varied pictures of adequate or inadequate monitoring. Two appear to be well advanced: the programme in Strasbourg in particular, and the Eindhoven project. Both determined benchmarks in advance, and with the help of zero-measurement and regular monitoring are trying to correct if necessary. Strasbourg is endeavouring to achieve comprehensive monitoring through the coupling of different types of data. In the projects submitted by Helsinki and Utrecht relatively little is done with the monitoring instrument. Hardly any benchmarks have been formulated, no zero measurements have been taken, hardly any regular monitoring has been performed so that there was no way to make adjustments on the basis of evaluation results. The quality of monitoring in the remaining four programmes is somewhere between the two extremes. Malmö and Stockholm do work with benchmarks and regular monitoring, but perform little comprehensive monitoring and make too few adjustments on the basis of evaluation results. Antwerp has indeed set up an extensive monitoring system, but the aspects evaluated so far lack the concreteness required for actual adjustment. In Rotterdam, relatively many measurements of elements of the social policy are performed, but little is done with the results. The conclusion must be that monitoring has had hardly any adjusting effect. That financial donors tend to ask for separate measurements is one more explanation for the fact that in spite of the (intended) comprehensive approach, there has hardly been any comprehensive evaluation.

Translation of qualitative improvements into measurable indicators Many effects of social policy programmes cannot immediately be quantified, such as the perception of the quality of life and safety in neighbourhoods. Admittedly, the formulation of measurable indicators, benchmarks, and methods to evaluate qualitative aspects is more and more the object of thinking and discussion. In Malmö the degree of integration of foreigners in the Swedish community is measured, among other criteria, by the results of interviews conducted every six months with people of foreign extraction. The (independent external) evaluators try to find out whether people have come to like their neighbourhood better since the stimulation of social networks among inhabitants. In Rotterdam-Hoogvliet, the perception of quality of life is evaluated by regular surveys among the residents. A potential pitfall is that such surveys are strongly affected by incidents. A robbery, for instance, may temporarily distort the residents' perception of quality of life.

The development of benchmarks alone can be a stimulus towards more result-orientation In Antwerp, new indicators have been evolved for various elements of the social policy. For several policy elements benchmarks have been formulated that can be measured on a regular basis (see the figure on the monitoring instrument in the Antwerp case). In some instances the suggestion was made that those involved do not know exactly what and how to measure. However, merely to think about indicators is considered inspiring towards a more opportunity-oriented social policy. Until a short time ago, the hours of contact with clients were recorded as output, but not much else. It has now been accepted that it is necessary to check whether the objectives of the projects are actually attained.

A public information system has several advantages In Strasbourg, much attention is given to the creation of an adequate monitoring system. Some associative and governmental actors work together in the so-called social observatory. Anybody can provide information to that system or use its results. The idea is that to have the same access to the same high-quality information will help social actors to cooperate better with one another. The envisaged goal is to develop a common analysis instrument to set up common actions. With the help of the observatory, social problems can be recognised at an early stage and customers served more coherently. Moreover, the system is a powerful tool to evaluate the results of the new type of social policy.

Have the analysed projects been successful? Whether a project is a success or a failure is hard to assess. A possibility is to compare the financial results with the social investment made. However, nowhere has a societal cost-benefit analysis of social strategies been performed that could enlighten us as to the final return on the means invested. One aspect worth evaluating is how far objectives stated in advance have been reached (effectiveness) and how efficiently that has been done. An important question in that respect is: could they have done better? The answer to that question may reveal how far in the circumstances the policy implementers have done a good job. To understand the actual achievement of the actors, a specific social problem has to be related to its context. For instance, in the current flourishing economy, an employment policy (as in Stockholm and Malmö) is far easier to carry out than a measure to reduce the nuisance caused by drug addicts (as in Eindhoven). A complication is that most programmes have not yet been completed, so that any conclusions must be tentative.

10.4 Evolution of Social Policies in Urban Areas

From the results of the comparative study, there is evolution noticeable regarding social policies. In the course of that evolution, changes occur in the approach to social policy (top-down versus bottom-up) and the dominance of the actors involved (private and public actors and the third sector). Three stages can be distinguished (see Figure 10.3):

1 *The direct action stage.* Within urban areas, social policy often begins with small-scale bottom-up initiatives taken by private actors and/or the third sector. People will accept, for instance, the need to help those in danger of social exclusion, and help them to start up small-scale projects. At this stage, the city recognises social problems and tries to solve them, without bothering about their backgrounds or the conditions for their solution. The behaviour of the municipality is instrumental and direct, but policy making remains limited. Projects tend to fit the urgent needs of people with social problems, since they have been set up as an immediate response to specific troubles. However, as long as the social policy consists of individual actions of individual actors, the projects will hardly show any coherence at all.

2 *The institutionalisation stage.* The municipal government will not stop at admitting and recognising the problems. It will try to optimise its own social policy by improving existing structures, processes and services. The municipality acquires the knowledge and skills it thinks necessary for its social policy. The institutionalisation of social policy is initiated, with at first interplay between public and private actors. Local – bottom-up – initiatives are institutionalised for the sake of a better overall framework and more coherent projects. The municipal government sets up its own separate organisations to get to grips with the wide range of social problems. Social workers are supposed to specialise. Finally, public actors are taking over the policy field, and social policy is developed and carried out almost entirely from the top down. The result is that the relations between social projects and immediate needs become tenuous. Owing to the functional

organisation of the social field, social employees will work more and more in isolation, and island-like structures will arise in the social arena.

3 *The activation stage.* The city looks for and acquires active access to options for solving municipal social problems. To that end it does not confine itself to its own municipal departments. On the one hand, attempts are made to strike a balance between a bottom-up approach responding adequately to the prevailing social problems, and a top-down approach favouring, among other things, the internal coherence of the social policy and the achievement of adequate structures. On the other hand the city will adjust its policy to that of other actors in the social field by seeking to balance nicely the government intervention and that of private actors (who are able to respond more professionally and faster to concrete social needs). The upshot will be that the city redefines its own function in terms of responsibilities and roles. Cities will for instance choose the role of director, without immediate concrete input. The accent is on the development of an adequate vision and on the relation of the municipal government with other parties. At a more advanced phase of this stage, innovations are carried through. The municipal government is now capable of creating effective formulas for existing as well as new social problems. It switches between several domains of policy – physical, economic or social – and between different roles and tasks of partner organisations, as seems at any time most fitting for taking problems in hand or seizing opportunities.

The search for new equilibria is represented in the right-hand picture of Figure 10.3. To carry out the new desirable approach, other organisation structures can be created. The mostly functionally appointed public organisations can be converted into area-oriented or divisionally-controlled organisations that are more apt to cooperate with private actors.

Three prominent features of the activation stage can be distinguished:

1 *Awareness of insufficient grip on the problems.* The government is becoming aware of the fact that, as a consequence of bureaucracy and rigidity, it more and more loses its grip on the approach to social problems.
2 *Vision development for social policies.* New ideas (visions) may also evolve about the approach to certain problems. An example is the idea that in principle every citizen should be able to fend for himself. That is a fundamental change from the idea of the twentieth-century welfare state. The combination of physical restructuring with social policies can also be considered innovative, as can the chain approach to drug addicts.

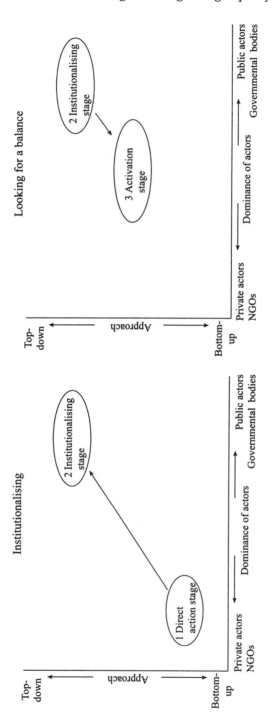

Figure 10.3 Evolution of social policies within urban areas

3   *Organisational changes in social policy.* To realise the new ideas, organisational changes of the social policy can be desirable, combined with training of personnel in new skills.

The relationship between Figure 10.2 (the theoretical framework of organising capacity) and Figure 10.3 (evolution of social policies) is that in each of the distinguished stages, another substance can be given to the elements of organising capacity. Furthermore, during the evolution of social policies a difference of stress on different elements is noticeable. For instance, in the first and the second stage vision development plays a secondary role, while it is the leading element in the 'activation stage'. An example is the strategic networks. In the 'direct action stage' they are in particular constituted by private actors, while during the 'institutionalisation stage' they consist especially of public actors, while in the 'activation stage' these networks comprise of a mix of public and private institutions.

From the limited number of projects and programmes that have been studied in each city, no pertinent conclusions can be drawn about the position of the cities investigated in the stages discussed above. Nevertheless, the impression is that the Dutch cities, inspired by the national policy, are at the transition from stage 2 to stage 3; Rotterdam, the city with the worst social problems, seems to be ahead thanks to its longer experience with municipal social problems. The Swedish cities are at stage 2 but taking steps towards stage 3. In Helsinki, social policy seems to be still at stage 1. By learning from experiences elsewhere, possibly the city can jump stage 2 and thanks to new international insights take steps towards stage 3. Antwerp and Strasbourg seem also on their way to stage 3. Significant organisational changes are being carried through to achieve that transition.

10.5   Main Conclusions

From the investigation, the combination of elements that we have referred to as organising capacity appears to have a clear impact on the quality and the results of social policy programmes and projects. The problem statement was primarily commented on in each of the eight case studies (chapters 2 to 9), of which a summary has been given in section 10.2. The analysis of section 10.3 comments on the objectives of gaining insight into the role of organising capacity and of generating practical knowledge and tools to strengthen the social organising capacity in social policy strategies.

This section summarises the principal conclusions as more extensively presented in section 10.3. As already pointed out in section 10.1, the conclusions are perforce based on a limited number of programmes and projects, which in turn had been selected from a multitude of local programmes and projects. That makes unequivocal conclusions hardly meaningful. Nevertheless we believe, supported by the unique material that this investigation has collected, that the outcomes can contribute to the further development of strategies of social policy and all its implications. We are particularly hopeful that the results of this investigation will encourage the critical observation of the contribution of elements of organising capacity to programmes and projects.

Conclusions regarding Vision Development

Without a vision linking social problems with opportunities, social policies will not lead to lasting results Vision is the key element in this research. It is the embodying of the opportunity-oriented approach of social policies. The visions in the case studies were all aimed at one objective, namely to make the target groups self-supporting (or emancipated). Ultimately, the idea is that social programmes are temporary, but solutions lasting. When the stated aims are achieved, other urgent problems have to be solved with the help of new programmes.

National policy remains a catalyst for structural changes in municipal social policy Dedicated impulses to cities will encourage them to choose new ways to take their social problems in hand. When demands of linking problems to opportunities (visions), integrality and partnership are imposed on social policy, such impulses may act as a lubricant towards a new approach.

Cities get more influence on vision development on the level of the social policy field Three levels for vision development were distinguished: the city or functional urban region, the social policy field and the social programme or project. The intermediate one was determined mainly by national governments, and essentially divisional, spatially undimensional and oriented to solving problem but not responding to chances. Under the influence of a decentralising tendency, cities are more and more filling in their visions on social policy themselves.

Proficiency in the national language is the basis for successful integration policy On the labour market, in particular, the potential of foreign labourseems to be poorly exploited, as is apparent from the persistently high unemployment rates among them. Thus, much attention is given to integration projects. Knowledge of the national language is indispensable in that context. Without it, integration is virtually impossible.

Attention for the quality of the housing and living environment is increasingly recognised as important for overcoming social arrears. The attention for neighbourhood identity, image and physical differentiation is emerging as a component of urban revitalisation The anonymous, monotonous structure of certain backward regions, the frequently poor differentiation of the housing stock, and the lack of services induce residents who can afford it to leave, so that mostly those without prospects remain behind. Further impoverishment and a poor image, especially among outsiders, are then unavoidable.

Opportunity-oriented approach particularly successful in times of a tight labour market The opportunity-oriented approach appears to be popular, mostly coupled to a customer-oriented approach. The final aim is to equip people for a position on the labour market. The popularity seems due in part to the tight European labour markets. In times of considerable unemployment this approach will be less effective. Nevertheless, even in bad economic circumstances, the opportunity-approach seems preferable to the problem-oriented approach.

Conclusions regarding Strategic Networks

The poor cooperation among municipal departments is a significant handicap to a comprehensive policy The need for a comprehensive approach is admitted (on paper), but its execution is obstructed by rigid structures and traditional work cultures impeding cooperation.

Private parties are still hardly involved in social policy The activities in the sphere of social policy appear still largely reserved to public networks. Despite the fact that opportunity-oriented policies try to seize economic opportunities, the participation of the private sector is remarkably low.

Sectorial political responsibility: one of the obstacles to comprehensive approach Political governors are accountable for the policy fields in their portfolio. That stimulates the divisional approach and impedes the comprehensive approach.

Cooperation is readily achieved on the level of neighbourhoods On the district level communication lines are shorter and the relevant actors are quicker to see that cooperation is necessary if solutions are to be achieved. The impression is that for a customer-oriented or area-based approach, the municipal level is (too) far removed from the facts.

Striking a balance between top-down and bottom-up The closer to the problems, the simpler it is to achieve cooperation. On the other hand, the closer to the problems, the harder it is to keep the whole picture. What matters is to find the optimum scale.

Conclusions regarding Leadership

Leadership must be anchored on several levels: the required operational skills and tactical and strategic insights are not the same at all levels Leadership on the level of projects addresses implementation and therefore should be operationally strong. On the level of policy making and (political) decision-making, strategic and tactical insight is most expected.

The contents of the leadership function and its effectiveness often appear to depend on personal qualities Inspiring leadership motivates others and strengthens trust in the approach. To leave others enough elbow-room for their own initiatives also works well.

Without political backing or distinct objectives, leadership may grow diffuse The lacking of political leadership impedes the adequate implementation of programmes. Powerful political support is indispensable to, for instance, drastic organisational reforms. If the leadership has insufficient content, disappointing results are looming.

A comprehensive approach makes high demands on the communicative skills of programme leaders In a comprehensive approach within a divisional structure, leadership on the level of programmes requires intensive consultation, negotiation and adjustment with other programmes and with the public and private parties involved. Communicative skills are crucial in such a situation.

The weak side of voluntary projects which depend on personal appeal is their discontinuity More financial security and moral backing by authorities reinforce the continuity of valuable projects. The commitment of leaders/ initiators of voluntary work often determines its quality. Some degree of formality need not be harmful to the private initiative.

Conclusions regarding Support and Communication

Explicit support by responsible governors turns the signals to green. Poor political support may hamper the implementation An explicit and convincing attitude of aldermen as propellers of a programme or policy facilitates the implementation, especially when without such support the implementation cannot count on much applause.

Societal support is won by explicitly involving the clients in the decision-making: trust is of the essence Good listening to and taking account of the (real) desires of the customers enhances their trust in the plans. Within the field of social policy, clarity and trust are fundamental conditions for support among the target groups.

The lack of societal support for 'positive discrimination' of backward neighbourhoods or certain groups in the community constitutes a great handicap to the implementation of certain policy programmes Sometimes parts of the population look askance at plans to grant certain neighbourhoods or groups in the community advantages above others. Integration and equipment programmes are negatively affected by such feelings, which are often due to unfamiliarity with the advantages.

Trust in policy does not evolve until results become visible: seeing is believing Only when improvements can be seen with their own eyes will people begin to trust in the approach. That is why in some cities much store is set by physical improvements in backward neighbourhoods as a condition for approval on the accompanying, less noticeable policy measures.

When the private sector takes an active part, political support appears to increase A more generous input from the private sector in employment projects seems to be a condition for getting politicians interested. On the other hand, the private sector expects a clear, business-oriented approach to projects, for instance based on a business plan.

Communication is among the most underappreciated aspects of social policy
Societal or political support often depends on the manner of communication.
The tendency is for communication to come at the bottom of the list. Even
within the local public organisation or within one and the same department,
people often do not know what others are doing, nor do they know the opinion
of the target group.

Conclusions regarding Strategy Implementation and Output

A comprehensive approach calls for much mutual communication The
comprehensive implementation of social programmes implies frequent
communication. The communication may take up so much time that little is
left for other policy matters.

Adjustment of the policy concept in the process Because so little is yet known
about comprehensive, opportunity-oriented social policy, and because the
problem fields are so dynamic, 'learning by doing' or 'trial-and-error' are the
order of the day. As long as there is a clear overall concept that directs the
implementation of the policy, all may be well.

*New organisations and other skills are required for an opportunity-oriented
social policy* Bureaucracy and a conservative culture hardly open to innovation
invoke tensions between the existing and the desired organisation structures.
In a modern approach, different skills and a different mentality are required
from those working in social policy. That implies investment in training and
schooling of those involved.

Conclusions regarding Monitoring and Outcome

Results of monitoring and evaluation are not always duly exploited The reports
on monitoring vary greatly. Some programmes are far advanced, in others
monitoring is a neglected aspect. In some cases there is some monitoring but
hardly anything is done with the results. Sometimes financial donors make
their own evaluation claims, to the detriment of a good evaluation of the
(intended) comprehensive approach.

Translation of qualitative improvements into measurable indicators
Sometimes effects are not quantifiable, for instance the degree of integration
of foreigners. Sometimes an inquiry is held into their 'school marks'. A pitfall

is that such inquiries are very sensitive to incidents. The possibilities of measurement are facilitated by formulating benchmarks in an early stage.

The development of benchmarks alone may stimulate more result-orientation To work in a result-oriented way demands the formulation of indicators for measuring results. In particular when matters like quality of life or security are at stake, it stimulates thinking about what results to aim for.

A public social information system offers advantages A 'social observatory' to which anybody can contribute information and the results are available to all, can help towards better communication. Social problems will be recognised earlier and customers can be served more coherently. Such an observatory can also be a powerful tool to evaluate the results of the new approach.

Have the analysed projects been successful? Whether a project has been a *success or a failure* is difficult to assess. One way is to consider the social benefits, expressed in money, of (social) investments. Not once have we recorded an attempt to compute, for instance by a cost-benefit analysis, the profitability of a social strategy.

Finally: What makes Social Policies more Effective and Efficient?

1   To achieve a more efficient and effective social policy, attention to all tools of organising capacity distinguished in this research is essential, for all of them – vision, communication, strategic networks, leadership, political and societal support and communication – are of great importance. Should one of them receive too little attention, inevitably the goals stated will fail to be attained, or fail to be attained efficiently.

2   The analysis of eight social strategies has revealed that *vision* appears to be the most important element, while *communication* is probably the most underappreciated one. Without a vision, programmes or projects are unguided missiles, often not oriented to opportunities. Without a well developed communication strategy the message of the vision will not receive the attention and support requested. Too often the role of communication as binding agent of organising capacity is underestimated.

3   Opportunities tend to be offered in other policy fields than that of social policy. Therefore, to design an opportunity-oriented social policy, comprehensive strategies should achieve a link with, for instance, economic – or spatial – housing – or quality-of-life – policies.

4   Social policies can be observed to be progressing. In many cities, social policy is passing from a so-called 'institutionalisation stage' to an 'activation stage'. Important elements of the transition are attempts to strike a balance between top-down and bottom-up approaches, and between the dominance of public and of private actors. The objective is a better match between individual social needs and new opportunities, a sound internal coherence of policies, as well as adequate, more flexible, organisational structures.

5   A central aim of most social programmes is to make target groups self-supporting (or emancipated). To that end, sustainable (lasting) solutions to social problems should be found. So, in principle social programmes give temporary support to certain areas or groups, and can be concluded as soon as the aims are achieved, so that other urgent problems can be taken in hand.

6   Rigid structures and traditional work cultures are obstructing effective cooperation in strategic networks, both between municipal departments as well as with parties outside the public domain. Despite the fact that opportunity-oriented policies try to seize labour-market opportunities, involvement from the business sector is remarkably missing.

7   Bureaucratic organisations appear to be the most serious handicap for reaching the aims of comprehensive social programmes. Dependent on the vision evolved, sometimes the administration has to be restructured to make room for an area-based, functional or categorical approach. Whatever the organisational structure chosen, flexible structures and flexible attitudes are invariably needed. This appears to be a big challenge for city governments.

8   Ultimately, the implementation of the chosen strategies falls to the employees of the public and private organisations involved. If they lack the necessary education or skills, the envisaged aims will not be achieved. Therefore, adequate training and education of the staff involved will always be a prominent precondition for organising capacity.

Discussion Partners

Report on Antwerp

Mr Jos Goossens, Civil Servant, Integration City of Antwerp
Mr Marc Wellens, Alderman, Social Policy
Mr Jan Deceuninck, Coordinator, SIF – OCMW
Ms Dominique Peirs, Coordinator, Business centre 'Noord-Oost Antwerpen'
  and Telecentre
Mr Dries Willems, Coordinator, Planning Department
Ms Kris Cleiren, Coordinator, Regional Institute for Neighbourhood
  Development
Mr Jan Goorden, Coordinator, SOMA
Mr Bie Bosmans, Coordinator, Borough Development Organisation
Mr Dirk Diels, Coordinator, Urban Employment

Report on Eindhoven

Mr J. Beniers, manager, Municipal Health Services (GGZE)
Mr J. van Corven, researcher, Municipal Health Authority (GGD)
Mr P. Dijkstra, Novadic, District Manager, Eindhoven Region
Mr A. van Gerwen, Care Department, City of Eindhoven
Mr T. van der Heuvel, Welfare Department, City of Eindhoven
Mr R. Jansen, director, Municipal Health Authority (GGD)
Mr E. van Merrienboer, Coordinator, Major Cities Policy, City of Eindhoven
Mr R. Pullen, Administration and Policy Advice, City of Eindhoven
Mr E. Slaats, Neighbourhood Association, Tongelre
Mr N. van der Spek, Alderman, Social Development, City of Eindhoven
Mr P. van der Ven, Police Commissioner, Police Zuidoost Brabant
Ms I. Verduin, Neighbourhood Association Woensel West
Mr L. Vermeulen, Secretary, Business Assocation De Kade
Mr J. Vosters, President, Business Assocation De Kade

Report on Helsinki

Mr Lasse Halme, Pastor, The Parish Union of Helsinki (Lutheran church)
Mr Eero Holstila, Managing Director, City of Helsinki Urban Facts
Mr Aulikki Kananoja, Managing Director, Social Services Department, City of Helsinki
Mr Marko Karvinen, Secretary of the Partnership Working Group, City of Helsinki
Mr Hannu Kurki, Activist and Researcher, Maunula Forum, Local development initiative in northern Helsinki
Ms Jaana Löppönen, Coordinator, Horisontti Project, The Job Seekers' Association of Helsinki West
Ms Leena Mikkola, Social Worker, Social Services Department, City of Helsinki
Ms Paula Sermilä, Acting Director of Education, City of Helsinki
Mr Jyrki Tiihonen, Project Coordinator, City of Helsinki Education System
Group of citizens involved in the Maunula Neighbourhood Association

Report on Malmö

Mr Mats Andersson, Malmö City Office
Mr Anders Ardmar, Statistical Officer, Malmö City Office
Ms Britta Strom, Project Manager, Malmö City Office
Mr Alf Merlov, Head of Department of Employment and Training, Malmö City Office
Mr Krystof Laczak, Quality Controller, Malmö City Office
Mr Freddie Akerblom, Chairman of the Hyllie District City Council
Mr Bo Sjostrom, Head of the Hyllie City District Administration
Mr Inger Bjorkquist, Development Manager, Hyllie City District Administration
Mr Peter Bodis, Planning Secretary, Hyllie City District Administration
Ms Eva Kärfve, Lecturer, Faculty of Sociology, Lunds University
Mr Berit Andersson, Lecturer, Faculty of Sociology, Lunds University
Ms Anne Schmid, Programme Manager, Hyllie Work and Development Centre
Mr Lars Ekstrom, Manager, Hyllie Work and Development Centre
Mr Mats Bjork, Staff Member, Hyllie Work And Development Centre
Ms Eva-Lena Palm, Staff Member, Hyllie Work And Development Centre
Mr Johan Petrici, Staff Member, Hyllie Work And Development Centre

Ms Paula Hart, Staff Member, Hyllie Work And Development Centre
Ms Gunilla Berg, Staff Member, Hyllie Work And Development Centre
Mr Matti Laukkanen, Staff Member, Hyllie Work And Development Centre
Mr Hazrat Mohmand, Staff Member, Hyllie Work And Development Centre
Ms Elvira Haxhiagaj, Staff Member, Hyllie Work And Development Centre
Mr Hussein Sadayo, Staff Member, Hyllie Work And Development Centre
Ms Hamida Nabi, Staff Member, Hyllie Work And Development Centre

Report on Rotterdam

Mr Theo Eikenbroek, Department of City Planning and Housing (dS+V), Social Programme Leader, IAA Office, City of Rotterdam
Mr Jon van Eenennaam, Housing Corporation 'Maasoevers', Director, Strategy and Development, responsible for Project Hoogvliet
Mr Hans Elemans, Chair, Borough of Hoogvliet
Mr Jan Lagendijk, Coordinator, Urban Vision, City of Rotterdam
Ms Mirjam van Lierop, Project Manager, IAA 'Hoogvliet Plus'
Ms Elisabeth Poot, Department of City Planning and Housing (dS+V), Manager Programme Implementation, IAA Office, City of Rotterdam
Mr Eric Trinconi, Director, Welfare NGO, Hoogvliet

Report on Stockholm

Mr Stig Hanno, Chairman, central steering group TEP/Coordinater TEP Stockholm
Ms Elisabeth Anderson, Unit Manager, Maintenance Support Unit, Social Welfare Department
Ms Margareta Sörqvist, Head of Employment Agency/member of TEP Norrmalm Local Control Group
Ms Lena Rogeland, Project Manager and Managing Director, Millennium Bruk AB
Mr Jan Valeskog, Social Democratic councillor at the Norrmalm Local Council
Mr Crollis MacConnel, participant in 'New Ways to Work' Project
Ms Ulla-Britt Fingal, Administrator, TEP in Stockholm
Mr Mats Granath, Project Manager, TEP in Norrmalm
Mr Gustav Blix, Conservative councillor, Stockholm Municipal Council
Mr Johan af Winklerfeldt, participant in 'New Ways to Work' Project

Report on Strasbourg

Ms J. Couval, Directeur Général Adjoint in charge of l'Action Sociale, Department of Social Action, City of Strasbourg

Mr J. Maillard, Adjoint au Directeur, Department of Social Action, City of Strasbourg

Mr Aubert, Grand Projet de Ville, Department of Social Action, City of Strasbourg

Ms M. Latzer, responsible for l'Unité Territoriale, Department of Social Action, City of Strasbourg

Ms J. Bret, Chargée de projet, Polygone District, Department of Social Action, City of Strasbourg

Ms A. Sobler, Insertion RMI, Department of Social Action, City of Strasbourg

Ms H. Rihn, Chargée de projet – Logement, Department of Social Action, City of Strasbourg

Mr Guery, Department of Social Action, City of Strasbourg

Mr Schalck (Compas Tis), Department of Social Action, City of Strasbourg

Mr Chenderowski, Direction des Etudes et de la Prospective, Department of Social Action, City of Strasbourg

Mr Chappaz, Directeur de la Caisse d'Allocations Familiales de Strasbourg

Ms M.H. Gillig, Adjointe au Maire en charge des Affaires Sociales, Vice-présidente de la Communauté Urbaine de Strasbourg, Député européen

Ms Gustin, Directrice, Direction Départementale des Affaires Sanitaires et Sociales (service de l'Etat), partenaire de la Ville de Strasbourg

Mr J.M. Kuczkowski en charge de la Coordination Partenariale du Centre Communal d'Action Sociale (CCAS) de la Ville de Strasbourg

Report on Utrecht

Mr Marc van Zon, Project leader 'De Leeuw'

Mr Wim van Berkel, Rayon manager, Housing Corporation Mitros

Mr Theo van Wijk, Architect

Mr Arthur van Loon, Development Corporation, City of Utrecht

Ms Atie Versteeg, project leader, District Service Centre, Department for District Management and Urban Renewal, City of Utrecht

Ms Annelies Stevens, Director, UNO Centrum

Mr Marlon Alvares, Head 'Wijkgericht Werken' (District-oriented Approach)

Mr Paul Hartman, Former District Manager

Bibliography

General

Bhalla, A. and Lapeyre, F. (1997), 'Social Exclusion: Towards an analytical and operational framework', *Development and Change*, Vol. 28, No. 3, pp. 413–34.

Byrne, D. (1997), 'Social Exclusion and Capitalism: The reserve army across space and time', *Critical Social Policy*, Vol. 17, pp. 27–51.

Castells, M. and Hall, P. (1994), *Technopoles of the World*, London, Routledge.

Cheshire, P.C. and Hay, D.G. (1989), *Urban Problems in Western Europe*, London, Unwin Hyman.

Clasen, J., Gould, A. and Vincent, J. (1997), *Long-term Unemployment and the Threat of Social Exclusion*, Bristol, The Policy Press.

Eurocities Social Welfare Committee (1993), *European Social Policy and the City*, Brussels.

European Commission (2000), *The Urban Audit 2000*, Vols 1 and 2, European Communities.

Geddes, M.(2000), 'Tackling Social Exclusion in the European Union? The Limits to the New Orthodoxy of Local Partnership', *International Journal of Urban and Regional Research*, Vol. 24, No. 4, pp. 782–800.

Jacobs, J. (1984), *Cities and the Wealth of Nations*, Penguin Books, Harmondsworth.

Levitas, R. (1998) *The Inclusive Society: Social exclusion and new labour*, London, MacMillan.

Liebfried, S. (1993), 'Towards a European Welfare State? On Integrating Poverty Regimes into the European Community', in Jones, C. (ed.), *New Perspectives on the Welfare State in Europe*, Routledge, London.

Madanipour, A. (1998), 'Social Exclusion and Space', in Madanipour, A., Cars, G. and Allen, J. (eds), *Social Exclusion in European Cities*, London, Jessica Kingsley.

Mingione, F. (ed.) (1996), *Urban Poverty and the Underclass: A reader*, Blackwell, Oxford.

Musterd, S. and Ostendorf, W. (1998), *Urban Segregation and the Welfare State*, London, Routledge.

OECD (1996), *Strategies for Housing and Social Integration in Cities*.

Perry, I. (1997), *Escaping Poverty: From safety nets to networks of opportunity*, London, Demos.

Porter, M.E. (1995), 'The Competitive Advantage of the Inner City', *Harvard Business Review*, May–June, pp. 55–71.

van den Berg, L., van Klink, H.A. and van der Meer, J. (1993), *Governing Metropolitan Regions*, Avebury, Aldershot.

van den Berg, L., Braun, E. and van der Meer, J. (1997), *Metropolitan Organising Capacity*, Ashgate, Aldershot.

Wacquant, L. (1999), 'Urban Marginality in the Coming Millennium', *Urban Studies*, Vol. 36, No. 10, pp. 1639–47.
Young, J. and Lemos, G. (1997), *The Communities we have Lost and can Regain*, London, Lemos and Crane.

Report on Antwerp

European Commission (2000), *The Urban Audit 2000*, Vols 1 and 2, European Communities
Kesteloot, C. (1996), *Atlas van Achtergestelde Buurten in Vlaanderen en Brussel*, Ministerie van de Vlaamse Gemeenschap.
Ministerie van de Vlaamse Gemeenschap (2000), *Voortgangsrapport 1999, SIF-beleidsovereenkomst tussen de Vlaamse Gemeenschap en het gemeentebestuur en O.C.M.W. van Antwerpen.*
SIF beleidsplan 1997–99, final version, 1 July.
SOMA vzw (1997), *Handleiding bij de uitvoering van het Sociaal Impulsfonds*, Beleidsplan 1997–99.
Sociaal Impulsfonds Antwerpen (1997), *Beleidsplan 1997–1999*, 24 March.
Stad Antwerpen/OCMW Antwerpen (1999), *Sociaal Impulsfonds Antwerpen*, Evaluatierapport SIF 1997–99, Antwerpen.
Stad Antwerpen, Burgerzaken en het Ontwikkelingsbedrijf (2000), *Scheve stad in sterke positie*, Sociaal-Economische Nota 2000.
van den Berg, L., Braun, E. and van der Meer, J. (1998), *National Urban Policies in the European Union, Responses to Urban Issues in the Fifteen Member States*, Ashgate, Aldershot.
van den Berg, L. and Pol, P.M.J. (1999), *The High-Speed Train Station and Urban Revitalisation: A comparative analysis of station areas in the cities of Amsterdam, Antwerp, Berlin, Cologne, Dortmund, Lille, Munich, Rotterdam and Utrecht*, Euricur.
van Hove, Erik and Stefan Nieuwinckel (1996), *Het BOMboek, het verhaal van de buurtontwikkelingsmaatschappij Noordoost-Antwerpen*, Offset Vandevelde.

Report on Eindhoven

Adang, A.V.J.M. and J.M.P. van Oorschot (1996), *Regio in bedrijf, Hoofdlijnen van industriële ontwikkeling en zakelijke dienstverlening in Zuidoost-Brabant.*
Bieleman, B., J. Snipe and E. de Bie (1995), *Drugs Inside the Borders; Hard Drugs and Crime in the Netherlands; Estimations of the Extent*, Intraval, Groningen.
City of Eindhoven (2000), *Onderzoek Handvatten voor Herstel* (Research Handles for Recovery), Department General and Public Affairs.

City of Eindhoven (2000), *Stadsvisie, in het licht van de toekomst* (*City Vision, in the Light of the Future*).

City of Eindhoven (2000), *Stedelijk ontwikkelingsprogramma* (*Urban Development Programme*) 1999–2003/4.

Gemeente Eindhoven (2000), *Kerncijfers Eindhoven 2000*.

Novadic (1999), *De keuzes verantwoord: jaarverslag 1999* (*The Legitimation of Choices: Annual Report 1999*).

The Netherlands Ministry of Foreign Affairs (2000), *Q & A Drugs: A guide to Dutch Policy*, Foreign Information Division in co-operation with the Ministry of Health, Welfare and Sport, The Ministry of Justice and the Ministry of the Interior and Kingdom Relations, Zuidam & Zonen, Zaandam.

van den Berg, L., Braun, E. and van der Meer, J. (1998), *National Urban Policies in the European Union, Responses to Urban Issues in the Fifteen Member States*, Ashgate, Aldershot.

van Gerwen, A. (2000), *Verslavingszorg; Bouwen en werken aan een kaartenhuis*, Dienst Maatschappelijke en Culturele Zaken, Gemeente Eindhoven.

Report on Helsinki

City of Helsinki Urban Facts (2000), *Statistical Comparisons*, City of Helsinki Information Management Centre.

City of Helsinki Urban Facts (1999), 'The Information Sector as the Flywheel of Economy in Helsinki', *Statistics 1999*, p. 16.

European Commission (2000), *The Urban Audit 2000*, Vols 1 and 2, European Communities.

Helsinki City Office (1997), *Report on Social Exclusion and Social Segregation*, Publication Series A, 15/1997.

Helsinki City Office (1999), *Helsinki Today – Policy Priorities for an International City*, Publication Series A, 7/1999.

Holstila, E. (1998), 'National Urban Policy in Finland', in van den Berg, L., Braun, E. and van der Meer, J. (eds), *National Urban Policies in the European Union*, Ashgate, Aldershot.

Katajamaki, E. and Nevala, S. (1997), 'Helsinki, a City of Services', *Helsinki Quarterly*, Kvartti 3/1997, City of Helsinki Urban Facts.

Kattelus, K. (1996), 'Helsinki, a City of Work and Unemployment', *Helsinki Quarterly*, Kvartti 3B/1996.

Nordstat (1999), *Major Nordic Cities and Regions – Facts and Figures*, Elanders Graphic Systems, Sweden.

Partnership Working Group (2000), *Final Report from the Partnership Working Group*, City of Helsinki.

Tuominen, M. (1997), 'Broken Windows – the Case of Helsinki', *Helsinki Quarterly*, 3/1997.
van den Berg, L. and Pol, P.M.J. (1999), *The High-Speed Train Station and Urban Revitalisation: A comparative analysis of station areas in the cities of Amsterdam, Antwerp, Berlin, Cologne, Dortmund, Lille, Munich, Rotterdam and Utrecht*, Euricur Report, Erasmus University Rotterdam.

Report on Malmö

City of Helsinki Urban Facts (1999), *Comparative City Statistics*, major cities of Scandinavia: Tallinn, Riga, Vilnius and St Petersburg, Helsinki, Finland.
City of Malmö (2000a), *Revised Programme for 2001 Hyllie City District Council Metropolitan Initiative.*
City of Malmö (2000b), *Goals for Labour Market Policy Measures in Malmö in the Year 2001.*
Commission on Metropolitan Affairs (2001), *Metropolitan Policy in Sweden*, www.storstad.gov.se.
Hyllie City District Council (1998), *Report and Continued Action Plan for Special Initiatives in At-risk Neighbourhoods*, 16 October.
Malmö City Administration Office (2000), *Breaking the Cycle of Segregation*, revised program for the Metropolitan Initiative in Malmö.
Nilsson, J.-E. (1998), 'Sweden', in van den Berg, L., Braun, E. and van der Meer, J. (1998), *National Urban Policies in the European Union, Responses to Urban Issues in the Fifteen Member States*, Ashgate, Aldershot.
Nordstat (1999), *Major Nordic Cities and Regions – Facts and Figures*, Elanders Graphic Systems, Sweden.
Status Report Metropolitan Initiative Programmes in Hyllie.
www.malmo.se.

Report on Rotterdam

City of Rotterdam (1998), *Met Raad en Daad*, Collegeprogramma 1998–2002.
COS, Centre for Research and Statistics (1998), *Buurten in Cijfers.*
COS, Centre for Research and Statistics (1999), *Kerncijfers voor Rotterdam 1999.*
COS, Centre for Research and Statistics (2000), *Kerncijfers voor Rotterdam 2000.*
Deelgemeente Hoogvliet (1999), Strategische IAA 2010 *Visie op toekomst Hoogvliet Investeringsplan* (September 1999).
European Commission (2000), *The Urban Audit 2000*, Vols 1 and 2, European Communities.

Meijer, H. (1999), *Waar bemoeien wij ons mee? Sociaal Investeren: Hart van de Rotterdamse IAA*, Toespraak tijdens congres IAA: het Grote-Stedenbeleid in Rotterdam, 3 November.

Miedema, F. and Oude Engberink, G. (1999), *Urban Development and Social Polarisation*, case study on Rotterdam, Research for the EU, DGXII (http:// www.ifresi.univ-lille1.fr/PagesHTML/URSPIC/Index.htm).

Ministry of VROM (Housing, Planning and the Environment) (2001), *Ruimte maken ruimte delen*, Part A of the 5th Memorandum on Spatial Planning.

Rotterdam City Development Corporation (RCDC) (1998), *Trendbericht Rotterdam 1998*; Sociaal-economische rapportage.

Uitvoeringsprogramma IAA (1998), *Plan van Aanpak*, concept 22 September.

van den Berg, L., Braun, E. and van der Meer, J. (1998), *National Urban Policies in the European Union, Responses to Urban Issues in the Fifteen Member States*, Ashgate, Aldershot.

van den Berg, L., van der Meer, J. and Otgaar, A.H.J. (2000), *The Attractive City; Catalyst for economic development and social revitalisation; an international comparative research into the experiences of Birmingham, Lisbon and Rotterdam.*

van der Vegt, J. (1998), *Rotterdam Orgware*, Rotterdam City Development Corporation.

Report on Stockholm

City of Stockholm (1997), *How the city is governed*, February 1997.

European Commission (2000), *The Urban Audit 2000*, Vols 1 and 2, European Communities.

European Social Fund and City of Stockholm (1998), *Territorial Employment Pact, More Jobs in Stockholm*, Action Plan 1998–99.

Hanno, S. (2000), *Proposed Action Plan for Employment*, 3 March.

Murdie, A. and Borgegard, L. (1998), 'Immigration, Spatial Segregation and Housing Segmentation of Immigrants in Metropolitan Stockholm, 1960–95', *Urban Studies*, Vol. 35.

Nordstat (1999), *Major Nordic Cities and Regions – facts and figures*, Nordstat, Sweden.

TEP pacts, www.stockholmspakten.stockholm.se.

USK Statistic Stockholm.

van den Berg, L., Braun, E. and van der Meer, J. (1998), *National Urban Policies in the European Union, Responses to Urban Issues in the Fifteen Member States*, Ashgate, Aldershot.

www.stockholm.se.

Report on Strasbourg

City of Strasbourg (1999), *L'intervention sociale de la Ville de Strasbourg, Le guide de l'Action Sociale*, Strasbourg.

Direction de l'Action Sociale (1996), *Schéma Directeur de l'Intervention Sociale de la Ville de Strasbourg*, 1ère phase: Redéfinition de l'Intervention Sociale dans les quartiers, Communication au Conseil Municipal du 25 mars 1996, Strasbourg.

Direction de l'Action Sociale (1997), *Mise en oeuvre du Schéma Directeur de l'Intervention Sociale*, Juin 1997, Strasbourg.

Direction de l'Action Sociale, City of Strasbourg (2001), *Social Revitalisation of Urban Regions*, Document préparatoire aux journées de travail des 7 et 8 Fevrier, Strasbourg.

European Commission (2000), *The Urban Audit 2000*, Vols 1 and 2, European Communities.

van den Berg, L., Braun, E. and van der Meer, J. (1998), *National Urban Policies in the European Union, Responses to Urban Issues in the Fifteen Member States*, Ashgate, Aldershot.

Report on Utrecht

Gemeente Utrecht, DMO (1999), 'Jaarverslag Wijkgericht Werken', *Proeven van wijkgericht werken*, Utrecht.

Gemeente Utrecht, Programmabureau Betrokken Stad (2000), *De Betrokken Stad, Bewogen Samenleving*, Utrecht.

Gemeente Utrecht, Programmabureau Betrokken Stad (2000), *De Betrokken Stad, Halfjaarverslag*, Eerste helft 2000, Utrecht.

Gemeente Utrecht, Programmabureau Betrokken Stad (2000), *Evaluatie Wijkservicecentra*, Utrecht.

KPMG-BEA (1998), *Nieuwe sleutelprojecten*, Hoofddorp.

UNO, Gemeente Utrecht, Mitros Wonen, Politie district Paardenveld, Bewonerscomité Staatslieden, Projektorganisatie Wijkservicecentra (1999), *Globaal ontwerp Buurt Service Punt De Leeuw*, Utrecht.

van den Berg, L., Braun, E. and van der Meer, J. (1998), *National Urban Policies in the European Union, Responses to Urban Issues in the Fifteen Member States*, Ashgate, Aldershot.

van den Berg, L. and Pol, P.M.J. (1999), *The High-Speed Train Station and Urban Revitalisation: A comparative analysis of station areas in the cities of Amsterdam, Antwerp, Berlin, Cologne, Dortmund, Lille, Munich, Rotterdam and Utrecht*, Euricur Report, Erasmus University Rotterdam.

Wijkservicecentrum De Leeuw (2000), *Startnotitie pilotproject*, 17 February.

Index